Telling the Story of Translation

Bloomsbury Advances in Translation Series

Series Editor: Jeremy Munday, Centre for Translation Studies, University of Leeds, UK

Bloomsbury Advances in Translation Studies publishes cutting-edge research in translation studies. This field has grown in importance in the modern, globalized world, with international translation between languages a daily occurrence. Research into the practices, processes, and theory of translation is essential, and this series aims to showcase the best in international academic and professional output.

Other titles in the series:

Collaborative Translation
Edited by Anthony Cordingley and Céline Frigau Manning

Community Translation
Mustapha Taibi and Uldis Ozolins

Corpus-Based Translation Studies
Edited by Alet Kruger, Kim Wallmach, and Jeremy Munday

Global Trends in Translator and Interpreter Training
Edited by Séverine Hubscher-Davidson and Michał Borodo

Music, Text and Translation
Edited by Helen Julia Minors

Quality in Professional Translation
Joanna Drugan

Retranslation
Sharon Deane-Cox

The Pragmatic Translator
Massimiliano Morini

Translation, Adaptation and Transformation
Edited by Laurence Raw

Translation and Translation Studies in the Japanese Context
Edited by Nana Sato-Rossberg and Judy Wakabayashi

Telling the Story of Translation

Writers Who Translate

Judith Woodsworth

BLOOMSBURY ACADEMIC
LONDON · NEW YORK · OXFORD · NEW DELHI · SYDNEY

BLOOMSBURY ACADEMIC
Bloomsbury Publishing Plc
50 Bedford Square, London, WC1B 3DP, UK
1385 Broadway, New York, NY 10018, USA

BLOOMSBURY, BLOOMSBURY ACADEMIC and the Diana logo
are trademarks of Bloomsbury Publishing Plc

First published 2017
Paperback edition first published 2019

A catalogue record for this book is available from the British Library.

A catalog record for this book is available from the Library of Congress.

ISBN: HB: 978-1-4742-7708-2
PB: 978-1-3501-0103-6
ePDF: 978-1-4742-7710-5
ePub: 978-1-4742-7709-9

Series: Bloomsbury Advances in Translation

Typeset by Integra Software Services Pvt. Ltd.

To find out more about our authors and books visit
www.bloomsbury.com and sign up for our newsletters.

Contents

List of Figures

Acknowledgements

A book of this kind cannot be put together without ample assistance. In addition to the dusty library shelves that I so love to peruse, modern technology has enabled me to lay my hands on print and electronic resources from around the world. My sincere thanks go to Andréa Harland, the head of Interlibrary Loans at Concordia University's Webster Library, and her extremely cooperative team, who have facilitated my quest for material going back decades and more. That such an efficient service is still available at no cost to individual researchers is truly a miracle.

I am equally grateful for the opportunity I had to consult the extensive collection of Gertrude Stein manuscripts at the Beinecke Rare Book Room, at Yale University, where I spent many hours. The documentation I obtained digitally and on microfilm made it possible to continue my sleuthing from home. Archivist and curator Timothy Young took the time to discuss my project with me, and the Beinecke personnel were very helpful. I also wish to thank staff at the New York Public Library for giving me access to the Paul Auster manuscripts held by the *Henry W. and Albert A. Berg Collection of English and American Literature.*

As I was beginning my work on Gertrude Stein, two eminent Stein scholars extended a warm welcome to me. Barbara Will, a professor in the Department of English at Dartmouth College, hosted me at her home in Hanover, New Hampshire, where she offered me excellent home baking, print materials from her private library, and, above all, her encouragement. Edward Burns, professor emeritus at William Patterson University, invited me to his New York City apartment. I have derived much benefit from the documents he lent me and from his indisputable expertise.

I am indebted to Paul Auster for responding so generously when I reached out to him as a Park Slope grandmother, hoping for a few moments of his time to chat in a nearby café about translation. Instead, I had a leisurely conversation with him in his stately Brooklyn brownstone, where he shared his experience and fascinating perception of a topic so important to him and so dear to me. Jennifer Dougherty was wonderfully efficient in making our meeting possible.

Christine York, my colleague in the translation studies programme at Concordia University, shared a paper she had given on Paul Auster's translation of Pierre Clastres, which proved to be indispensable to my project. She later read and critiqued the corresponding portion of manuscript. Her advice has been invaluable and her friendship much appreciated. I also extend my thanks to Professor Csaba Nikolenyi, Director of the Azrieli Institute of Israel Studies, who enthusiastically provided financial support to attend my first 'transfiction' conference, held in Tel Aviv in 2013 on the topic of translators and their authors. I presented my first paper on Gertrude Stein and Paul Auster at that event, which kindled my interest in the topic of this book.

I owe a huge debt of gratitude to Carmen Ruschiensky, a doctoral student at Concordia University, who has worked as a research assistant on a number of my projects. We have enjoyed many hours of conversation, during which she has been good enough to listen intently as I have chattered away about my work. She has willingly assisted me in gathering information, and has cast her eagle eye on different versions of my manuscript. As she has grown into a translation specialist in her own right, I have come to rely not only on her inestimable technical assistance but also on her scholarly acumen.

Amazing colleagues have sparked my curiosity and provided stimulation in conference sessions or informal conversations. Rainier Grutman's ideas on self-fashioning authors, Bella Brodzki's thoughts on translation and memorialization, and Teresa Caneda's work on modernist writers were all enlightening. Esther Allen, always warm and generous, brought Idra Novey to my attention. Rachel Weissbrod was kind enough to invite me to speak in Israel, a country where I continue to draw inspiration. It was Clarence Epstein's suggestion that I visit the exhibition 'The Steins Collect' at New York's Metropolitan Museum; I thank him for that advice as well as for the discussions we had about the restitution of spoliated art. Many friends, new and old, have been boosters along the way: Véronique Béghain, Judie Benjamin, Ann Carson Tempier, Marthe Catry-Verron, Jean Delisle, Sue Harrison, Dana Hearne, Jonathan Levinson, Anne Pallen, Enn Raudsepp, Sherry Simon, Janet Stern, and Christine Yeager. Heartfelt thanks go out to Patrick Woodsworth for his enduring friendship. His expertise in Germanic literatures and intimate knowledge of the German language were invaluable to me in understanding the subtleties of Shaw's handling of the Trebitsch play.

My family has once again provided unfailing support. Un gros merci à mon gendre, Laurent Martin, qui pendant une période difficile a gracieusement offert de venir donner un coup de main à la maison, me permettant ainsi de passer une partie de mon congé sabbatique à l'étranger, où, loin des soucis quotidiens, j'ai pu m'avancer dans mes travaux de recherche. Thanks to Patrice, always caring, who encouraged him to come.

In addition to filial love, Michael Woodsworth brought his penetrating insights as a young academic and his skills as a brilliant writer to bear on the manuscript of his devoted mother. All the while, Amy Farley cheered us on. I am nurtured and inspired by the affectionate disposition and clever observations of my grandchildren, from the youngest Brooklynites Eleanor and Will Woodsworth to the eldest, Julien Crysler-Martin, who lived with us for most of the book's gestation period, and who always said as he came and went, 'Good luck with your writing, Grandma. How's your work?' My companion of a quarter-century, Lindsay Crysler, has given me infinite attention and once again graced my pages with his editor's touch. I offer him my deepest appreciation and boundless love.

Introduction: 'One More Possession of Beauty'

English literature lives on translation, it is fed by translation; every new exuberance, every new heave is stimulated by translation, every allegedly great age is an age of translations.

–Ezra Pound, *How to Read*

Translation in the modernist age

By the time Ezra Pound published these words in 1931, in what has been called a 'primer for Modernism' (Yao 2002: 2), he had already completed much of what would become an astonishing (and contested) body of work as a translator. He had translated the poetry of fourteenth-century Italian poet Guido Cavalcanti, transposed medieval Chinese poetry into a collection entitled *Cathay* (relying on the notes of Orientalist Ernest Fenollosa), and generated a verse tribute to Latin poet Sextus Propertius, to name a few examples. Several other prominent writers of the early twentieth century had similarly employed their talents: James Joyce, W.B. Yeats, T.S. Eliot, Virginia Woolf, and D.H. Lawrence, among others, had turned their attention to what had long been viewed as a subservient art. As this work flowed from their pens, new perspectives on the very idea of translation emerged. For the modernists, translation was a 'generative' art, rather than a secondary one.[1] Pound held the view, as Paul Auster would later point out, that translation was good training for original writing. It also contributed to the renewal and enrichment of English literature by providing new models, by allowing English writers to 'make it new'.

As translators become more visible conduits for interlinkages between countries, the motivation and work of writers devoted to translating each other is of increasing interest. The phenomenon of cross-pollination is fertile ground in the context of emergent transatlantic or transnational literary studies. Translation is not only a mode of writing but also a way of being, a way of knowing; it is a practice, a subject, and a trope in literature.

Telling the Story of Translation presents studies of three writers, three points along the modernist spectrum: Bernard Shaw, Gertrude Stein, and Paul Auster. Bernard Shaw straddled the nineteenth and twentieth centuries, his life spanning nearly a century from Victorian times to the nuclear age. Described as 'the modernist that never was' (Grene 1996), he was a progressive Edwardian at the 'dawn of the modernist era' who incarnated the *Zeitgeist* of the early twentieth century (Wright 2003: 383). Gertrude Stein, self-proclaimed creator of the twentieth century, exemplified modernism in her experimental handling of language and genre, as well as in the choices of artists she promoted and collected. The apartment she shared, first with her brother and then with Alice Toklas, was considered a 'fulcrum for the movement known as modernism' (Wineapple 1996: 2). Contemporary author Paul Auster, although he does not personally like the designation, came of age as a writer in the postmodern period. Elements of intertextuality, metafiction, and playful use of language in his multilayered fiction, combined with his 'detective-novel' story lines, have earned him the label of 'postmodern gumshoe'.

Shaw, Stein, and Auster are not the only writers who translate, nor the first. Six centuries before them, Geoffrey Chaucer combined translation with other forms of text production at a time when the lines between translating and original composition were not drawn as neatly as they subsequently became. Described as the 'father and founder of the English language' by printer and translator William Caxton, Chaucer is cited again by Pound as marking the beginning of the 'great ages' of English literature: 'Le Grand Translateur, translator of the *Romaunt of the Rose*, paraphraser of Virgil and Ovid, condenser of old stories he had found in Latin, French, and Italian' (1931: 44). A writer who mixed original writing, translation, and compilation, Chaucer is known for his metaphor of ploughing old fields to produce new corn – in other words, of making new books from old ones (*Parliament of Fowls*). In keeping with this principle, his *Romaunt of the Rose* is a literary product based in part on a translation from the French, and his iconic *Canterbury Tales* are inspired by classical and Italian sources (Virgil, Dante, and Boccaccio). *Confessio Amantis*, the most famous work of Chaucer's contemporary John Gower, is a poem of consolation inspired by Boethius, with a structure borrowed from Boccaccio; while written in English, Gower's tales are influenced by other classical and medieval sources.

Chaucer's productive use and view of translation were eclipsed subsequently, as cultures began to recognize the supremacy of original authorship and the preeminence of original texts over translations. In contrast to writers, who have tended to live public lives and achieve recognition as singular geniuses, translators have largely remained in the shadows. Even seventeenth-century poet, playwright, and literary critic John Dryden, who was a key figure in the history of translation, famous for his versions of Virgil, regarded translation as imitation, a derivative art, and even a form of 'drudgery'.

Yet it is also true that authors who, like Chaucer, have included translation among their creative activities have continued to flourish. Such writers have, to varying degrees, integrated translation practice and thinking on translation into their body of writing, raising complex questions of linguistic identity and cultural affiliation. Writers for whom translation has been a form of tribute, veneration, or even idolatry have imported works of foreign literature with missionary-like zeal. Think of Edgar Allan Poe's French translators. Charles Baudelaire is of note in the light of recent theories of agency in translation – specifically, the way in which his widely circulated translations of Poe's tales were accompanied by laudatory prefaces that contributed to the construction of a myth of Poe as a great American writer, a legacy that ultimately changed the course of literary history in France. Paul Valéry followed in the footsteps of Stéphane Mallarmé, eminent poet and translator of Poe's poems. Valéry idolized Poe, whom he read in French translation. Describing Poe as the 'the only writer – with no sins' ('le seul écrivain – sans aucun péché'), Valéry tackled what was left – Poe's idiosyncratic *Marginalia* – and took credit for a translation he did not actually do himself.[2]

As notions of authorship and originality have shifted over time, so, too, have the different motives that lie behind each act of translation. Dante Gabriel Rossetti shared his views on translation in a preface to his 1861 volume, *The Early Italian Poets*. The only true motive for translating a work of foreign literature, he says, is to provide a fresh nation 'with one more possession of beauty' (Rossetti 1992: 65). Both the idea and the act of translation served as inspiration for Rossetti's entire body of work. Despite the fact that he refers to translation, or a certain form of rhymed translation, as a 'tributary art', his view of translation as a source of new models led the way for the modernist authors, like Pound, who followed in his footsteps.

Translation paradoxically flourished amid the upheavals of twentieth-century Europe. Stefan Zweig, whose books were banned and burned by the Nazis, is said to have been the most translated author of his day; his life and writings were 'translated' to the screen by Wes Anderson in the 2014 film *The Grand Budapest Hotel*. Zweig was also a translator. Writing about his translation of the Belgian symbolist poet Émile Verhaeren, in his autobiography, *The World of Yesterday*, he stresses the importance of 'service'. Although it cost him two years to serve Verhaeren, he concludes that the 'moral task' had a dual benefit, not only to the man whose work he translated but to himself: 'In all sacrificing service there is more assurance for the beginner than in his own creation, and nothing that one has ever done with devotion is done in vain' (1964 [c. 1943]). Boris Pasternak, laureate of the 1958 Nobel Prize in literature, took refuge in translation and earned a living as a translator of Shakespeare and Goethe's *Faust* when he was under attack by the Soviet regime and his original work was not being published. He used translation as a tool to 'exact some sly revenge', taking advantage of the revision of his translation of *Hamlet* to slip in harsh words about the political situation in his own country (Finn and Couvée 2014: 60). While deliberately hijacking translation in this way, he affirmed the importance and feasibility of translation: 'Translations are conceivable because for centuries before our time whole literatures have translated one another; translations are not a method of becoming acquainted with individual works, but a medium for the age-old intercourse of cultures and peoples' (Pasternak 1976: 97).

The ultimate examples of writers who translate are the self-translators, among whom Samuel Beckett and Nancy Huston stand out for the ease with which they have both composed and translated their own work both from and into their mother tongues (or rewritten it in the other language).[3] Since the later twentieth century, eminent translation scholars have illustrated the way in which translation practice can nourish and complement theoretical reflection. The Belgian André Lefevere and Israeli Gideon Toury are but two such cases.[4] A recent publication, *Writing Translators, Translators Writing*, pursues this thread; it pays tribute to American theorist and practitioner Carol Maier in a collection featuring studies by translation studies scholars – Suzanne Jill Levine and Peter Bush, for instance – who are also actively engaged in the practice of literary translation (Massardier-Kenney, Tymoczko, and Baer 2016).

The case study method employed in *Telling the Story of Translation* has inevitably involved a selection of specific examples. Other choices might have been possible, some of which have been the subject of previous studies. A number of scholars have already addressed the fascinating case of Ezra Pound; Joyce and other modernist writers are well known and have been amply investigated.[5] Shaw, Stein, and Auster, on the other hand, are ones who have achieved relatively little recognition within the sphere of translation. Their work as translators has been only incidentally scrutinized by literary scholars, and their practice and theorization of translation have not received the attention they deserve from the translation studies community. Yet translation does occupy an important place in their literary careers, and an exploration of those careers will further our understanding of the intersection of language and culture in the modern era.

While quite distinct in provenance, in ideology, and in literary styles, Shaw, Stein, and Auster share similar traits. Each of them either originated in or moved in multilingual spaces, where they were engaged in the dialectic of the familiar and the foreign, of mother tongue and alien languages, and in the problematization of the self in contact with others. All three have been involved in translating the other and in 'translating' themselves not only literally but in the metaphorical (geographical) sense. Shaw left the 'cultural as well as economic and political backwater' that was Dublin at the time (Gibbs 2005: 6) to move to London, although he remained essentially an Irishman as well as an internationalist. Stein spent over half her life in self-imposed exile, navigating between America, her 'country', and Paris, her 'home town'. Auster, like Stein, spent considerable time as an apprentice expatriate writer in Paris before settling in cosmopolitan Brooklyn.

They are acclaimed and prodigious writers. The designation 'literary decathlete', coined in relation to Auster, could equally be applied to the other two.[6] Literary giants, they have all tried their hand at a variety of genres; they have expounded upon a range of subjects, with confidence, some might say arrogance, but always with an air of authority. Shaw is the only author to have won both a Nobel Prize and an Academy Award, Stein was notorious for her salon and experimental writing until *The Autobiography of Alice B. Toklas* made her truly famous as a writer, and Auster has seen his widely celebrated work translated into more than forty languages.

Each of the writers discussed in the book is linked in one way or another to Rossetti's declaration. While busy churning out a vast *œuvre*, they have nonetheless, at some time or another, devoted time to both the practice and conceptualization of translation. We may well ask why. Their motives, although different, converge in ways that have the potential to shed light on key aspects of literature and translation alike. Taken together, they also point the way to a teleology of translation, which poses the question: *What is translation for?* For the writers themselves, translation is a productive starting point, a means of flexing one's creative muscles. Writers have always regarded translation as an exercise, as a prelude to and preparation for original work, in short as *pre-text*. Alternatively, they have seen it as a *pretext* for something else, as a way of paying tribute to an admired foreign writer, as an infusion of elements of a foreign culture into their own culture, or as a mechanism for strengthening personal or collective identity. Just as translation affords opportunities for individual training, it helps, on a collective level, to build the resources of the receiving language, literature, and culture. Introducing foreign objects of beauty serves to enrich a national literature and language, and to broaden the horizons of its authors and readers. In the words of critic Israel Cohen, writing about the development of modern Hebrew, translation 'forges the national language, hammers it, forces it to scour its treasures, to plumb its depths, to find equivalent expressions'.[7]

This book delves into the complex lives and extensive bibliographies of these mega-figures in the history of modernist writing and translation, yielding insights into the act of translation, how it plays out, what it means, and how it is interpreted. The book focuses on the person, but the narrative moves from the purely biographical level to an approach that takes into account the broader context in which these writers operated. Attention is paid not only to their specific reasons for translating, and the ways in which they viewed the translation process, but also to their insertion within specific linguistic, aesthetic, and cultural communities, and to their movement within what has been referred to as the 'world republic of letters' (Casanova 2007). Sociological aspects are also considered: the writer-translators as agents, examined in association with the acolytes, facilitators, and other agents in their entourage, all operating within specific fields that were to greater or less degrees receptive to the introduction of foreign works by means of translation.

The following chapters will highlight the position of the Self in relation to the Other, and the role of translation in this negotiation. I propose a reading of their texts, including a sampling of translated texts and their originals, not so much for the purpose of evaluating the skill of each translator or the adequacy (according to the age-old criterion of faithfulness) of the translation as to indicate the approach that the translator has taken in each case. I also offer a close reading of texts in which the authors reflect on translation. With the development of translation studies as a discipline in its own right, and in the wake of new contributions to literary studies more generally, translational discourse has taken on new importance. The paratext is no longer a place in which the 'poor drudge' of a translator offers excuses (apologies for not finding exact equivalents, I will do better next time, etc.), but rather a medium for presenting the ideological and aesthetic parameters underlying the translation

(Simon 2000).[8] In other words, translation strategy aside (e.g. opting for either 'foreignization' or 'domestication' or 'transparent' translation, to use Venuti's terms), these texts serve to give the translator an opportunity to become more 'visible'.[9]

Self-reflexivity is the hallmark of all three subjects. Shaw, Stein, and Auster are writers writing about writing, at the same time questioning the status, authority, and legitimacy of the translator. In his translation, *Jitta's Atonement*, for example, Shaw makes writing the subject of the drama; 'forty years before Roland Barthes', as Gahan observes, 'Shaw is predicating his play on "the death of the author"' (2004: 155).[10] In addition to embedding such reflections in the literary work itself, all three writers are fond of stepping up to the podium. They take the floor and express themselves in a wide range of paratextual material – prefaces, interviews, lectures, correspondence – in which they comment on their work, and at the same time craft their identities as translator-authors, thereby pushing back the boundaries between translation and writing. The 'self' is larger than life for Shaw, who viewed himself as omniscient and omnipotent. As one reviewer commented: 'For him the world's not a stage but the big top with the three rings. His only regret is that he cannot cut his capers and perform his tricks in all three rings at the same time' (*The New York Times* 1926: 2). He endeavoured to exercise control over the work of his biographers and translators, trying (in vain) to hang on to the denouement of his plays as they were being deflected, refracted, and adapted for the stage and screen. Gertrude Stein declared herself a genius, using the literary device of putting words into Alice B. Toklas's mouth, and then went on tour of her native USA, explaining what her writing was about. Paul Auster has repeatedly told his life story in fiction, essays, and memoirs, in the first person, the second person, and the third person – to get it right.

Self-fashioning, an idea articulated by Stephen Greenblatt (1980) in relation to the Renaissance, and pursued by Jérôme Meizoz (2007), who formulates notions of *posture de l'auteur* and *mise en scène*, is a useful concept that applies to all three of our authors, who are preoccupied with positioning themselves in relation to other literary figures and literary norms. They work hard at resisting their *habitus* and shaping their authorial personae, fashioning an image, or even myth, of themselves as writers.[11] In each case, the figure of the translator is woven into these tapestries of authorial identity. Thus the book pays special attention to the phenomenon of translation in the authors' *own words*, from their perspective, accompanied, in addition, by an inquiry into the reception or afterlife of their translations.

The writer's space

Just as Gertrude Stein considered her translation of Georges Hugnet a 'different way to write', translation, at the hands of these writers, is perhaps a 'different way to translate'. Because of a certain tradition of subservience, translators have been reluctant to adopt an authorial stance. Writers, on the other hand, even when involved in the act of translation, are more inclined to be authorial, or 'author-itative'. Whether commenting on translation, generally, or their own particular translation efforts – as in Shaw's prefaces, Stein's autobiographies, or Auster's prefaces or interviews – they do so as writers. In other words, they take advantage of the writer's space to tell a story, which allows them the freedom to construct their personalities as writers, and to present the act of translation in ways that are different from 'regular' translators. Writers give themselves permission to express themselves (*prendre la parole*) in more ways than one: they take more liberties, perhaps, in their translational strategies, and they use their work as translators as a platform for giving voice to their ideas, aesthetics, and personal preoccupations. They take more space; their words spill over into the liminal space of the text. They stretch the boundaries of the translation proper, and in some cases hijack the act of translation to serve their own ends. At the same time – and this is the question posed by our study – they may well be conferring greater prestige on the beleaguered art form, giving it more credibility by virtue of the fact that they, as eminent writers, have taken time out to engage with translation as a literary act in its own right, indicative of the place that translation is taking in the consciousness of artists in an ever more destabilized and hybrid world.

As Shaw, Stein, and Auster tell their stories of translation, they reveal what is to be gained in translation, from personal to cultural enrichment. What also emerges is an occasionally bleak glimpse into what it means to be a translator: tales of loss, counterfeit, separation, hardship, and hard labour. In investigating the various uses (and abuses) of translation at the hands of these distinguished writers, who also bring into play assorted fictions of translation, the studies that follow highlight the shifting relations between author and translator and the evolution of the translator's voice and visibility.

Figure 1 Autographed drawing of G. Bernard Shaw by Edouard Loévy, dated 1908. Reprinted from Hamon's *Le Molière du XXe siècle: Bernard Shaw* (1913).

Lost Masterpieces:
Bernard Shaw and Translation

It is not for me to say how far English drama is indebted to Herr Trebitsch for its present prestige abroad. It **is** *for me to say that my personal debt to him is incalculable....I could do no less than take advantage of the fact that Trebitsch had written plays of his own, to translate one of them from German into English for the man who has translated so many plays from English into German.*

–Bernard Shaw, *Translator's Note*

The author of himself

Bernard Shaw was a prodigious writer, well known for the volume and scope of his work as well as for the breadth of his intellectual faculties. He was born in Dublin on 26 July 1856. By the time of his death, on 2 November 1950, he had produced over sixty plays and a body of work extending over almost forty volumes; in addition, he had generated a correspondence estimated at a quarter of a million letters and postcards. Described as 'a boundary crosser and a polymath' (Switzky 2015: 4), he was not only an influential playwright but a novelist as well; he was a prolific music, art, and drama critic, and a distinguished essayist who took up the major issues of his time. Not averse to mounting a soapbox at Speaker's Corner in Hyde Park, he expressed boldly and publicly his sometimes radical, often eccentric, ideas on politics, economics, religion, and the arts.[1]

Yet, despite his biographer's claim that he 'added to his other areas of expertise the art of translation' (Holroyd 1989: 50), Shaw is noticeably absent from the roster of writers associated with translation. His 'Translator's Note' has not been reprinted or cited in any of the principal anthologies of writings on translation; nor has it been listed in bibliographies pertaining to translation. Shaw is referred to only incidentally in what have come to be standard works on translation studies (in the English language at least), such as that of George Steiner, for example – who does cite authors the likes of Goethe, Pound, Nabokov, Gide, Valéry, and Octavio Paz. He is missing from some of the more recent encyclopaedias or 'handbooks' of translation.[2] Shaw's translation of *Frau Gittas Sühne* (*Jitta's Atonement*) by his German translator, Siegfried Trebitsch, as well as his relations with his translators have elicited the interest of Shavian scholars.[3] However, those working in the field of translation have largely ignored Shaw's interest in and engagement with translation.[4]

This chapter fills the gap by examining and contextualizing Shaw's links to translation: his association with his translators, his conceptualization of translation, and his own achievements as a translator. We concentrate, in particular, on his relationship with Trebitsch, whose own story forms an intriguing subplot in the drama of Shaw's life. The ties that Shaw had with some of his other translators are also of note, for he was an author who took a keen interest in how his work was translated, even to the point of interfering with the process. Some twenty years after first meeting Trebitsch, Shaw undertook to translate his translator, and wrote a 'Translator's Note' as a preface. The views expressed therein complement the other nuggets on translating that can be mined from his voluminous body of writing and correspondence. Taken together, they make up a vision of translation that is both complex and sophisticated. Nothing less could be expected from an intellectual of the stature of Bernard Shaw.

Unlike Stein and Auster, who are noted for their self-writing, Shaw did not produce an autobiography as such. His reminiscences and confessions take the form of letters, prefaces, essays, and interviews. The closest he came to authoring an autobiography is a two-volume work intriguingly entitled *Shaw. An Autobiography*; in it, editor Stanley Weintraub presents selections from Shaw's work, including this condemnation of autobiography itself: 'All autobiographies are lies … deliberate lies …. my goods are all in the bookshop window and on the stage' (Weintraub 1969: vol. 1: 2–4). Since his creative work was based on himself and his own life, there was no need for an explicit life story. Yet, in a striking example of the proximity of autobiography and translation, as well as authorial self-fashioning, Shaw was intimately involved in the work of those who attempted to write the story of his life, in much the same way as he tried to control how his work was translated into other languages. He wrote copious letters to his first biographer, Archibald Henderson, and in fact came close to writing the biography himself. He also provided substantial information to subsequent biographers Frank Harris and Hesketh Pearson. Thus Shaw became, in the words of Michael Holroyd, 'the very author of himself' (Holroyd 1988) – a vast, yet not-always-trustworthy, source of insights into his complex links with the art, craft, and idea of translation.[5]

'I know so little German that I have to guess everything'

Astonishing for someone who defined himself as an internationalist, who was well travelled and whose work bore the influence of foreign cultures, Shaw was not well versed in foreign languages. He propagated something of a myth about himself: in his usual self-deprecating way, he would sometimes overestimate his incomprehension or blunders, and then at other times he would exaggerate his command of a foreign language. Archibald Henderson's assessment is typical:

> Indeed, it is one of Mr Shaw's foibles to insist that he is short of many accomplishments which are fairly common, and in some ways an obviously ignorant, stupid and unready man. Certainly it is not a little strange that with all his remarkable knowledge of modern art, music, literature, economics and politics, he speaks no language but his own, and reads no foreign language, save French, with ease. I remember hearing someone ask Rodin whether Shaw really spoke French. 'Ah! no!' replied Rodin, with his genial smile and a faint twinkle of the eyes; 'Monsieur Shaw does not speak French. But somehow or other, by the very violence of his manner and gesticulation, he succeeds in *imposing* his meaning upon you!' (Henderson 1918: 500; emphasis in the original)

Shaw may not have been able to converse in French, but he had a sustained interest in French literature, philosophy, and art. He read Karl Marx's *Das Kapital* in French translation, as well as many well-known French authors in the original. He also took French lessons, resulting in his earliest work for the stage – a small 'playlet' in French called *Un Petit Drame* (Pharand 2000: 1–7).

While Shaw had some knowledge of written French, what he knew of German, by his own admission, did not amount to much: 'I can read French as easily as English; and under pressure of necessity I can turn to account some scraps of German and a little operatic Italian' (Preface to *Misalliance* in *Complete Prefaces* vol. 2: 20). When he announced to Trebitsch that he had begun to translate *Gitta*, he confessed that his principal difficulty had been that he did not know German; undeterred, however, he went ahead, relying on guesswork and instinct (Letter of 15 September 1920, Weiss 1986: 212).[6]

Trebitsch confirms Shaw's lack of proficiency in German; unable to read German himself, Shaw had a secretary who was fluent in German read the play to him and tell him about it (Trebitsch 1953: 263). Shaw was in a position to undertake the translation of Trebitsch's work from German to English, but only with the secretary's literal draft translation to rely on, a dictionary to hand, and a good dose of 'divination'.[7]

Lawrence Langner, who was considering producing *Jitta* in the United States, asked Shaw how he had been able to translate it without knowing German, to which Shaw apparently replied: 'I have a smattering. Besides, translating isn't just a matter of knowing the language. The original play was a tragedy – which was all right for Austria where they like tragic endings – but it would never go that way in England and America, so I turned it into a comedy!' (Langner 1963: 94).

In a posthumous tribute to Shaw, Thomas Mann credits Trebitsch for Shaw's success in Germany, but also points out that the alleged influence of German culture on Shaw is a 'vast exaggeration', quite simply 'meaningless'. And he borrows the following self-satirizing anecdote from Shaw's essay 'What I Owe to German Culture' to emphasize how little German Shaw knew:

> 'Everyone ought to learn German', Shaw said, and he himself was determined to do so. But since he was only fifty-five there was no hurry. He never did learn it, and when Germans who knew no English visited him he would let them talk until they ran out of breath. Then he would put his hand to his heart and say, '*ausgezeichnet*' [excellent]. He did not know what this word meant, he said, tongue in cheek, but it always made the Germans happy. (Mann 1997: 396–7)

Given this level of ineptitude, it is surprising that Shaw became so involved in the work of his translators, and even more so that he actually translated anything himself. The utterances of the theatrical, inscrutable, and mercurial Shaw cannot always be taken at face value, however. The truth lies somewhere in between – between the lines of a linguist who was not as 'hopeless' as he often claimed and who was, moreover, highly sensitive to cultural differences (Pharand 2000: 7–8).[8]

The 'conqueror of the stage throughout the world': Shaw in translation

The meeting that took place between an already middle-aged Shaw, who had yet to make his mark on the London stage, and a younger, eager, but markedly undistinguished man who would be his translator was a 'fortuitous' one – in both senses of the word. It was unexpected, from Shaw's perspective at least, and a fortunate coincidence for both men. While their relationship was fraught from the beginning, it was to pay considerable dividends. Shaw regarded Trebitsch as a 'young lunatic' whereas his translator-to-be looked upon him as a 'crazy Irishman'. The story was told, retold, and to a great extent mythologized by each of these men of letters. Their collaboration over a period of nearly five decades had both ups and downs: high points of loyalty and friendship, in addition to low points ranging from harsh criticism doled out by an increasingly illustrious, and imperious, author to bitter disappointment on the part of the subservient translator. While success did not come easily or immediately, German audiences came to recognize Shaw's importance through Trebitsch's perseverance and efforts. This, in turn, contributed to Shaw's reputation at home. Other translations followed; performances of Shavian drama abroad ensued, although not without some notable twists and turns, disagreements and disputes.

A young lunatic carries the citadel by storm: Shaw's encounter with Trebitsch

Siegfried Trebitsch was born in Vienna on 22 December 1868, to a wealthy, assimilated Jewish family. He frequented the avant-garde group of young intellectuals known as *Jung-Wien* (Young Vienna) or *Die Moderne* (The Moderns), who gathered in the coffeehouses of Vienna in the late nineteenth century, although he does not appear to have occupied a central position within that circle. While working in the family's silk trade business, Trebitsch wrote theatre reviews, along with some fiction and poetry. With the publication of a novella in 1901, entitled *Genesung* (Convalescence), he declared to his family his intention to become a full-time author (Weiss 1986: 5–6).[9]

Trebitsch wrote several accounts of how he became Shaw's translator, beginning with a lecture given in honour of Shaw's seventieth birthday and ending with his autobiography, published after Shaw's death. Over the years, Trebitsch's story was revised, altered, and sometimes embellished. Shaw also contributed his version of events. Despite some discrepancies between versions and inconsistencies of time, season, and so on, the actual events can be reconstructed with some degree of accuracy.[10]

Trebitsch first learned about Shaw through William Archer, Ibsen's English translator and a friend of Shaw. At the suggestion of one of his Viennese colleagues, Trebitsch got in touch with Archer in late 1900, when travelling to London to do business on his father's behalf. He was promptly invited to tea at the National Liberal Club. Archer, according to Trebitsch, had read his theatre reviews and agreed with him that English theatre was disappointing. He urged Trebitsch to look instead into lesser known playwrights. 'The most important writer among them', he said referring to Shaw, 'one with whom I am on terms of close friendship, is a dramatist to his finger-tips, but a West End theatre would never put on a play of his'. At the time, many of Shaw's plays were published, but not performed. Archer recommended three titles and gave Trebitsch the name of a bookshop where they could be found. Trebitsch left for home with three volumes, *Plays Unpleasant, Plays Pleasant*, and *Plays for Puritans*. On the train trip home, he read *Candida*; he then went on to read all ten plays with enthusiasm and resolved to 'campaign' for Shaw in Germany and Austria. Trebitsch realized that he was not going about this in the accustomed manner, something that Shaw acknowledges in his 'Translator's Note'. When a theatrical agent saw a foreign play he considered to be potentially successful in his own country, he would usually purchase the rights and then commission a professional translator to translate the newly acquired foreign work for a fee. Trebitsch, who tried to convince theatrical agents and publishers to take on Shaw's work, was just a translator by default: 'I was not a professional translator, only a cobbler who would not stick to his last'. At first, he encountered only opposition and even derision. As one experienced publisher advised, 'keep your hands off foreign plays that have not the slightest chance of success now or at any other time' (Trebitsch 1953: 95–8).

Trebitsch returned to London and once again met with Archer, who this time provided him with a letter of introduction to Bernard Shaw. Some time in mid-March 1902, Trebitsch appeared at the London residence of Bernard and Charlotte Shaw. Trebitsch recalls first being received by Charlotte Shaw, who chatted with him about matters of little importance, all the while observing him and sizing him up. Shaw then made an 'impatient appearance', having in the meantime read the letter of introduction from Archer. Charlotte disappeared and left the two men alone. Trebitsch took note of Shaw's 'unusual stature', describing his own demeanour as 'shy' as he spoke to Shaw about his plays. Shaw demanded to know what Trebitsch intended to 'do with him'. Trebitsch's reply, as conveyed in his own accounts, is couched in language that belies his alleged shyness: 'I said roundly and boldly that I was determined to translate his plays into German and had set myself the aim of conquering the German stage for him' (Trebitsch 1953: 123).

Charlotte's role as a mediator between Shaw and his German translator was critical. By the time Trebitsch appeared on the scene, Charlotte Shaw was trying to give a new direction to her husband's career by strengthening his position in politics and building his reputation as a playwright abroad (Holroyd 1997: 285). In the absence of theatre royalties or sufficient remuneration as a journalist, Shaw was dependent on his wife's income. Trebitsch was to come along at precisely the right moment. G.B.S. let his wife deal with him: 'Charlotte, here's a young lunatic Archer's sent to whom I won't be able to make see reason! You come and try to calm him down'. After some discussion with the would-be translator, Charlotte is alleged to have said to her husband, 'Why should the German theatre, which has made Shakespeare into a German poet, not also give you the satisfaction that is still denied you in your own country?' Shaw then turned to Trebitsch and exclaimed, 'So you want to be my Schlegel and Tieck, do you?' (Trebitsch 1953: 123–4). They went on to discuss copyright matters, which preoccupied Shaw and of which Trebitsch knew little. Trebitsch had also brought along galley proofs of his first novel in French translation (since he knew that Shaw had little German), and Shaw examined these. A meal was served, although according to some accounts, this did not happen until several days later when Mrs Shaw invited Trebitsch back for lunch.[11]

Trebitsch offered to translate three plays within a year, agreeing that if he had not found a publisher or stage producer for the works within that time, he would hand back the rights to Shaw (Trebitsch 1953: 125). This arrangement was confirmed in a letter to Trebitsch of 10 April 1902, in which Shaw agreed not to sanction the publication or performance of a translation or adaptation by anyone else before April 1903 (Weiss 1986: 7). Both Shaw and Trebitsch were on their way to achieving their goals.

A pilgrimage made with a heavy heart: From original writer to Shaw's translator

Trebitsch's attitude to his task as Shaw's translator and Shaw's reaction to him are expressed in both religious and military terms – Trebitsch uses the term 'pilgrimage' when describing his first meeting with Shaw, while Shaw refers to him as an 'apostle' in the 'Note'. Interestingly, this phraseology has endured, and was used as recently as a 2001 theatre review in which the author states that Trebitsch 'became his young apostle in Europe, helping Shaw conquer the new territory of the Continent' (Levett 2001: 27). This discourse is not uncommon among translators, who have often perceived the work of introducing foreign literature to their own culture as a 'mission'. When Trebitsch says in the above-quoted passage that he was 'determined to translate [Shaw's] plays into German and had set myself the aim of conquering the German stage for him' (Trebitsch 1953: 123), he recalls Baudelaire, who considered Edgar Allan Poe a 'spiritual brother' and saw it as his mission to bring his work to the attention of the French public. The imagery of conquest and warfare in Trebitsch's statements is also noteworthy: 'my first thought was to campaign – at least in Germany and Austria – for this man, in whom I saw an epoch-making personality and the future conqueror of the stage throughout the world' (Trebitsch 1953: 96).

Trebitsch's quixotic behaviour is corroborated by Shaw in his own narrative, which highlights Trebitsch's desire to become his 'interpreter and *apostle* in Central Europe'. G.B.S. underlines his '*explosive* contempt' for the excuses of Mrs Shaw, and his ultimate success in carrying 'the citadel by *storm*' ('Translator's Note', emphasis added). However, by the time he wrote the *Chronicle*, Trebitsch also evoked a certain reticence. In the following excerpt from his autobiography, the dramatization of the event is evident:

> It was with rather a heavy heart that I set out on my pilgrimage to the man whose personal acquaintance I was now positively burning to make. Because of the great distances to be covered in London, one often has time to become hesitant and turn back before reaching one's goal. Shaw was at that time living in Adelphi Terrace, in the heart of that city of so many millions, and I was standing outside his door before my qualms had become clear to me or been settled. When, as I went up the steps, I thought of my own poor plans, for an instant I started back.... An inner voice was still holding me back as I stretched out my hand to the knocker. Then I recalled an infinitely beautiful poetic passage from *Candida* that I had already translated, by way of experiment, into German. This rapidly silenced all my doubts. I felt that a decisive hour had struck in my life, and I knocked at the door. (Trebitsch 1953: 122)

These words contradict Trebitsch's early enthusiasm and reveal the ambivalence that plagued him, later in his career. He had become Shaw's translator, rather than Trebitsch, the writer.

When Trebitsch embarked on his project to translate Shaw, he had no intention of giving up his own literary pursuits. When they first met, he had brought some of his own work to show G.B.S., who encouraged him at various times to continue with his own writing. Furthermore, as Weiss points out, he could not have approached Shaw with such a 'heavy heart' since he had already translated Georges Courteline and Georges Rodenbach: 'I was evidently born with an unusual delight in discovering men of genius' (Trebitsch 1953: 77).

It is true, nonetheless, that Trebitsch's original production declined over the years. After *Frau Gittas Sühne* and a further historical play, he abandoned drama. He attributed this decision not to his own lack of success, but to the risk of endangering his relationship with G.B.S. 'I would not express myself in drama any more', he would write in 1953. 'It would have been bound to lead to the most unpleasant feelings and incidents and would in the end also have imperilled my friendship with Bernard Shaw, if I had gone on submitting plays by both of us' (Trebitsch 1953: 184). After Shaw's Nobel Prize in 1926, Trebitsch was increasingly identified with Shaw. And so, after a half century of devoting himself to the success and promotion of Shaw, as what he terms his 'harbinger' and 'herald', Trebitsch contemplated this 'odd depreciation' and yielded to 'depression'. Forced to admit that his own identity as a writer had been eclipsed, he concluded that his work as a translator had led to negative consequences. 'I was badly cornered', he wrote in his memoirs:

> A horrible expression was coined for referring to me publicly, one that the reviewers cannot bring themselves to drop even to this day. And this expression is 'Shaw's translator'. ... I thought that with my endeavours for Shaw I was adding a plus to my own work, but, alas, it was a minus. (Trebitsch 1953: 272–3)

Toward the end of Shaw's life, Trebitsch tried to go to London to see him. Shaw refused, repeating in more than one letter that he didn't want to see him or anyone else. By this time, Trebitsch had become the 'translator as parasite': in the eyes of some, he had not only blundered his way through the translations of Shaw's body of work, but he had mismanaged Shaw's business in the German-speaking world (Weintraub 1996: 210–11). Thus, a lifetime of collaboration, if not exactly an intimate friendship, ended on an abrupt and sour note.

A roundabout route to success: The reception of the German translations

Trebitsch, then, made an appearance in Shaw's life and met his personal needs at a particularly crucial time. By all accounts, he contributed to Shaw's success abroad and, subsequently, on the London stage. Both Trebitsch and Shaw were inclined to overstate or oversimplify what appears to be Shaw's almost miraculous rise to fame in Austria and Germany. The titles of their essays alone tell the story: Trebitsch's lecture, 'How I Discovered Bernard Shaw', and Shaw's preface to the German edition of his plays, 'What I Owe to German Culture'. But it didn't happen that easily. The agency of a determined Trebitsch as both the 'translator and trumpeter' (Gibbs 2005: 272) of the great Irishman is noteworthy, but other factors were at play. Beyond the *habitus* of each man, beyond the relationship they forged with one another, lie a set of circumstances and a network of individuals and institutions that paved the road along which Bernard Shaw was to make his triumphant entrance into the culture of the German-speaking world, and then his own.

For one thing, Bernard Shaw was known to a certain group in Vienna, not for his literary works, but for his social and political views, a decade before Siegfried Trebitsch began translating and promoting the first three plays. A 'prime example of a writer who links the spheres of art and politics', as Schweiger points out in his study of *fin-de-siècle* Vienna (2005: 145), Shaw had already published articles in political periodicals, and is even credited with having contributed indirectly to the establishment of the first Fabian society in Austria in 1891. Ironically, it was the man who later led the assault against Shaw and his German translator who helped grease the skids for G.B.S. in Vienna.

Dr Leon Kellner (1859–1928) was an erudite Viennese scholar. An English lexicographer, grammarian, and Shakespearian scholar, he had spent time in London where he researched and translated William Caxton for his *habilitation* degree. He wrote literary criticism for the *Frankfürter Zeitung* and was a professor at the University of Czernowitz until the beginning of the First World War. Prevented from occupying a chair at the University of Vienna because of his Zionist activities, he became a translator for the president of the Austrian Republic. Every year, Kellner would return to England for two months. There, he was introduced to the Fabian Society by Bernard Shaw and became acquainted with influential intellectuals, such as William Archer, who were also in Shaw's circle. He brought Shaw to the attention of the Viennese readership in the early 1890s when he wrote about the Fabians in the *Neue Freie Presse*, a liberal newspaper. These articles were to lead to the initiation of a Viennese Fabian Society, which included among its members the editors of the paper *Die Zeit*, in which Shaw published his first article in German, 'Die Illusionen des Socialismus' (The Illusions of Socialism) in 1896 (Schweiger 2005: 136–7).[12]

Kellner had written the first article in German on Shaw in 1899. He had also offered to translate some of his work. Shaw did not accept the offer on the grounds that he preferred to find someone to translate his entire *œuvre*, rather than isolated works (Letter to Archer of 7 June 1906, *Letters* vol. 2: 626).[13] Kellner was to become one of Trebitsch's most vehement critics, although he was not the only one. In the words of Crawford, Shaw's rejection of Kellner's advances, followed by the appearance of an 'approved candidate', set off a 'heavy assault by a rat pack led by a pedantic scholar ... a clamorous cabal of which Kellner was kingpin' (2000: 180).

But the ground had been laid for the introduction of the crazy Irishman into the culture of Vienna and then Berlin. There was already a place for Shaw in the literary and cultural field of Vienna when Trebitsch published his first article on Shaw in the *Neue Freie Presse* – the same newspaper that had run Kellner's piece on Shaw several years earlier. He then translated *The Devil's Disciple*, *Candida*, and *Arms and the Man* and circulated the plays among publishers, theatrical people and producers. After some hurdles, Trebitsch succeeded: the Raimund Theater in Vienna agreed to stage *The Devil's Disciple* (*Teufelskerl*) in February 1903. That same year, all three plays were brought out by the Stuttgart publishing house Cotta as *Drei Dramen von Bernard Shaw*. In 1904, the Deutsches Volkstheater in Vienna produced *Candida* and *Arms and the Man*.

Trebitsch had thus fulfilled his initial obligation to Shaw. As he would later recall, Shaw was pleased that he had kept his word; they then entered into a lifetime partnership, dedicated to building Shaw's reputation (Trebitsch 1953: 130). Within the next three years, *You Never Can Tell*, *Mrs Warren's Profession*, and *Man and Superman* were produced in German by leading directors. Trebitsch went on to introduce the German-speaking public to almost the entire body of Shaw's literature.

'A donkey of a translator'

Trebitch's work as a translator was by his own admission more hurried and superficial than it should have been (Trebitsch 1953: 130). This pace, coupled with his lack of familiarity with colloquial English and English culture and customs, contributed to a number of errors. Despite his resolve to produce a new edition eventually, his blunders sparked a debate in the German-language press about the quality of his translations.

Kellner was the first to attack Trebitsch's translations. In an article entitled 'Eine verunglückte Übersetzung' (An Unsuccessful Translation), published on 22 January 1903 in the *Neues Wiener Tagblatt*, he singled out numerous errors in the first German edition of *The Devil's Disciple*, *Candida*, and *Arms and the Man*. Criticism of the Shaw translations was to continue throughout the decade. Shaw consoled Trebitsch by laughing off Kellner's reaction, but in a letter dated 26 January 1903, he also admitted that the criticism was justified and advised his translator not to reply (Weiss 1986: 38–40).

Do not think me unfeeling – but I have laughed myself almost into hysterics over Kellner's onslaught … A reply to Kellner is impossible, because he is perfectly right on the points which admit of argument. You cannot *prove* that your translation is artistically good, any more than you can prove that Rembrandt was a great painter. Artistic qualities are matters of taste.

'You made the mistakes', Shaw goes on to say in the same letter, 'and you made an enemy at the same time. To remedy this you must not lie awake and get neuralgia; you must correct the mistakes and disarm the enemy'. He suggested that instead of reacting to the review in writing, Trebitsch offer, in the 'grand style of fighting', to purchase Kellner's copy of the plays, corrections included, so that he could use them in preparing the next edition. The preface to the revised edition would then include the following acknowledgement: 'I am indebted to Dr Leon Kellner, who was the first to draw the attention of the German readers to the works of Bernard Shaw, and whose knowledge of contemporary English local life and political organization is unrivalled, for several important corrections in this edition' (Weiss 1986: 38–40). It is ironic, but completely in character for Shaw, to want to disarm his adversary while giving him his due, recognizing the role that Kellner had in fact played by ensuring the success of Trebitsch's efforts to launch an Anglo-Irish playwright.

Shaw did not shrink from entering the fray himself, however. On 22 February 1903, one month after Kellner's article and just as *The Devil's Disciple* was about to open in Vienna, he published a piece in *Die Zeit* entitled 'Ein Teufelskerl: Selbstkritik' ('A Devil of a Fellow: Self-Criticism'), to which we return below. Kellner responded with a clever portrait of Shaw, but continued to dismiss Trebitsch as an 'idle Fifth-former'. In 1911, after the publication of a revised edition of Shaw's plays, Kellner conceded that Trebitsch had developed a 'certain command' of his craft, although he was still too literal and insufficiently colloquial. Other critics, including Max Meyerfeld, Oscar Wilde's German translator, continued to critique Trebitsch's work as a translator and to produce lists of errata (Weiss 1986: 11).

Shaw was well aware of the deficiencies of Trebitsch's translations. In the early stages, as he points out in a letter to Archer of 7 June 1906, Trebitsch rushed through and was not well acquainted with certain aspects of British society. Nevertheless, Shaw felt that he needed to declare publicly his satisfaction with the translations, having learned from Archer's experience that the case against Trebitsch rested on mistakes that did not matter rather than on actual incompetence. He also blamed the hostility toward Trebitsch on envy on the part of the attackers, whom he considered 'would-be rival translators' (*Letters*, vol. 2: 626–7).

In a preface to the 1911 German edition of his collected plays, entitled 'Was ich der deutschen Kultur verdanke' ('What I Owe to German Culture'), Shaw offers his strongest defence of Trebitsch. He expresses 'exasperation' at insinuations that he has derived his own thought from Schopenhauer and Nietzsche, but he does recognize a deep debt to German music, citing Bach, Mozart, Beethoven and Wagner, for example. He expresses sympathy for his 'friend the translator', who has 'expiated the crime of having discovered my works and made them successful in Germany by suffering all the insults and misunderstandings which afflict an original author complicated by the disparagements which fall on the head of the translator' (Shaw 1970: 15). He concludes with the following tribute:

> [T]here is no man in Europe to whom I am more deeply indebted or with whom I feel happier in all our relations, whether of business, or art, or of personal honor and friendship. And I conclude this long preface by my best bow to the German nation, and a very cordial shake-hands with Siegfried Trebitsch. (Shaw 1970: 16)

The attacks on Trebitsch's work persisted, as did Shaw's public support of the translator and routine dismissal of his critics as envious. As late as 1925, in an unsigned open letter to Shaw, the writer (presumed to be Meyerfeld) says, 'You were informed time and again fifteen years ago from the most competent sources that your plays were not translated but Trebitsched' (Weiss 1986: 13). Yet by the 1920s, every play Trebitsch translated opened to 'vast plaudits' in Germany and Austria. By the end of the 1920s, Shaw had acquired the 'status of a German classic'. His plays were studied and performed throughout the German-speaking countries. Trebitsch greeted this success with his characteristic ambivalence, for it signalled his own failure to earn a reputation as an author in his own right.

After the hiatus resulting from the Second World War, Shaw's plays, in Trebitsch's German translations, were welcomed enthusiastically. Shaw regained popularity in both East and West Germany, although praised in each of the countries for different ideological virtues. The culmination of Trebitsch's efforts was a collected edition of Shaw's plays and prefaces issued by the Swiss publisher Artemis.

Trebitsch tells the story of how he was nearly awarded an honorary degree by the University of Oxford. His candidacy was put forward by Professor

Hermann G. Fiedler, Professor of German Language and Literature, on the grounds that he had discovered Bernard Shaw and brought him to the attention of Central Europe. Unanimous approval was required. Eleven voted in favour and one against. The person who cast the dissenting ballot regarded Shaw as a playwright who had 'made it his life's work to expose and ridicule our manners and customs, our way of living, our way of thinking, in short, to ridicule and expose us English and all we stand for, at every opportunity'. Trebitsch, in sum, was a candidate who had done only harm in promoting Shaw (Trebitsch 1953: 209).

Why Shaw put up with such a bad translator remains somewhat of a mystery. Weintraub, among the harshest critics of Shaw's translators, portrays Trebitsch as 'a donkey of a translator' and a 'writer of stupefying mediocrity' (1996: 211). However, Trebitsch's alleged blunders or awkward dialogue notwithstanding, he did contribute to the success of Shaw abroad and, indirectly, at home. His accuracy improved through successive revisions, and by the end of his career he had earned respect as Shaw's translator. Thanks to Trebitsch's translations, Germany came to recognize the literary value of Shaw, whose fame in England came to him only by a 'roundabout route', as Thomas Mann so famously remarked. In addition to the agency of Trebitsch, Mann points out, the literary and cultural field in the German-speaking world had been more 'receptive' to Shaw's drama than England was at the time, complementing the ideological affinities shown above between Shaw and noted intellectuals in Austria and Germany.

> Germany recognized his importance to the modern stage, indeed to modern intellectual life as a whole, earlier than the English-speaking world. His fame actually reached England only by way of Germany, just as Ibsen and Hamsun conquered Norway, and Strindberg Sweden, by the same roundabout route ... for the simple reason that at that time the German stage was ahead of its British counterpart ... less frozen in the bourgeois mould, more receptive to new things. (Mann 1997: 396)

Augustin Hamon partage toutes mes idées politiques: Shaw's French translators

In the 'Translator's Note', which he wrote when he was on the brink of receiving the Nobel Prize in literature, Shaw says that he was able to attract a hundred translators ('Note', 4). That was not always the case. Yet, preoccupied as he was with the business of writing, Shaw had always known how important it was to have translators. As he points out in a 1904 letter to Trebitsch, a book needed to be translated within ten years of publication for the author to be able to secure copyright (Weiss 1986: 73). Once his partnership with Trebitsch was under way, Shaw set out to find translators in other countries, even underwriting the costs of publication himself in some cases in order to protect his copyright, although he was not averse to turning down prospective translators if he sensed that they would not make a commitment to producing versions of all his work in a foreign language. He had already rejected Kellner's offer to translate some of his work, and had also refused to grant Count Auguste Gilbert de Voisins, French writer and translator of Robert Browning, permission to translate *Arms and the Man*.

Looking whenever possible for a man with an English or American wife, he chose his translators 'eccentrically', because they 'charmed him, touched his sense of humour or presented impeccable political credentials'. One such choice was his French translator, Augustin Hamon, who was not a man of letters but who would indeed be assisted by his rather more fluent wife. In the words of Henderson, 'Few odder things have ever happened in the history of the theatre than Shaw's pouncing on Hamon, who was no more concerned with the theatre than with polar exploration, and much less interested in it, and forcing him to take up the rôle of a French Bernard Shaw' (1932: 824). Thus, Hamon joined Trebitsch as one of the principal members of Shaw's 'family of translators over whom he exercised great power and generosity' (Holroyd 1997: 288–90). Once the Hamons became his authorized translators, Shaw looked after them, providing them with a house at Port Blanc en Penvénan, in Hamon's native Brittany, where they spent the next four decades translating his works (Pharand 2000: 106).[14]

Augustin Hamon (1862–1945) was a social psychologist who embraced contemporary anarchist, socialist and communist tendencies. He had sent Shaw a copy of his book, *Psychologie du militaire professionnel*, which may have inspired Shaw's antimilitaristic play *Arms and the Man*. After the assassination of French President Sadi Carnot in 1894, Hamon's anarchist views put him in a vulnerable position, and he fled to London. He met Shaw at a Fabian congress there in 1894. After returning to France, Hamon asked Shaw to contribute an article to his journal, *L'Humanité nouvelle*. Instead of writing a new piece, Shaw proposed the essay that had already appeared in *Die Zeit*, 'The Illusions of Socialism'; the piece was published in 1900, in a French translation by Henriette-Marie-Hortense Rynenbroeck, a Belgian who was to become Hamon's wife the following year. This marked a turning point in the precarious life and career of the Hamons. At a time when the journal was failing and their financial prospects deteriorating, Shaw asked the Hamons to translate his body of work into French. Desperate, Hamon took on a task for which he was fundamentally unsuited (Pharand 2000: 101–2).[15]

Shaw was attracted by the political orientation of his French translators, and less concerned by their linguistic inadequacy and potential marginalization. He acquired a dictionary, as he had done to lend Trebitsch a hand, with a view to becoming what Holroyd has called a 'co-translator of his plays into the French language' (1997: 289). Hamon did his best, setting out to become the interpreter and collaborator of his English-speaking author: 'Le traducteur devient interprète de l'auteur, altérant en somme le texte pour conserver l'esprit. C'est une vraie collaboration' (quoted in Pharand 2000: 104). Although Hamon says that he aims to retain the spirit while changing the text, or the wording, it is interesting to note the echo of Cicero's term, *fides interpres*, signifying a literal, or word-for-word, translator in opposition to the *orator*, or sense-for-sense translator. Hamon was attacked precisely for his literal and hence awkward translations.[16]

Shaw would laboriously revise and annotate the French translations, which the translators would then re-revise and return to him. He was as critical of Hamon as he was of Trebitsch, pointing out the importance of adapting the language of the play, but of making a text that could be spoken and performed on stage. At one point, he offered Hamon the following admonition:

> Remember that the great failing of the Frenchman is his respect for the academic. Every Frenchman is a born pedant. He thinks it a crime to repeat a word – the crime of tautology. He wants to have in every sentence a subject, a predicate, a noun, a verb, a complete grammatical structure. Now on the stage, where the word is spoken, and so much depends on the way it is spoken, grammatical completeness does not matter at all. If a string of interjections or broken phrases will give the meaning, so much the better. So far from its being a crime to repeat words and phrases, it is the worst of crimes to vary them, since the effect is often lost by doing so. Ne cherchez pas le style: cherchez toujours la vie. (Letter to Hamon of 4 December 1906, *Letters* vol. 2: 664)

Shaw not only corrected the Hamons' version but also provided meticulous explanations to help them grasp the meaning of his rich and varied language, including literary and biblical references, puns and colloquial expressions. Hamon's wife, who had a better command of English than he did, did much of the translation work, although she 'remained a silent partner, while poor Augustin was bombarded by Shaw's queries and corrections' (Pharand 2000: 113–4).

Hamon was regarded as conscientious, but he was judged to be plodding and, despite his avowed intentions, unable to convey the spirit of the original (Moore 1933: 191). Like Trebitsch, the Hamons were criticized for more than just inelegant translation; they committed actual errors of meaning and misinterpreted many of Shaw's ideas. Critics also found that the literal translations the Hamons produced failed to capture the fine points of Shaw's style, humour and wit. Hamon is said to have been surprised when his translation of *Candida* elicited laughter from Belgian and French audiences, so insensitive was he to the humour in Shaw's script (Grindea 1956: 4). Through a complex back-and-forth process, Hamon and his wife submitted successive versions to Shaw for editing, correcting, and repeated revisions, without producing a satisfactory end-product. Rather, these multiple revisions resulted in a text that ultimately remained 'ambiguous and confusing' (Pharand 2000: 109).

Not only did Hamon and his wife translate Shaw's plays – albeit with errors – they acted as agents on his behalf. Less effective than Trebitsch, they nonetheless played a role in having the plays staged and in promoting Shaw's reputation. Hamon is credited with bringing about Shaw's first French-language production, a performance of *Candida* that took place at the Théâtre du Parc in Brussels. Hamon extended his activities to lectures in both Brussels and Paris, and also wrote essays, reviews, and promotional texts in newspapers and other publications. In 1913, Hamon published a collection of lectures he had given at the Sorbonne. The very title of his book puts Shaw on an equal footing with France's favoured playwright: *Le Molière du XXe siècle: Bernard Shaw.*[17] The letter he addresses to Shaw ('Épître Dédicatoire'), which serves as a preface to the book, summarizes his efforts to promote G.B.S. (1913: 8–13). Hamon's dedication has been described in religious terms, not unlike the way in which Trebitsch's devotion to Shaw has been portrayed. Grindea calls the Hamons' undertaking a 'fierce crusade aimed at introducing the Shavian gospel into France and Belgium' (1956: 5) and Pharand refers to Hamon's Molière book as 'the apex of his Shaviolatry' (2000: 119). Shaw, however, soon became concerned about the kind of image his translators were projecting. Anxious to control his reputation in the same way as he oversaw the translations of his work, he warned Hamon about 'distorting his views' (Pharand 2000: 118).

And yet Shaw clung to his translators. His devotion to Hamon was ideological at the outset. Shaw shared Hamon's dedication to reforming society and felt, naively, that these common objectives would somehow translate into a faithful translation: 'Monsieur Augustin Hamon *partage toutes mes idées politiques. Il ne saurait donc me trahir*' (Augustin Hamon shares all my political ideas. He is therefore incapable of being unfaithful to me) (quoted in Grindea 1956: 5; emphasis in the original). Hamon expresses the same thought in his 'Épître Dédicatoire': 'Vous vouliez un traducteur qui fit mentir le proverbe "*Traduttore, traditore*", qui pût rendre toute l'âme révolutionnaire de votre œuvre' (You wanted a translator who would disprove the proverb '*Traduttore, traditore*', who would render the true revolutionary spirit of your work) (1913: 5). However, as with Trebitsch, the bond was also emotional: Shaw entered into an ambivalent 'love-hate relationship' with his translators. While critical in his private correspondence, he showed unusual loyalty, generosity and a paternal protectiveness toward Hamon and his wife. Above all, he felt compelled to defend his translators against all criticism.

According to an oft-quoted anecdote, the Vicomte Robert d'Humières, a dramatist and translator of Conrad and Kipling, and stage director for the theatre where *Candida* was presented in May 1908, sent Shaw a list of corrections and proposed revisions. Shaw replied, thanking the Vicomte, but insisting that the final decision regarding revisions should rest with Hamon. This prompted d'Humières's famous line: Shaw is 'attached' to his translators 'like a criminal is attached to the rope which hanged him'; this 'defiant and heroic act' would prove to be a 'suicide on the threshold of our admiration' (Henderson 1956: 497, n. 6).[18]

Indeed, despite his sustained interest in the literature, philosophy, drama, and art of France, despite his efforts to cultivate and mentor his French translators, Shaw was not well received in that country. The translations met with widespread criticism from theatre critics as well as other writers. In Langner's words, 'Shaw had been so badly translated into French by his authorized translators that his plays were seldom given in France, but his loyalty to these translators was so great that it was impossible to have better versions made by other translators' (1963: 96).

Shaw contributed to this situation by being provocative and by making disparaging remarks about the French. *The New York Times* calls him a literary '*fumiste*' (charlatan) – of which there were both French and foreign examples and with which the French public was well acquainted – citing the posters that announced the 1912 Paris premiere of *La Profession de Madame Warren*:

> Paris is always the last city in the world to discover and accept an author or composer of international reputation. London is twenty-five years behind

the times and Paris is ten years behind London. Paris is a marvelous city. But Parisians have not yet discovered Paris. It is not surprising, then, that they have not yet discovered me. In ten years, they will discover me. (Sanborn 1912)[19]

In short, 'the Irish Molière got the translators he deserved – although not the translations the French, or Shaw himself, required' (Pharand 2000: 128). Unable to gain the respect of the French, Shaw responded with arrogance and even rudeness. Despite the extensive efforts of his French translators, consequently, there were few Parisian productions of Shaw's plays – a 'mere baker's dozen… principally in coterie theatres… with abbreviated runs' (Crawford 2000: 185). *Sainte-Jeanne* appears to have been an exception. It was a hit in Paris in 1925, obviously because of the subject matter but mainly because of alterations made by its producers (Grindea 1956: 6).

'Infamous impostors': Shaw and his other translators

Shaw's translators were the subject of continual criticism and, generally, he seemed to take a certain delight in shrugging off the attacks. 'It is always the same song', he wrote in a letter to Trebitsch on 10 December 1919, apparently in response to an article by a Viennese journalist:

> Trebitsch, Vallentin [Sweden], Brouta [Spain], Hevesi [Hungary], Hamon [France], Agresti [Italy] are all infamous impostors: how can I possibly allow my works to be so horribly misrepresented? I always cut this sort of thing short exactly as the Viennese journalist describes, by saying 'I know what you are going to tell me. I have heard it all before. Every living German thinks that he, and he alone, should translate my plays; and therefore every living German agrees that Trebitsch's translations are atrocious. No doubt they are not translations at all. He writes original plays, and puts my name to them. But as they seem to please the German public, and make money for me, I let him have his own way.' I cannot argue with a German about his own language; and so I make fun of it… (Weiss 1986: 208)

Shaw may well have been right to detect jealousy on the part of the critics. He was also perceptive, as the words below indicate, in attributing the successful reception of translations of his work to the power exercised by individual translators (Agresti, Vallentin, Hevesi, Musek) and to their status within the literary circles of their respective countries. This illustrates how keenly Shaw was able to perceive the complex ways in which translation is inscribed within a specific cultural and social context, although it also reveals his blindness to the fundamental weakness of some of his translators.

> All this has become very tedious to me because I have been through it so often. Trebitsch, my German translator, had articles and books written showing that his translations were an European scandal.... Exactly the same thing is happening now in Spain. My translator Brouta, after waiting for many years, suddenly found himself attacked by a conspiracy to oust him now that my affairs in Spain are beginning to move at last ... I have escaped this in Italy only because Agresti, being on the staff of La Tribuna, could revenge himself signally on both the cliques and the publishers if they attacked him; and the same thing saved me in Sweden, where the late Hugo Vallentin, being the editor of a satirical paper, and a man of influence, could have wiped the floor with any literary assailant. Hevesi in Budapest, and Musek in Prague, are powerful in the theatre; and the cliques, with their desks full of unacted (and mostly unactable) plays, are on their knees to them. But in every case where the translator is not feared in this way the story is always the same. (Letter to Hamon of 26 July 1922, *Letters* vol. 3: 779–80)

Shaw supported his translators in various ways, not the least of which was financial. 'I have now invested more money in Poland than I am likely ever to get back', he wrote to his Polish translator, Floryan Sobieniowski (Letter of 26 September 1924, *Letters* vol. 3: 883). Sobieniowski was somewhat of a scoundrel, known to have committed fraud and blackmail. But he did contribute to Shaw's triumph on the Polish stage. *Pygmalion*, which opened in a Polish version at Warsaw's Teatr Polski one month before its first London performance, was a great success, and Shaw also authorized the Polski to stage the world premiere of *The Apple Cart (Wielki Kram)* on 14 June 1929. The theatre gave nearly a thousand performances of his plays, although almost none were published, as was the case in other European countries (Crawford 2000: 195).[20]

The question remains, though: why did Shaw suffer such bad translators? It may have stemmed from his 'obsessive need to control', as Peters puts it.

> Had he hired talented translators, his plays might have slipped out of his hands, taking on – as with all good translations – artistic lives of their own. With Trebitsch and Hamon he could play the schoolmaster, correcting and recorrecting their work, certain that his version would remain the work of genius. Shaw put up with an execrable biographer [Henderson] for the same reason .... (Peters 1997: 260)

Despite it all, Shaw's influence extended across Europe to audiences in Scandinavia, Spain, Italy, Hungary, and Russia. Shaw's stable of translators was populated by colourful characters who worked on his behalf, including the effective Hugo Vallentin, who was equipped with an American wife and who lived close enough to Shaw's London residence to be able to consult with the playwright in person, as Crawford (2000) shows in his detailed survey of Shaw's translators. Through the 1920s and 1930s, Shaw continued to pay close attention to his translation commitments, until he gradually turned over his affairs to agents in different parts of the world. By the late 1930s, when he was eighty, he was beginning to let go. His work was being translated into around fifty languages and dialects and, by the end of the Second World War, he had transferred his foreign licensing to the Society of Authors to administer on his behalf on a commission basis (Crawford 2000: 195–6).

On the threshold: Shaw on translation

Shaw expressed himself in myriad liminal texts, which served to mediate the interactions between his readers and his work. He published articles, maintained a copious correspondence, and made use of the page to complement the stage by means of his signature prefaces and notoriously elaborate stage directions. He took advantage of every kind of paratextual space available to comment on his work and articulate his views, at times in rather contradictory ways. His perceptions of translation are no exception: they emerge from a disparate set of writings that were contemporaneous with the foreign-language versions of his work at which his translators were labouring away, as well as the English translation he himself set out to do of one of Trebitsch's plays.[21]

Self-criticism

Shaw published an article about his relations with Trebitsch scarcely more than a year after meeting Trebitsch and only three days before *The Devil's Disciple*, Shaw's first play in the German language, was to open at the Raimund Theater in Vienna. With a title that plays on the word 'devil', 'Ein Teufelskerl: Selbstkritik' ('Devil of a Fellow: Self-Criticism'), the article devilishly turns the notion of self-criticism on its head.[22]

Shaw begins, modestly, by admitting that his plays will not be to everyone's taste. In answer to the possible question of why, then, his plays should be produced on a foreign stage, he lays the blame, so to speak, on Trebitsch. This is Shaw's first attempt to describe his encounter with the Viennese gentleman who quite unexpectedly called on him demanding authorization to translate his plays into German. In this version, which is not entirely consistent in small matters of detail with other versions, Shaw describes Trebitsch's initial meeting with Mrs Shaw, who explains copyright issues to the would-be translator and then invites him to return for lunch. On this second occasion, Trebitsch meets Shaw and then wins him over, or rather 'crushes' him.

In a brilliant piece of self-promotion, quite the opposite of 'self-criticism', Shaw puts words in the mouth of his newly acquired acolyte. Thus, appearing to be totally humble and 'guiltless', Shaw is able to cleverly proclaim himself to be an important playwright of outstanding talent, in much the same way as Gertrude Stein would later adopt the voice of her companion, Alice B. Toklas, to support her own claim to being a genius. Shaw writes:

> I never resist a man who is in earnest. [Trebitsch] professed strong conviction that I am a writer of European importance, a stimulating thinker, a fascinating playwright, with a magic touch in the theatre and a profound insight into human character and destiny. In this I most fully agreed with him. Such an opinion seemed to me to stamp him as a man of rare and penetrating judgment. He has my fullest authority to propagate his views about me in all the German-speaking countries and elsewhere. I am too modest to say such things about myself; but when I find another man intelligent enough to say them, I am far too polite to contradict him. (Shaw 2000: 248)

In this brief introduction to his first play in German translation, Shaw goes on to talk about Trebitsch's work as a translator. He emphasizes the fact that he himself is not skilled in foreign languages (a point he made on various occasions throughout his life, including when he took on the task of translating some twenty years later). He admits to being 'congenitally incapable of acquiring foreign languages', although he paradoxically claims that he has been so steeped in German music (Mozart, Beethoven, Wagner) that he feels he knows German and, consequently, is competent enough to discern the mistakes Trebitsch has made. Shaw nevertheless dismisses these errors, advancing the theory that translation must go beyond a mere command of language. A translator must have the skill of a playwright, he says, to capture the essence of a dramatic text. He lavishes praise on Trebitsch – whom he would later berate, when communicating with him directly, for misconstruing and misinterpreting not only the sense but also the spirit of his work. As the following lines show, Shaw is trying to defend Trebitsch publicly against his German-speaking detractors, Leon Kellner in particular, but the way in which he frames the act of translation and portrays the translator as a double of the author is particularly perceptive – and modernist *avant la lettre*.

> Good translation is a matter, not merely of knowledge of a language, but of divination. However skilled a man may be as a linguist, he cannot translate a work which he would be incapable of conceiving in the original. And if he cannot write dramatic dialogue he cannot translate another man's dramatic dialogue. Trebitsch has succeeded in both points. By divination and dramatic faculty combined he has assimilated and reproduced the meaning of the plays, dramatizing himself for the occasion as Bernard Shaw, and actually becoming a different person from the author of Genesung, Weltuntergang and the rest of his own works. Sometimes a certain refinement and charm in his own style adds itself to the occasionally rather raw pungency of mine; so that there are parts of his translation which are better than the original. (Shaw 2000: 248–9)

Shaw expresses surprise that a writer would also dedicate himself to translation – a point that could easily be made with regard to his own translation efforts, and those of all writer-translators for that matter: 'What astonishes me is that one who can write so well should neglect his own work to translate that of a foreign author' (Shaw 2000: 249). In later years, he periodically reminded Trebitsch not to neglect his own work, although he did so from the vantage point of the superior author, with Trebitsch at his service.

The rest of the article 'Devil of a Fellow' is devoted to his previous dealings with the vociferous and redoubtable Kellner, whom he accuses of taking revenge on Trebitsch. 'Every literary German believes he was created by God expressly to translate Candida', Shaw writes. 'Even the strongminded, well-informed Kellner was no exception; and when Trebitsch snatched Candida from him, he took a hideous revenge'. Shaw's reaction to Kellner's attacks, at least publicly, is to laugh, for in his view, Kellner identifies a mere half-dozen errors Trebitsch has made in translating stage directions, on the basis of which he concludes that the Austrian is 'wholly unacquainted with the English language' (Shaw 2000: 250).[23]

That Kellner's critique is a laughing matter was already stated in a letter that Shaw wrote to Trebitsch the day after Kellner's article on *Candida* appeared, in which Shaw also admitted that Kellner was right. Shaw concludes with words of comfort: 'Meanwhile dont worry, be magnanimous with Kellner, sleep well; and do not neglect your work to grieve over your mistakes. Even I – Bernard Shaw – make mistakes sometimes' (Letter of 26 January 1903, Weiss 1986: 38–40).

Translating in a new key: 'Translator's Note'

The 'Translator's Note' that Shaw wrote to accompany *Jitta's Atonement* was included in the programme when the play was first produced in the United States in 1923. It was published as a 'loosely inserted leaflet' in the programme for the first London performance of 1925 (*Complete Prefaces* vol. 2: 548), after which it was revised and reprinted as a preface when the play was published, along with some other items, in the 1926 volume *Translations and Tomfooleries*.[24]

Shaw was in the habit of writing substantial prefaces to his plays – in some cases even longer than the play itself. Whether the tone was autobiographical, journalistic or political, Shaw interacted with his reader in a 'podium performance', which is but a variation of the theatre of ideas for which he was famous.[25] When, for instance, *Jitta's Atonement* was resurrected in New York, nearly eighty years after its premiere, one reviewer wrote that the greatest 'drama' was not in the play itself, but in the translator's comments. Like Paul Auster's preface to a book-length translation, which is said to have drawn more attention than the translated book itself, Shaw's 'Note' makes for a good read. The reviewer refers to a note included in the programme in which Shaw himself describes the personal debt that both he and the theatre itself owed to Trebitsch and concludes, 'It is, perhaps, telling that one of the most dramatic moments of the evening occurs not on the stage, but in the program itself' (Murray 2001).

In writing the 'Translator's Note', Shaw is not only true to himself as a writer of prefaces; he also joins a long line of translators who introduce their work with a text providing a glimpse into issues of methodology, translation strategy and the art of translation itself. Taking up his pen as a writer to reflect on his relationship to the original author and the circumstances surrounding the translation, Shaw participates in the age-old tradition of crafting a narrative about the process. While not to be taken entirely at face value, it is interesting in itself for the perspectives it offers on his conception of translation and writer-translator relations in general.

Before the 'Note' itself, a title page is inserted, which is worth looking at since it reveals Shaw's efforts to establish Trebitsch's credibility as a writer and to enhance his status.

The page reads as follows:

JITTA'S ATONEMENT

By SIEGFRIED TREBITSCH

Author of Genesung, Weltuntergang, Das Haus am Abhang,
Tagwandler, Ein Muttersohn, Der Tod und die Liebe, Gefährliche Jahre,
Spätes Licht, Die Frau ohne Dienstag,
Der Geliebte, Die Last des Blutes, etc. etc.

TRANSLATED BY

BERNARD SHAW

This is a typographical tribute, in which not only Trebitsch's name, but also his literary bona fides are set out. It should be noted that in the preface that follows, Shaw specifies that Trebitsch has published 'eight novels and volumes of stories, and six or seven plays, including Frau Gitta's Sühne' ('Note', 3). Listing the majority of them here, therefore, and adding a double 'etc.' seems like overkill, and somewhat of an exaggeration. Unlike Gertrude Stein, Shaw does not baulk at putting his name below that of the author, albeit in a font of equal size. Thus, the title page serves to complement the laudatory tone of the 'Translator's Note'.[26]

In the 'Note', Shaw begins by labelling the Austrian a 'well-known' writer and credits Trebitsch with the production of a substantial body of 'original work'. He stresses the word 'original', which he repeats three times in the first paragraph, precisely because Trebitsch has undertaken the enormous task of introducing to the German-speaking world his entire body of work, an extraordinary feat for a writer who also has the potential to enjoy a literary career of his own. As someone who was introducing the first translation of his career, made when he was well over sixty, and who had previously commented on the time-consuming nature of supervising translators of his own work, Shaw seemed to genuinely admire Trebitsch's 'extraordinary' devotion to the task of translating.

In this preface, Shaw reminds readers of the particular circumstances surrounding Trebitsch's decision to become his translator. When Trebitsch first came along, Shaw did not yet enjoy a good reputation in the English theatre. Occupying instead a position of 'infamy', he was regarded as an 'absurd pamphleteer, who had been allowed to display his ignorance of the rudiments of stage technique, and a hopeless incapacity for representing human nature dramatically or otherwise, in a few performances at coterie theatres quite outside recognized theatrical commerce' ('Note', 3). Shaw stages the tale of how he met Trebitsch in the context of his failure to get sufficient recognition in his own country. In two pithy sentences, he demonstrates Trebitsch's importance to him: 'Trebitsch knew better. He also knew English'. The account differs slightly from the earlier version given in 'Devil of a Fellow', mainly in that in this text Trebitsch's two visits are combined into one. Their encounter, as we have seen, is depicted by both parties in both religious and military terms, with a good dash of hyperbole and drama. Thus assaulted – and flattered – Shaw surrenders to Trebitsch's proposal to become his apostle. At a time when English-speaking audiences did not look upon him favourably, to say the least, and critics were urging him to 'cease my vain efforts to enter a profession for which Nature had utterly unfitted me', he finds himself a 'successful and respected playwright' in the German language ('Note', 3–4).

Shaw's route to success in Britain, via Germany, was corroborated by Thomas Mann, as we have seen, although the reasons for his success go beyond the dedication of the indefatigable Siegfried Trebitsch. In this preface, nonetheless, Shaw recognizes that he owes a debt of gratitude to his German translator. He also presents a second reason for having undertaken the translation: in a more political vein, he alludes to the 'horrible catastrophe' of the First World War, which had 'torn Anglo-German relations to shreds'. Through his translation of one of Trebitsch's plays from German to English, he proposes to contribute to the process of finally mending those relations ('Note', 4).

Like many a translator before him, G.B.S. elaborates on some of the particular 'technical difficulties' he faced. His difficulties would appear to be greater than most since his knowledge of German was limited, although he dismisses this challenge as a 'minor matter'. He paints the picture of a reasonably competent tourist able to purchase something in a shop or ask directions when visiting Bayreuth, but when confronted with one of Trebitsch's plays, he is driven to the dictionary. Even at that, he must resort to a 'telepathic method' whereby he would 'divine, infer, guess, and co-invent the story of Gitta, or Jitta' ('Note', 4–5).[27]

In 'inventing' the new version of Gitta, in fact, Shaw is working from the word-for-word translation provided by his secretary, as mentioned above. Although this may seem inconceivable in the world of translation in general, it is not uncommon, in the more specialized field of dramaturgy, for a stage version to be an adaptation from an existing translation or from a literal translation of a foreign work. The other attitude at play here is the view held by writers of the time, in opposition to the 'men of learning' evoked by Shaw (5), that a profound knowledge of a foreign language was unnecessary: in fact, it was thought to be possible, or even desirable, to translate from foreign languages without any scholarly, or philological, foundation in that language. This was the position of Pound and other modernist translators, who – astonishingly – felt capable and confident enough to undertake translations with a limited understanding of the languages in which the originals were written, often achieving remarkable results. Not only were they willing to dispense with the scholarly approach taken by their nineteenth-century predecessors, but they even considered classical training a 'barrier to authentic translation', as Yao points out (2002: 11–12).

Shaw opined that the real 'business' of translating a play consisted not in 'mere translation', by which he meant producing a 'literal translation', but rather in translating 'the audience as well as the play' – that is, in translating Vienna into London and New York. Shaw recognized, long before the translation theorists of the later twentieth century, to what extent it was important to adjust the work to the literary conventions of the target culture. For Shaw, translation was a form of 'rewriting'. However literary his manner of expressing it, as shown in the following excerpt from the 'Note', he is not far at all from theories of 'refraction' that would be advanced by André Lefevere in the 1980s.[28]

> Vienna is still romantic in the manner of Verdi's operas, and modern in the manner of De Maupassant and Baudelaire. And as the conqueror always acquires some of the qualities of the conquered, even now that he no longer eats him, there is a touch of the east in Vienna, not only brought by the winds along the Danube, but left by the Turks when Sobieski drove them back from the gates. Add to this that Vienna has never weaned itself from the sweet milk of eighteenth-century art, when even woe was a luxury, and the heroine could not die in gloom too deep to please the audience…. To preserve this delicious anaesthesia there must be no bringing down to earth of the business by the disillusioning touch of comedy.
>
> In England and America nowadays, such romance is privileged only in Italian Opera, and is not tolerated without the music. The Anglo-American audience wants a happy ending because it wants a credible ending…. ('Note', 5–6)

Having so deftly described the divergent cultural contexts of Vienna and London or New York, Shaw suggests that he has had no choice but to change the ending of Trebitsch's play. In an evocative rapprochement of the theme of marital infidelity and the treasons of translation, he concludes that his audience would not tolerate the 'miserably-ever-after' fate of Trebitsch's married couple. He contrives, instead, to make them 'settle down on reasonable human terms'. Shaw's references to the art of translation are couched, as is frequently the case, in metaphorical language. He admits to resorting to translator's 'treacheries', thus conjuring up the well-known Italian adage, '*traduttore, traditore*'.[29]

Shaw frequently revised his prefaces as new editions of his work were issued. This one is no exception. The original 'Note' (as printed in Mander and Mitchenson 1955) differs from the one published in 1926. Shaw made some minor editorial and factual emendations. One interesting alteration, made perhaps to satisfy a more sophisticated, or at least different, readership, is as follows: The original statement 'Vienna is still romantic in the manner of Victor Hugo and Théophile Gauthier' (Mander and Mitchenson 1955: 201) is replaced in the 1926 version by 'Vienna is still romantic in the manner of Verdi's operas, and modern in the manner of De Maupassant and Baudelaire' ('Note', 5). The most substantial revision occurs in the paragraph on conjugal infidelity. In the 1923 version, Shaw writes:

> I may as well confess at once that though in the original play Jitta lives miserably ever afterwards, and her husband hardly escapes for a moment from the strictest Spanish tradition of jealousy cruel as the grave, I have permitted myself to suggest, by a few slight touches, that they may quite possibly settle down on reasonable human terms and find life quite bearable after all. (Mander and Mitchenson 1955: 202)

This is revised in the 1926 version to read as follows:

> I may as well confess at once that in the original play Jitta lives miserably ever after, and that her husband bears malice, and presents a character-study much subtler and more elusive than you will gather from my frankly comedic British version of him. Also Trebitsch, being a German poet, has a certain melancholic delicacy which escapes my comparatively barbarous and hilarious occidental touch. I could not help suggesting, by a few translator's treacheries here and there, that the ill-assorted pair settle down on reasonable human terms, and find life bearable after all. ('Note', 6)[30]

In this excerpt, Shaw compares his 'comedic' and 'hilarious' version of the character of the cuckolded husband to Trebitsch's original one, which has been conveyed with subtlety and 'melancholic delicacy'. It is not until the published version that Shaw comes up with the term 'translator's treacheries' to refer to the changes he has made in adapting the play. These variations, he specifies, affect not the story, but the 'key in which it ends', although in the earlier version, he says the 'key in which it is played', thereby suggesting in the revised note that the adaptation applies not to the whole play, but merely to its ending ('Note', 6–7).

'Dear Trebitsch, You are perfectly mad ...': Letters to translators

Shaw's correspondence with Trebitsch began in June 1902, just after Trebitsch was entrusted with the translation of Shaw's plays; it continued for nearly a half century, until Shaw's death in 1950. It is clear from the vast number of letters exchanged between the two men that Shaw became instantly engaged in the work of his German translator and that his involvement was sustained over his lifetime. Privately, Shaw took every opportunity to draw attention to Trebitsch's numerous errors: for example, he says of *Arms and the Man* that it was 'full of hideous and devastating errors' (Weiss 1986: 30) and of *Candida*, Trebitsch's favourite, 'You didn't understand the play: you only wallowed in it' (Weiss 1986: 32). Trebitsch improved as time passed, and their correspondence came to reflect the practical side of their relationship with one another: concerns over money, film rights, control over stage productions in which Shaw's plays were cut or otherwise altered – to his continual chagrin – as well as the way in which European politics, especially through two world wars, affected their professional arrangements and the personal circumstances of the Austrian-Jewish Siegfried and Tina Trebitsch.

The early letters, mainly, paint a picture of a sometimes harsh, sometimes patronizing, but always solicitous, author protecting his subservient translator. They set the tone for their working relationship and also echo Shaw's thinking on translation. There is evidence from the earliest extant letter, dated 26 June 1902, that Shaw micro-managed Trebitsch's work and that he expected his translator, in turn, to ensure that the plays were performed exactly as they were written. 'I wont have the two last acts run into one. I wont have a line omitted or a comma altered', Shaw stipulated (Weiss 1986: 17). Shaw carefully revised Trebitsch's translations, with the use of his 'huge Muret-Sanders dictionary'. He even intimated that he might have to translate the plays himself. Having 'spent a month revising a translation in a language that I have never learnt', he wrote that 'in future I will make the translation and you shall revise it' (Letter of 16 August 1903, Weiss 1986: 59). What Shaw was proposing (facetiously, perhaps, but there is a grain of truth to what he says) resembles the kind of self-translation undertaken by Gertrude Stein, who was so anxious for her work to be translated accurately and so loath to relinquish authorial control, that she supplied a crib to her translators, as will be seen in the following chapter.

Shaw spent time dealing with public criticism of Trebitsch's work, by Kellner notably. Although he tried to comfort Trebitsch and coach him in how to respond to criticism, he did not hesitate to express both dismay and disappointment when writing to Trebitsch directly. Trebitsch's problems stemmed from his inadequate knowledge of English. Despite the words of praise with which his letters were laced, Shaw often began with a merciless castigation of his translator: 'Trebitsch, Trebitsch, du bist ganz und gar unverbesserlich (you are completely incorrigible)' (Letter of 4 August 1903, Weiss 1986: 56) and 'Dear Trebitsch, You are perfectly mad – mad as a hatter' (Letter of 10 August 1903, Weiss 1986: 57). While preoccupied with Trebitsch's missteps, he also says (contradicting himself): 'Mistakes dont matter: they can always be corrected, and they dont kill a play even if they are left uncorrected'. More important, in this case, is the fact that Trebitsch, who was working on *Caesar and Cleopatra*, was not familiar with 'Roman history, Roman politics & Roman institutions' (Letter of 16 August 1903, Weiss 1986: 59). In other words, he appeared to be ignorant of the underlying cultural and political context of the play, which is now considered so important in translation.

After checking Trebitsch's translations, Shaw would often call for an 'exact translation', insisting, as well, that his translator pay close attention to his revisions. The following excerpt, from a letter of 18 August 1906 with regard to *Man and Superman*, illustrates the spirit of their interactions:

> The Superman dream has been very troublesome because it requires exact translation. You have in several places thought I was writing poetry when I was writing the most rigidly scientific psychology... It is quite amazing how well you have succeeded; but it is still more amazing that, understanding it so well, you should have let one or two passages pass as sheer nonsense. I rub this into you because you must not underrate the importance of my corrections. (Weiss 1986: 109–10)

At the same time, he warns Trebitsch against trying for too much artistry:

> You are thinking about nothing but the artistic side of the business. About that I never concern myself: it is in the hands of Providence. As a work of art, your translations seem to me better than the originals in several ways, and to have a certain charm of style and character... But all this we may leave to the critics & the public. There is a mechanical side to the business that can be mastered only by experience and by drudgery. (Letter of 10 December 1902, Weiss 1986: 26)

This attitude is reminiscent of the image of the translator as a 'drudge' in John Dryden's 'Dedication' to his 1697 translation of the *Aeneid*. 'But slaves we are, and labour on another man's plantation; we dress the vineyard, but the wine is the owner's; if the soil be sometimes barren, then we are sure of being scourged:

if it be fruitful, and our care succeeds, we are not thanked; for the proud reader will only say, the poor drudge has done his duty' (quoted in Lefevere 1992a: 24). This conception of the translator as a slave, a servant to the original text and author, was to endure for nearly three centuries. Ironically, though, both Dryden and Shaw felt free enough to take liberties in their own translation practice.

In yet another metaphorical description of translation, Shaw uses the looking glass trope to rebuke Trebitsch for his faithful yet untrue rendering of meaning, for conveying the sentence while failing to grasp the broader picture:

My dear Trebitsch-Spiegelmann
    Why do I call you Spieglemann? Look at the corrections to Candida and you will understand. What is a Spiegelmann? A Mirrorman. A Looking Glass man. What is a Looking Glass? A thing that reflects what is before it with exquisite fidelity, but that has neither Rücksicht [hindsight] nor Vorsicht [foresight], neither memory nor hope, neither reason nor conscience. And that is what you are as a translator. You translate a sentence beautifully, but you do not remember the last sentence, do not foresee the next sentence, and when you finish the play it goes out of your head just as your head vanishes from your mirror when you have finished shaving. (Letter of 7 January 1903, Weiss 1986: 32)

Shaw assumed the role of educator and mentor to his translator – understandable as he was the older, and more established, writer of the two. 'I want to complete *your* education', he wrote to Trebitsch in 1902, 'You must begin where I leave off & surpass me ...' (Letter of 26 December 1902, Weiss 1986: 31; Shaw's emphasis). He urged Trebitsch to take a leaf out of his own book and write a translator's preface (prefaces, we have seen, are a hallmark of Shaw's work), to explain his 'departures from custom' (Letter of 4 August 1903, Weiss 1986: 56).

All of this criticism, advice and even fulsome praise reflect the preoccupations of a superior, perhaps arrogant, author, anxious that his own work not be betrayed in translation. Shaw's attitude to translation as a subservient art is further illustrated by his advice that Trebitsch stick to his 'own' work. Shaw opens his letter of 26 June 1902 with: 'I am amazed at your industry. But why dont you write plays of your own?' and ends with: 'Once more, dont neglect your own work. Translation will not teach you half so much as original composition' (Weiss 1986: 17–18). On another occasion, in words again echoing those of Dryden ('another man's plantation'), Shaw writes, 'You may easily be led into a frightful waste of your life on another man's work, and my conscience is not at peace on the subject. Can you not arrange to set aside only a part of your time to translate?' (Letter of 7 October 1903, Weiss 1986: 64). While Shaw is grateful to Trebitsch for his devoted service as his agent and translator, he is also prescient. Early in their relationship, he anticipates the conclusion Trebitsch would ultimately reach at the end of his career, when he would become conscious of the secondary role he has played and the 'depreciation' to which he has been subjected (Trebitsch 1953: 273).

What emerges from these missives is a tangle of views on translation, which are nuanced but inconsistent. They vary depending on whether Shaw's own work was being either translated into other languages or transposed to other media, or whether, on the contrary, he was the one who was doing the translating. While he railed against the 'tampering' and 'ridiculous mutilations' wreaked upon *Saint Joan* in Vienna in 1928 (Letter of 16 May 1928, Weiss 1986: 289), he gave himself permission to rescue the character Jitta from the 'hopeless gloom and despair' to which Trebitsch had condemned her in his original version (Letter of 2 October 1921, Weiss 1986: 225).

While less extensive, Shaw's correspondence with the Hamons reflects a similar obsession with the quality of the French versions the couple were producing. He appears to advocate a certain degree of adaptation, but since his own plays were concerned, he didn't want it to be too extreme. At the same time, he suggests that they enrich the French text with borrowings from English, thereby shocking classically oriented French.

> You must write my plays as I would have written them had I been a Frenchman.... I have no doubt that you will, after practice, create a style which shall be both Shavian and French, both English and Hamonique. But do not be too much afraid of neologisms & turns of expression borrowed from English. Languages enrich each other in that way. Classicism, pedantry, is the besetting sin of the Frenchman. Do not hesitate to épater les académiques. (Letter to Hamon of 26 December 1905, quoted in Pharand 2000: 104)

Later, as Hamon was working on an adaptation of *Pygmalion* for French audiences – it was 1922 and Shaw had just translated Trebitsch's *Gitta* – Shaw advised Hamon to be flexible and avoid the kind of literal translation that fails to tell the story adequately. He argued that Hamon should 'prevent the absurdity of English people speaking French'. On the other hand, Shaw writes that he is opposed to any attempt to 'disguise Pygmalion as a French play about French people' (Letter of 13 June 1922, *Letters* vol. 3: 772–3).

'When I had a spare moment ... I devoted it to you': Shaw as translator

In 1913, Shaw had talked of translating one of Trebitsch's plays, but war intervened. When Trebitsch sent him a copy of *Frau Gittas Sühne*, shortly after the war, Shaw decided that this was the work he would translate. In 1920, then, in an unusual reversal of roles, Shaw undertook his only translation, seeking to become Trebitsch's 'translator-agent' by placing him on the English-language stage (Weiss 2000: 212).[31]

Shaw first wrote to Trebitsch about translating *Gitta* in a letter dated 15 September 1920:

> From time to time, when I had a spare moment in the evening, I devoted it to you by translating scraps of Gitta ... I do not know what you will say to it; but it will amuse you anyhow; and you can decide whether I am capable of finishing it. The difficulty has been partly that I do not know German, and mainly that apparently you do not know it either; for not one of your words could I find in the little pocket dictionary I travelled with (you have invented a language of your own) and I had to guess what it was all about by mere instinct. It is therefore possible that you may find the whole thing absurdly wrong from beginning to end. I have made some changes purposely .... (Weiss 1986: 212)

Shaw accomplished this task within a year, during which he was also occupied with his own projects. Of note in this case are the circumstances surrounding the translation and, in particular, Shaw's motives. It is also interesting to look at the manner in which Shaw actually translated, or adapted, the play, as well as the afterlife of the translated work, on the stage and in the eyes of the critics who assessed the job that Shaw had done.

Shaw's translation project: Neglecting his own work

Shaw was well occupied with his own work as a playwright, critic, and essayist, not to mention the task of churning out a correspondence of a quarter of a million letters. He had expressed reservations about the potential burden associated with simply overseeing the translation of his work into foreign languages. It is legitimate to ask, therefore, what prompted him to undertake the translation of one of Trebitsch's plays, and why *Frau Gittas Sühne*, in particular. What drove Shaw to translate and how did he conceive of his translation project?[32]

The tensions between original writing and translating, felt in this case by both writer and translator, are linked to the question of motivation. Shaw was ever mindful of Trebitsch's work as an original writer. As shown above, he urged him not to neglect his own work: 'Keep writing: that is your business – your own stories first, and the translations when you are tired of original invention' (Letter of 16 October 1902, Weiss 1986: 22). Trebitsch was also sensitive about being reduced to the status of 'Shaw's translator'. When Berlin critic Alfred Kerr interviewed G.B.S. in 1913, he reported that the playwright would have preferred to have French poet and novelist Anatole France, rather than Hamon, translate his works into French, to which Shaw had added, 'whoever has something to produce himself doesn't translate'. Trebitsch, obviously offended by the article, wrote about it to Shaw, who attempted to placate him by saying, 'As to you, you have "given your proofs": besides, I am going to translate a play of yours; so we shall both be tarred with the same brush' (Weiss 1986: 166 and 166n).

Shaw's motives for trying his hand at translation were at once personal, financial and political. In an attempt to repay his translator, he was prompted to reciprocate by translating one of Trebitsch's plays. Trebitsch also regarded this translation as 'compensation' for his efforts, although his estimation of its success was somewhat at odds with the opinion of others: 'Bernard Shaw, who had in any case always sought an opportunity to compensate me for many a trouble of my youth, adapted this play … and brought about a great success for it both in his own country and also in America' (Trebitsch 1953: 184).

In the years following the First World War, Shaw was genuinely concerned about the financial situation of Trebitsch, 'now ruined by the war'. He suggested that Trebitsch keep all royalty monies from the German translations to use for himself and his wife. Translating *Gitta* into English would be a way of earning extra money for Trebitsch. This is substantiated by the drawn-out communications between Trebitsch and Shaw following the translation, production and publication of *Jitta* with regard to royalties and movie rights (there never was a film based on the play), which indicate the extent to which Trebitsch regarded the work as a kind of 'pension'. In the opinion of Weintraub, who saw Trebitsch not only as an inadequate translator, but also someone of 'unmitigated whimpering selfishness' and even 'dishonesty' (1996: 211), Shaw's translation of Trebitsch's play was essentially a business matter. It was not even an authentic translation, in Weintraub's eyes: 'adapting one of his plays into English, a feeble Viennese melodrama that Shaw turned into an English farce. Making *Jitta's Atonement* … out of *Frau Gittas Sühne* was more like another of

Shaw's lengthy corrections of Trebitsch's German than a proper translation' (1996: 202).

In referring to the 'vital European necessity' for mending torn Anglo-German relations, Shaw is also suggesting political motives ('Note', 4). Ties between the British and Germans had obviously been affected by the First World War, during which Shaw's dealings and correspondence with Trebitsch were curtailed. Even after the war's end in 1918, relations were strained. Shaw's personal indebtedness to Trebitsch, who by this time had spent two decades translating and promoting his work, was coupled with Shaw's further debt to Germany (all the more striking in the context of German debt to the rest of Europe following Versailles). By 1920, political efforts were being made to heal the wounds of the First World War. In keeping with his position on public policy, Shaw made a point of investing his private income, earned in the form of German royalties, in German industry (Holroyd 1997: 515).

Behind the reasons given in the 'Translator's Note' and corroborated by Trebitsch, lie various, more obscure, motives. Charlotte Shaw was also a translator, and this might have had an influence on her husband, who aided her in her efforts. She was very fluent in French, so much so that she helped Shaw write letters to his French translators. In admiration of Eugène Brieux's play *Maternité*, she felt compelled to translate it, as she writes in her foreword to the published version: 'I felt an event had occurred, and a new possession come into my life. I knew at once that I must translate the play into English to make it accessible to those of my countrymen and women who could not read it in the original French' (Brieux 1921: i). Charlotte's Shaw's translation project is not untypical: she regarded translation as a means of paying tribute to a particular cause or author, in this case a foreign author committed to social justice. With the help of her husband, who would have been attuned to her missionary-like sensibility, the play was performed in English in London and published in the volume *Three Plays by Brieux* in 1911.[33]

Another factor is the affinity Shaw would have felt with some of the themes of the Trebitsch story. This particular play, while certainly not of a literary calibre equal to that of his own work (although considered the most successful of Trebitsch's dramas), was particularly fruitful. It therefore lent itself to this, Shaw's only foray into translation. First, like the characters in the play, Shaw had been involved in extramarital relationships, in particular a love affair with actress Mrs Campbell who had played some of the lead roles in his plays (the role of Eliza Doolittle in *Pygmalion*, for example, was written for her). Yet Shaw, again like the Trebitsch characters, ended up remaining in his marriage.

Interestingly, betrayal and infidelity, which are topics of the play, are also tropes used in the discourse of translation; this creates several layers of meaning in the actual text and in the metatext surrounding its translation. Shaw engages in the performance of translation as a kind of transgression of Trebitsch's original, which parallels the theme of adultery and transgression of the marriage contract on which Trebitsch's *Gitta* is based (Gahan 2004: 130 and 165, n. 51).[34]

Further, the backdrop of the play is the emerging field of psychoanalysis. Shaw was not only aware of the new discipline; he was also interested in developments resulting from Sigmund Freud's findings. As Gahan points out, 'echoes of Freudian psychology permeate the text'. Shaw's detailed stage directions emphasize the eroticism of the plot far more than Trebitsch had done (2004: 141). The focus on reading and writing, and the position of translation in that dynamic, would also have resonated with Shaw. In the play, the character Bruno Haldenstedt tries to ensure, before dying, that the manuscript on which he has been working, entitled 'Fetters of the Feminine Psyche', will have an afterlife, that it will be published and read and not an 'orphan'. As a way of making amends to the man he has cuckolded, he wants the husband of his mistress to take credit for the book by pretending to be its author. The notion of a 'stolen' manuscript, or of a fraudulent author, would have struck a chord in a man whose work was being translated and transported into other cultures by 'impostors'. In Trebitsch's play, Gitta assumes the role of (false) mother to Edith by virtue of her affair with Edith's father, Bruno, replacing a somewhat shallow, therefore unworthy, mother in the person of Agnes. The problem of authorship, associated with the theme of infidelity and parenting, or rather false parenting, would have appealed to Shaw, who remained childless despite a long (perhaps platonic?) marriage to Charlotte. There are obvious parallels in the world of translation, in which the translator 'steals' the work of an author and 'gives birth' to a new work of art. *Jitta's Atonement* can be read as a reflection on the relations between writing and translation, and on the ties between Shaw and Trebitsch as writer and translator, or writer and co-author (Gahan 2004: 156).

Lives of their own: Exercising control and getting even

By amending and adapting *Frau Gittas Sühne* to produce *Jitta's Atonement*, Bernard Shaw was settling scores in a way. In other words, he was taking his own turn at hijacking someone else's work and giving it a literary 'life of its own'. Preoccupied with authorial control, Shaw agonized about what others did to his work. One of the most obvious illustrations of a text that eluded him is

Pygmalion, which was subjected to profound alterations from the beginning, 'major transformations' in the plot, and eventually even further shifts as it was adapted to the screen and Broadway stage. As Gibbs has observed, this is 'the story of a lost masterpiece – or, if not lost, substantially altered and obscured.... a fascinating example of the ways in which texts ... take on lives and meanings of their own once they are launched into the world' (Gibbs 2005: 330).

Trebitsch, who arranged for the premiere of *Pygmalion* in Vienna in 1913, and then a production in Berlin, was the first to give a new twist to Shaw's play by intimating that the romance between Higgins and Eliza would end in marriage, a conclusion Shaw had not intended and about which he in fact protested. Shaw had talked of translating Trebitsch as early as 1913. Was he already thinking of getting back at his translator? In any case, a review that appeared in *The New York Times* after the premiere of *Jitta* suggested that Shaw deliberately transformed the play of his translator, in order to 'get even' (*The New York Times* 1923b). This point has also been made in later scholarly writing about the translated play. Because Trebitsch had been disloyal to him and to his plays, because others had similarly caused his original masterpieces to slip through his fingers, and perhaps, too, because the inconstant Mrs Campbell had eluded him, Shaw is said to be taking revenge through this transfiguration of his translator's play.[35]

'It is much better than the original'

When Shaw first submitted a draft Act I of *Jitta's Atonement* to Trebitsch, he wrote to say that given his lack of familiarity with German, the English translation might be 'disappointing'. He asked Trebitsch not to tear it up, though, since any translation was likely to be just as disappointing. But Trebtisch replied positively, 'It is much better than the original and I beg you by all means to continue and finish your version' (Weiss 1986: 217). Gertrude Stein's young acolyte and translator, Georges Hugnet, would similarly judge Stein's translation of *his* work to be better than the original, when it was quite clearly a significant departure from what he had written. Trebitsch's response was similarly respectful, to be sure, and Shaw adds his own touch of (feigned) humility in the 'Translator's Note'. Trebitsch is 'amiable', Shaw says, not to reproach him for having been 'shamefully unable to do justice' to the original ('Note', 6–7). Trebitsch did not reveal his true feelings until he wrote in his autobiography, published after Shaw's death, that Shaw actually 'took liberties that he himself would scarcely have forgiven his translator' (Trebitsch

1953: 264). Two ideas converge here: that the translation is 'better' than the original, and that Shaw betrayed Trebitsch in creating *Jitta*. Both imply that the translation is something *other* than the original. This merits closer examination, first through a brief synopsis of the play as written by Shaw, followed by an overview of some of the changes he made, the objective of which is not to critique his work as a translator, but rather to illustrate his approach to translation.

Synopsis of *Jitta's Atonement*

Like the German original, the play unfolds like a labyrinthine opera, twisting and turning around themes of love and betrayal and identities concealed and revealed. Act I opens with Jitta Lenkheim having an assignation with her lover, Professor Bruno Haldenstedt, in a flat they have been renting for this purpose. Haldenstedt has a heart condition, and fears he will soon die. He asks Jitta for her help in bequeathing his book on psychology, 'Fetters of the Feminine Psyche', to her husband, Professor Alfred Lenkheim, with whom he has collaborated and to whom he wishes to make amends. Haldenstedt proposes to leave the manuscript with Lenkheim's name on it, as if to suggest that Lenkheim has been the sole author. When her lover dies of a heart attack in the rented rooms, Jitta leaves him there and steals away so that her relationship to the dead man will remain a secret. (A housekeeper is aware of the tryst, but does not know who the woman is.) During Act II, Haldenstedt's widow, Agnes, and their daughter, Edith, express their grief in different ways, although they are equally anxious to discover the identity of the mystery woman in whose presence Haldenstedt has died. Jitta is guilt-ridden for having abandoned her lover. Lenkheim, who has been appointed Haldenstedt's executor, finds the book with his own name on the title-page and rejects the gift with contempt. In her anger at his attitude, Jitta reveals to him that she is the woman in question. She and her husband have a row, but agree to go on living together for the sake of appearances. In Act III, the various characters find out and come to terms with some elements of the truth. While sorting through the deceased's papers, Agnes is surprised to find that the book he has been working on is missing. Edith adored her father but feels disdain for her mother; she is drawn to the unknown woman her father was in love with. Jitta has a chat with Agnes and is able to persuade her that her husband had been having an affair with someone worthy of him. It is at this point that Shaw turns the potentially tragic ending into a comic one, because the two women end up laughing hysterically after Agnes says she has had her suspicions about Jitta. The widow is relieved. Jitta then reveals the actual truth to Edith. Both women are now happy: Edith because she knows and Agnes because she does not know, and because the missing manuscript, which Lenkheim in another comic moment has dismissed as 'tommy-rot' – although he will edit it – has been returned to the widow. The play closes with Jitta and her husband having come to some kind of reconciliation and going home together.

The translator's treacheries

Returning to Holroyd's comment, quoted above, to the effect that Shaw 'added to his other areas of expertise the art of translation' (Holroyd 1989: 50), it is fair to ask to what extent the attribution of 'expertise' to Shaw can be taken at face value. Is the biographer, like the subject himself, given to irony in this instance? In this particular experiment with translation, Shaw is quite possibly the opposite of an 'expert'. In other words, is Shaw merely 'dabbling' in translation, a practise to which he was unaccustomed, in a language he professed not to know, motivated by a plethora of factors that had little to do with an authentic drive to translate?

In the 'Translator's Note' summarized above, Shaw admits to 'a few translator's treacheries here and there'. Using a musical metaphor that is a fairly common topos in discourse on translation, he claims that his alterations are mere 'variations, which affect, not the story itself, but only the key in which it ends'. The translator takes more than a 'few' liberties, however, and the variations are far from insignificant, as Matlaw suggests, using a different metaphor:

> Shaw's imprimatur is superimposed over Trebitsch's play, like an inadequate new paint job that barely covers the old color. As would happen if a decorator of a new fashion were merely to rearrange some of the old furnishings, the result is discordant. (Matlaw 1979: viii)

Comparing the two scripts, Matlaw concludes that Shaw both exaggerates and understates his changes, which consist of dialogue that is more conversational, a greater emphasis on the erotic, and additions and omissions to the narrative that range from minor changes to more substantial ones (Matlaw 1979: ix). The most fundamental alteration is a modulation from the tragic, or sentimental, to the comic by the end of the play.

The play mimics other Shaw plays structurally. There are no scenes. Instead, Shaw runs Trebitsch's scenes together and keeps only the original division of three acts. (Trebitsch has three scenes in the first act, seven in the second, and fourteen in the third!) In Shaw, the characters are not always named: at the beginning, for example, Bruno Haldenstedt is called 'The Gentleman' and Jitta 'The Lady', whereas at other times their given names, Bruno and Jitta, are used. The name Lenkheim is sometimes used, and at other times the same character is called Alfred, the Christian name Shaw has given him (he is Alfons in the original). Finally, Shaw has expanded Trebitsch's minimal stage directions; he provides his trademark novelistic stage directions, including specific instructions for the actors to laugh: 'chuckling a little' (73); 'grinning' and 'more amused than ever' (74) – which help to transpose the action into a major key. In this particular case, Shaw's stage directions 'engage in a running meta-commentary on Trebitsch's original' (Conolly-Smith 2013: 113), which adds another layer of meaning to the script.[36]

In places, Shaw faithfully follows the constructions and turns of phrase of the original text. However, *Jitta's Atonement*, as most critics have remarked, becomes progressively more Shavian as the denouement approaches. In the first two acts, the translation is relatively close; in the final act, Shaw not only adds a lot of new material. (For example, as the presumed author of Haldenstedt's book, Lenkheim will become as famous as Einstein, 48–9.) He also turns the ending upside down, converting the tragedy to a comedy. Toward the end, the changes are so perceptible that it becomes futile to compare the translation to the source text.

Structural and substantive transformations aside, Shaw the translator commits his own 'blunders' at the micro-level, which are as serious as those that he and Trebitsch's most vocal critics, such as Kellner, decried in the German translations of his plays. The following examples, taken from the earlier portion of the play, illustrate the translation 'errors' that Shaw has made, deliberately or not. German quotations are taken from Trebitsch's original play (1920) and are designated 'ST'; the relatively literal English translation done by Myron Matlaw (1979) follows, designated 'MM'; and Shaw's version (from the published playscript of 1926) is given last, designated 'GBS'. Quotations from Shaw follow his spelling and punctuation, or lack of it (e.g. 'wont' for 'won't').

Example 1

There is a slight mistranslation in Shaw's English version of this excerpt, drawn from Act I. Haldenstedt has an attack of angina because he has walked up the stairs instead of taking the elevator. He has done so, it is suggested, to avoid running into somebody as he is entering the building to meet his mistress. When he sees Jitta, he observes that she looks like a fugitive, nervous about being found out.

Shaw has chosen to translate the German noun 'Mann', which can mean either 'man' or 'husband', as 'husband', making it look as if Jitta is afraid that her husband will see her. In the original German, on the other hand, the two characters are merely discussing the possibility of being seen by 'someone' ('ein Individuum'). The lines make sense, but do not translate what Trebitsch has written.

> Haldenstedt: Aber der Mann, von dem du dich stets beobachtet wähnst, stand diesmal hoffentlich nicht auf dem Treppenabsatz?
>
> Gitta: Scherze nur! Einmal wird so ein Individuum wirklich dastehen und nicht nur in meiner Einbildung. Dann wird alles ans Licht kommen – und – alles zu Ende sein. (ST 6)

> Haldenstedt: But the man you always imagine watching you did not stand at the foot of the stairs this time, did he?
>
> Gitta: Go ahead and joke! Some day such a person really will be there, and not only in my imagination. Then everything will be revealed – and – everything will end. (MM 6)

> The Gentleman: Why do you always look as if you were running away, and had just stumbled into my arms by chance?
>
> The Lady: I always feel as if my husband were lying in wait for me at the next turn. (GBS 13)

Example 2

In this instance, it would appear that Shaw has misinterpreted the sense of the German adjective 'reuelos' (which means 'rue-less' rather than 'ruthless', or to feel no sorrow or regret over something) and that he has added an additional attribute, 'shameless', to compound the mistranslation.

> Gitta: Wenn man glücklich ist, ist man auch reuelos. (ST 8)
>
> Gitta: When one is happy, one has no regrets. (MM 7)
>
> Jitta: When one is really happy, one is ruthless and shameless. (GBS 16)

Example 3

In the following line, Shaw has remained close to the original sentence structure, as he frequently does, especially early in the play. However, he stumbles over a word, which changes the sense of the exchange between the two lovers. In this case, in writing 'my most urgent prayer', he has probably confused 'bitten' (to ask or request) and 'beten' (to pray or entreat). He reinforces the latter sense by means of superlatives as well as stage directions: 'seizing her hands, but now pleading like a lover'.

> Haldenstedt: Es ist mein heisser Wunsch, meine inständige Bitte. (ST 12)
>
> Haldenstedt: This is my deep wish, my urgent request. (MM 11)
>
> Bruno: It is my deepest wish. It is my most urgent prayer to you, Jitta. (GBS 20)

Example 4

Following directly on the above error is another instance in which Shaw has altered the text, although this time more fundamentally. Bruno Haldenstedt has written a book, which might have made him famous, except that he does not expect to live long enough because of his poor health. He has destroyed the original manuscript and, on the typescript that he will leave behind, he has inscribed the name of Jitta's husband to make him look like the author. He is asking Jitta to be complicit in this fraud with him. In Trebitsch's original, there is a play on words, using 'schuld', which has the sense of 'fault', 'blame', 'guilt' and also 'debt', along with 'Mitschuldige', which means 'accomplices' or 'co-conspirators'. Shaw stretches the reference to guilt even further. He adds the word 'crime' to refer to the idea of fake authorship ('And I am to be your accomplice in such a crime!'), whereas Trebitsch alludes to it more vaguely ('Und ich soll deine Mitschuldige dabei sein?'). Shaw, for his part, is fixated on notions of 'infidelity': marital fidelity, in the more concrete sense, as well as betraying someone else's creative work or impersonating an author are all related to the act of translation in which the lines between author and translator are blurred. In the ensuing discussions around the identity of the late Bruno's mysterious lover, Shaw makes use of the words 'fidelity' (or 'infidelity') and their synonyms 'faithful/unfaithful' more frequently that in Trebitsch's original version.

> Gitta: Das verlangst du von mir? So Unerhörtes soll ich dir geloben? Dem, der mir alles schuldig ist, der uns hier aufgetrieben hat, ihm soll die Frucht deines Lebens in den Schoss fallen? Und ich soll deine Mitschuldige dabei sein? Nein, nein, niemals! (ST 12).
>
> Gitta: You demand that of me? Must I promise you such an unheard-of-thing? This man, who has remained my debtor in every respect, who drove us up here, is he the one into whose lap should fall the fruits of your life? And I should be your accomplice in this? No, no, never! (MM 11)
>
> Jitta: You ask me to do that! To promise you this unheard-of thing! This man who has no soul; who has been guilty of everything to me that a man can be guilty of to a woman except the infidelity that I would welcome with delight to

excuse my own (he's not man enough for that): the fruit of your life's work is to drop into his mouth! And I am to be your accomplice in such a crime! No. I cannot. Never. (GBS 20)

Example 5

By the second act, it becomes increasingly difficult to compare the translated version to the source text in the usual way. Shaw does continue to follow the original text, although there are many variations and additions. In our last example, Shaw completely changes the dynamic – through a mistranslation that may well be deliberate. In the original, Edith says about the her father's as-yet-to-be-revealed mistress, 'I am drawn to her'; in Shaw's version, this is turned around to become, 'she will be drawn to me'.

> Gitta: Können wir denn wissen, on sie nicht im Dunkel bleiben und in ihrem Winkel still verbluten will?
>
> Edith: Nein, mich zieht es zu ihr hin. Begreifen Sie jetzt, dass ich zu Hause keine Heimstatt mehr habe? Ich kann nicht leben ohne einen Menschen, dem es gegeben ist, mit meinem Herzen zu trauern … nur diese Frau hat meinen Vater so erlebt, wie ich ihn empfinde. Sie wird ihn mir lebendig erhalten. Ich werde ihr alle Rechte einräumen, die seine Liebe ihr gab. (ST 31)

> Gitta: How do we know whether she does not want to remain unknown [in darkness] and bleed to death in her corner?
>
> Edith: No, I am drawn to her. Don't you understand that I no longer can find a home in my house? I can not live without another person who can mourn as my heart mourns … only that woman perceived my father as I feel he really was. She will keep him alive for me. I will grant her all the rights to which his love entitles her. (MM 25)

> Jitta: No: she slunk away into the darkness. Let her be. She can bleed to death in her hiding-place.
>
> Edith: She shall not: she will be drawn to me: you will see. Remember that I have no longer any place at home. I cannot live with people who cannot feel about my father as I do; and there is only one such person in the world.
>
> Jitta: That woman?
>
> Edith: Yes. I will give her every right over me that the woman who returned my father's love should have over his daughter: the right I deny to my mother. I swear it. (GBS 38–9)

According to Matlaw, Shaw followed Trebitsch quite closely except for the ending, a few necessary plot adjustments to prepare for it, and occasional

'Shavian interpolations', which resulted in unevenness and incoherence. The 'unhappy amalgam of the two atmospheres and the characters' and the 'mixture of styles' help to explain the play's relative failure. It is included among his *Complete Plays*, but is the least known of Shaw's full-length plays (Matlaw 1979: xvi). Other observers have emphasized the way in which Shaw 'revels in the characters' sexuality', evidence of the role Mrs Campbell still played in his imagination (Conolly-Smith 2013: 110). Mainly, from what Shaw has said and what is reported by scholars and critics alike, Trebitsch's rather dreary Viennese drama has been transformed into a comedy, one in which serious ideas are staged and upon which the playwright has applied a decidedly Shavian stamp.

Tradaptation: Shaw as adapter

For Shaw, a man of the theatre, translation was performance. Just as he rewrote his biographies, just as he rewrote the work of his translators, he could not resist infusing the text he translated with new life. In much the same way as he became a 'co-translator' (with Trebitsch and the Hamons, in particular) of his plays, he became the co-author of *Jitta*.

The theatre, perhaps more than other genres, calls for continual transformations, not only at the interlingual level, but more immediately by directors and actors who translate from the 'page to the stage'. Shaw was uniformly regarded as an 'adapter', as the critical reception would show, but that doesn't mean that his work should not be treated as a 'translation'. In a relatively early commentary on *Jitta's Atonement*, Eric Bentley maintains that the play merely 'purports' to be a translation whereas Shaw in fact 're-writes the dialogue' (1957: 174). With the advent of new ways of conceptualizing translation in the later twentieth century, value judgements of this sort have been replaced by more nuanced positions. For example, 'texts which *refer to themselves as translations*' should be analysed as translations, rather than treated as something else, as Lefevere has pointed out (1992b: 96; emphasis added) – an approach that takes on particular meaning in the context of the 'manipulation school' whose position is that all translation is a form of rewriting.[37]

Where would Shaw position himself in the longstanding divide between faithful and unfaithful translation? To use Lawrence Venuti's framework, Shaw would fall within the 'domesticating' tradition that has long dominated British and American cultures (Venuti 1995: 16). From Shaw's observations on translation, from his exhortations to his translators as well as to the various producers of his plays (made indirectly at times through his German translator), it is clear that he is not in favour of word-for-word or literal translation; yet, his need to exert authorial control over his own creations prevents him from moving as far to the domestication end of the continuum as he does when he is the one who is translating, or adapting, *Jitta* for an English-language audience. He appears to be inclined, in the tradition of the French *belles infidèles*, to appropriate a foreign work in order to make it acceptable to his own culture. Wanting to 'translate' Vienna into London and New York, and 'to translate the audience as well as the play' ('Note', 5), Shaw is undeniably in the 'domestication' camp. He is 'unethically', as Venuti partisans would claim, erasing the foreignness of his original. However, whereas Venuti takes the Anglo world to task for 'producing the illusion of transparency' and favouring the kind of translation that 'masquerades as a true semantic equivalence when it in fact inscribes the foreign text with a partial interpretation, partial to English-language values' (Venuti 16), Shaw does not masquerade. In letters exchanged with Trebitsch, he carries out an extensive discussion about his choices as a translator and he proudly, publicly and transparently vaunts his 'treacheries' – all of which he considers necessary to the success of his translation when transported to the stage for consumption by English-language audiences.[38]

He was, in sum, a man of multiple views and many contradictions. In the words of Grindea, 'Shaw had the most complex character imaginable and enjoyed surrounding his over-involved self with constantly-changing fences of paradox, flippancy and exhibitionism – a hard dialectical core to be detected through the rapier points of his invective' (1956: 1). As a socialist, member of the Fabian Society, and sometime supporter of Stalin's USSR, he challenged his society's commonly held views on imperialism, colonialism, race, and gender. Nevertheless, he came of age and developed as a thinker and playwright in Victorian and Edwardian times, at the height of the British Empire. His *habitus* was inevitably influenced by his own upbringing and the imperial worldviews prevalent at the time. Shaw admired Queen Victoria and shared with her a belief in the 'benign exercise of power'; it has also been argued that he regarded Victoria as a mother figure, who was nurturing in ways his own mother was not, a Great Mother to her nation and to the British Empire (Peters 1997: 259).

The brilliance of Shaw resides in his ability to create through translation, to 'make it new', as the modernists would say. His translation is a form of rewriting and adaptation in its most positive sense. Recent theories of adaptation have shed light on the complexities of intertextuality or the dialogic relations among texts, and on 'the adaptive faculty, the ability to repeat without copying, to embed difference amid similarity, to be at once both self and Other' (Hutcheon 2006: 174). Not unlike his Victorian contemporaries, who were inclined to 'adapt just about everything' (Hutcheon 2006: xi), Shaw borrowed freely from previous works as well as real life. He did this most notably in the case of *Pygmalion*, the 'lost masterpiece' whose antecedents date back to ancient times, as well as a play written by W.A. Gilbert (of Gilbert and Sullivan fame). Shaw's play was adapted in turn, taking on a veritable life of its own in successive stage versions, as a film, as a Broadway musical, and finally as a second film, the smash hit *My Fair Lady*.[39]

Instead of measuring the value of the end product, using the criterion of fidelity – which often ends up devaluing the adaptation with respect to the 'original' – it is more productive to view adaptation as a creative process through which something is gained. Sanders (2006) makes a distinction between adaptation, which entails 'a relationship with an informing source text or original', and 'appropriation' – the better term she believes – because it involves moving away from the source toward a 'wholly new cultural product and domain' (26). What Shaw achieved – or attempted to achieve – in his translation of *Jitta* falls into this category. It could well be labelled 'tradaptation', to use a term coined by Montreal playwright and actor Michel Garneau to refer to his Québécois versions of Shakespeare. In this particular instance, the weakness of the work stems from the inherent flaws of the source text rather than from the skill of the adapter.

Jitta's Atonement on stage

Shaw had wanted the English version of *Jitta's Atonement* to not only enhance Trebitsch's literary reputation but also improve his financial situation. It was his intention to put Trebitsch in the limelight, as evidenced in a letter to a prospective producer (about whom more will be said later) in which he insisted, 'I do not want it suggested that it is 95% Shaw and 5% Trebitsch' (Langner 1963: 95). In spite of careful instructions, however, it was Shaw's name that was featured, usually in larger letters than that of Trebitsch. The critics, for their part, tended to regard *Jitta* as one of Shaw's plays, and to turn their attention to the unique way in which Shaw had handled it.

It may well have been treated as one of Shaw's plays, but unlike so many of the others, either in the original English or in translation, *Jitta* has enjoyed limited success on the stage. In his 'Note' of 1926, Shaw provides the following information on the premieres.

Frau Gitta's Sühne was performed for the first time at the great Burgtheater of Vienna on the 3rd February 1920.

Jitta's Atonement was performed for the first time at the Grand Theatre, Fulham, London, on the 3rd February 1925, with Violet Vanbrugh in the title part.

It was performed for the first time in America at the Shubert Theatre New York City, on the 6th January 1923, when Jitta was played by Bertha Kalich. ('Note', 7)

Theatre reviews published in 1923 indicate that *Jitta* was performed at New York's Comedy Theatre rather than the Shubert. When the volume *Translations and Tomfooleries* was published in 1926, the error was explicitly pointed out by a hair-splitting reviewer writing in *The New York Times*: 'as a matter of fact, Trebitsch's drama was performed at the Comedy Theatre. But what are facts in the life of Bernard Shaw? They are nothing. Facts for Shaw have the importance of dust on a withered leaf – not more' (1926: 2). The American producer of the play was Lee Shubert, who owned a number of theatres in New York City, New York State and elsewhere. This might account for the misunderstanding. The *Theatrical Companion to Shaw*, which documents performances of Shaw's plays, includes the following entry on *Jitta's Atonement*, indicating that Shaw and the above-mentioned reviewer were both correct to some extent:

> First presented by Lee Shubert at the Shubert-Garrick Theatre, Washington, 8 January 1923, and at the Comedy Theatre, New York, 17 January 1923 (37 performances).
>
> First produced in England by the Partnership Players at the Grand Theatre, Fulham, London, 26 January 1925 (16 performances).
>
> First presented in London (West End) at the Arts Theatre, 30 April 1930 (6 performances).
>
> There has been no public West End production. (Mander and Mitchenson 1955: 198)[40]

The world premiere of *Jitta's Atonement*, described as 'lackluster', actually took place in Stamford, Connecticut; it was followed by a week in Washington, DC, and then by a run on Broadway, where the play was 'plagued by mediocre reviews and bad luck' and 'effectively flopped' following the (real-life) heart attack of the actor who portrayed Alfred Lenkheim (Conolly-Smith 2013: 115). The Broadway run of *Jitta* was over by 17 February 1923, after which the play went on a three-week New York suburban circuit, which included Brooklyn and the Bronx. Shaw reported on the fortunes, and misfortunes, of the play to Trebitsch (Weiss 2000: 240 and 241, n. 1).

Shaw held off producing the play in London, hoping for a West End début, but in the end he was content with the suburban Grand Theatre, where it opened in January 1925 for a relatively short run, sixteen performances compared with 118 for *Pygmalion* a few years earlier. The West End appearance was not to come for another five years, although it was not in one of the major venues, as indicated above.[41]

There have been few productions of the play over the years. The Shaw Festival, founded in the Canadian town of Niagara-on-the-Lake in 1962, has never staged *Jitta*. The play has been only sporadically resurrected. In 1996, for example, it was presented at the Berkshire Theater Festival, a summer festival in Stockbridge, Massachusetts. In 2001, *Jitta's Atonement* returned to New York City. Nearly eighty years after it was first produced on Broadway, it was presented from 20 October to 3 November 2001 by the Lightning Strikes Theatre Company at the off-off-Broadway Altered Stages Theatre. In 2008, 'Project Shaw', which undertook to present every play Shaw ever wrote, one Monday a month for four years, included a performance of *Jitta* on 17 November 2008.[42]

'The Shaw is only skin deep': The critics react

Lawrence Langner, the founder of the American Theatre Guild, which served as Shaw's American agent, recalls his interest in *Jitta's Atonement* after reading it in 1922. Bertha Kalich had approached the Guild to play the part of Jitta, but since Langner was tied up with other business, she made arrangements to play the part at another theatre (Langner 1963: 94–5). There may or may not be a hint of sour grapes in his assessment, but he concludes: 'Alas *Jitta's Atonement* did not succeed even as a comedy, but the play stands as evidence of the kindness and loyalty of Shaw to his friends when in trouble, financial and otherwise' (Langner 1963: 96).[43]

Overall, the reception of *Jitta* has been less positive than that of other Shaw plays. The focus of most reviews, from the first production to the most recent, has been on the way in which Shaw altered the play through his translation, most frequently referred to as an 'adaptation'. The resulting assessments inevitably entail some form of critique of the unsuccessful melding of Shavian comedy with the dour drama penned by Trebitsch. The day after the play opened, for example, the *New York Evening Post* ran a rather negative review whose headline sums up what it calls the 'collaboration' between Trebitsch and Shaw: "'Jitta's Atonement". Queer Mixture. Old Triangle Theme From A

Modern Psychoanalytical Point of View. Chaotic Result of George Bernard Shaw's Emendation of the Austrian Author's Original Play' (Towse 1923).

On 18 January 1923, the day after the play opened on Broadway, *The Brooklyn Daily Eagle* referred to Shaw as the 'adapter'. Shaw is seen as a 'kind-hearted old gentleman with a sense of the humorous' who has repaid his debt to his translator. The reviewer mentions some of the changes made by Shaw, which result in a play that is 'happier in translation' than in the original. Despite some praise for Shaw's 'winning' lines, he reaches the conclusion that the play is a 'hybrid and not quite the sort of thing American audiences are eager to devour' (Pollock 1923: 6).

The New York Times (1923a) also published a piece entitled 'Bertha Kalich in New Role' with the notation in the subtitle 'Adapted by Shaw'. While not always 'plausible', *Jitta* is judged to be 'important' because it 'introduces George Bernard Shaw in the guise of adapter – a role that he has not hitherto filled in the theatre'. On the other hand, the reviewer finds, 'the Shaw is only skin deep'. In other words, his philosophy shines through only now and again, while the work bears the stamp of its original author. The implication is that although Trebitsch may well be 'not unimportant in his own country', he has less appeal for American audiences. The review's conclusion is that this is an 'artificial comedy' with an 'artificial character', which echoes Pollock's comment about its 'hybrid' quality.

A short piece appeared in *The New York Times* about one month later, entitled 'Shaw as adapter' (1923b). Pointing to the difficulty of the task: 'The way of the translator is not so hard, but adaptation is vexation', it describes Shaw's so-called 'method': 'The Shaw method, barring the stressing of the they-may-have-lived-happy-ever-after impression, which he admits frankly, seems to have been to read Mr. Trebitsch's play carefully, throw it aside, and reconstruct it from memory'. Interestingly, the writer suggests that since Trebitsch had taken liberties when adapting Shaw's plays for German-speaking audiences, Shaw was perhaps 'getting even' by altering the Trebitsch play to such an extent, thus perceptively putting his finger on one of the factors that may have motivated Shaw to translate this work in the first place. Similarly, *Life* magazine, reviewing the play around the same time, also refers to Shaw as the 'adapter', and declares that despite 'just about the worst first act in the history of the drama', the play ends with 'rather an amusing finish' (1923), which would suggest that the play improves the more Shaw departs from the source text.

The play was once again reviewed in *The New York Times* after it was published in 1926, along with Shaw's 'Translator's Note', as part of the volume *Translations and Tomfooleries*. In 'Mr. Shaw Frankly Dons The Cap and Bells', subtitled 'But Even His Collection of "Tomfooleries" Is Not Without Seriousness', the reviewer takes Shaw's preface at face value and foregrounds the notion that the translation has been Shaw's way of repaying his debt to Trebitsch for having made him popular on the continent. Trebitsch's original version, the article goes on to say, is 'a mawkish, involved and torturing piece of work', which Shaw has altered by turning the last act into a comedy. Sympathizing more with Shaw than with the unfortunate Trebitsch, the article concludes that 'All Shaw did was to open the windows on the fetid room and let in some greatly needed fresh air'. If he could confer an honorary doctorate on Shaw, the reviewer concludes, his citation would read: 'The Western World's Only Play Boy; Wise Man of England; Opener of Windows' (*The New York Times* 1926).

When the play opened in West-End London in 1930, it was received more favourably than it had been previously, although emphasis was placed on Shaw's transformation of the play. *The Daily Telegraph* points out that, while the programme announced a translation of Trebitsch by Shaw, 'it is pretty clear from internal textual evidence that Mr. Shaw conjugates the verb "to translate" very differently from most men'. Another reviewer is horrified at 'the shameful way the original author has been manhandled', but also recognizes what Shaw has accomplished: 'There may be those who will be shocked by such treatment of an original play by a "mere translator", but most of them will laugh with Mr Shaw, and the rest of the audience, and return thanks to him for the way in which he has returned his thanks to Herr Trebitsch' (*Nation and Athenaeum* 1930).

Decades later, the American summer festival edition of *Jitta*, which opened on 31 July 1996, was greeted with enthusiasm by *Variety*:

> Here's a rarity: George Bernard Shaw's translation/adaptation of a play by Austrian playwright Siegfried Trebitsch, the man who translated Shaw's plays into German. It's likely that the Berkshire Theater Festival production of 'Jitta's Atonement' is the first since Lee Shubert produced the world premiere on Broadway in 1923. And while the play is not a rediscovered masterpiece, it is a piece of high comedy that gets better and more Shavian as it proceeds, as does the production. 'Jitta's Atonement' is well worth reviving and brings some luster to New England's 1996 summer season. (Taylor 1996)

Another review of the summer festival version lavished praise on the company for 'pulling this little known George Bernard Shaw rarity out of mothballs'. The director, actors, and set designers obviously contributed to the play's success, but the reviewer underlines the quality of the play itself, which in her view is 'not just another old chestnut that should never have been unpacked from its seven decades of obscurity'. She sees it as a 'fascinating collaboration between the famous Irish playwright and an aspiring Austrian playwright named Siegfried Trebitsch, whose main claim to fame was and is as Shaw's German translator', although she opines that *Jitta* is an unlikely candidate for Broadway or even off Broadway since, in the final analysis, it remains merely 'half a Shaw' (Sommer 1996).

In his commentary on the 2001 Lightning Strikes production, the reviewer points out that the playwright is listed as George Bernard Shaw in 'a free adaptation of Siegfried Trebitsch's "Frau Gitta's Sühne"'. He adds that Trebitsch had become Shaw's 'apostle' in Europe, to help him conquer the new territory of the Continent. The 'thank-you present of a play', he concludes, 'is a curious collation of turgid Germanic domestic drama and Shavian compromises and practicalities'. Once again, it is the 'blending' that is called into question: 'That this odd mix of ingredients never blends is not surprising – as is the fact that the play has not had a New York production since it premiered here in 1923' (Levett 2001: 27). In another review, *Jitta* is considered weak in comparison to plays like *Pygmalion* or *Major Barbara*, with their 'wealth of complex relationships and gloriously flowering prose'. Granted, Trebitsch does not have the same 'flair for drama' as Shaw, it is pointed out, but Shaw himself is also to blame, for not having made it as 'compelling' as his own works (Murray 2001).

When *Jitta* was brought back to New York audiences as part of the project that ambitiously sought to resurrect each of Shaw's plays, it was described as a 'shocking Viennese 1920 amusement wickedly re-imagined by George Bernard Shaw'. Shaw is billed as an inspiring 'free-thinking humanist, dedicated to presenting the cause of human rights for all' (Broadwayworld.com 2008). In *Playbill*, the play is described as a 'rarely heard play', 'loosely translated' from a Viennese one in which the 'atonement isn't particularly profound but the wicked fun is' (Gans 2008).

What emerges from these commentaries, however divergent their appreciation of Shaw's work, is a recognition of the unique motivation driving Shaw to steal spare moments from his own creative pursuits to apply himself to the act of translating. Above all, the voices of the critics come together in a collective tribute to the exercise of translating for the theatre. In every case, translating for the stage is shown to entail a greater degree of adaptation than other genres. Although his experience was confined to this one instance of translating, Shaw proved to be both a lucid practitioner and theorizer of this challenging venture. One wonders, finally, what further attempts at *tradaptation* might have yielded had Shaw elected to tackle the work of a playwright of greater stature.

Conclusions: A writer's legacy and a translator's fate

It cannot be said unequivocally that Shaw had 'expertise' in the field of translation, either as a practitioner or as a theorist. He did, however, exert some influence on its practice through his own experience as a translator as well as his efforts to revise the translations of his work, made by Trebitsch and Hamon, in particular. The application of his prodigious intelligence and wit to the subject in the course of his long-time interaction and correspondence with Siegfried Trebitsch and others has generated fruitful and intriguing insights into the art of translation.

A Shavian legacy: The Nobel Prize in literature

Shaw also left his mark on the world of translation through a more concrete, less cerebral, act of philanthropy. In November 1926, it was announced that the 1925 Nobel Prize for literature would be bestowed upon Bernard Shaw for the 'idealism and humanity' of his body of work. Shaw's immediate reaction was to decline the Nobel Prize altogether, as he was quick to point out to his Swedish translator, Lady Ebba Low, who was the first to congratulate him (Letter of 14 November 1926, *Letters* vol. 4: 32). He was not interested in the monetary prize of approximately £6500, but Charlotte felt that such a distinction would bring honour to Ireland. After meeting with Baron Erik Kule Palmstierna, Swedish Minister to England, Shaw agreed to accept the award on the condition that the money be used to facilitate the translation of works by Swedish writers into English. On 18 November 1926, he wrote to the Permanent Secretary of the Royal Swedish Academy to inform him of the conclusions reached with Palmstierna. In his letter, Shaw describes the Nobel Prize as 'a very welcome reinforcement of the cordial understanding between British and Swedish culture' which 'will not be lost on my native country, Ireland'; he goes on to point out that he does not need the money, which he views as 'a lifebelt thrown to a swimmer who has already reached the shore in safety'. He underscores the importance of translation, but couches his arguments in his distinctive tongue-in-cheek style:

Some of the most advantageous sites in London are being rapidly filled up with agencies in which not only the British Dominions Oversea, but the European Powers, exhibit their choicest products and advertise the attractions and travelling facilities of their countries. Fruits, cereals, stuffed animals and birds ... The one thing that is rarely exhibited is a book. Sweden invites us to buy her paper; but there is nothing printed on it: the function of Swedish paper, it seems, is to wrap Australian apples in. And yet Sweden's most valuable export is her literature, of which we in Britain are deplorably ignorant.

Baron Palmstierna ... has informed me of Swedish books of great value which for lack of means cannot be translated and of organs working for the intellectual intercourse between us which are in need of support.

I therefore venture to propose to you that the money which accompanies the award be ... used to encourage intercourse and understanding in literature and arts between Sweden and the British Isles. (*Letters* vol. 4: 34)

Bernard Shaw accepted the award, but he did not attend the ceremony, which was held in Stockholm on 10 December 1926. The Nobel Prize, in his eyes, was a mere annoyance. As he wrote to Hamon, on 2 February 1927, it was 'a hideous calamity', almost as bad as his seventieth birthday, since he was solicited for loans and donations as soon as the news was announced. When it was revealed that he had not accepted the money, 'another million or so wrote to say that if I was rich enough to throw away money like that, I could afford to adopt their children, or pay off their mortgages on their houses' (*Letters* vol. 4: 39). None of the prize money went to these bold individual supplicants. Instead, it served to fund the Anglo-Swedish Literary Foundation, created to encourage 'cultural intercourse between Sweden and the British Islands through the promotion and diffusion of knowledge and appreciation of Swedish culture in the British Islands'. The Foundation supports the Swedish English Literary Translators' Association, an annual book grant for students studying Swedish at a British university, and the Bernard Shaw Translation Prize. This decision – a tip of the Shavian hat to translation and transnational literary exchange – had an impact that endures to this day.[44]

'Vicarious, reflected fame': The fate of the translator

In the shadow of the great playwright lurks the figure of an undervalued, embittered translator, 'depressed' by the fate dealt to him. The terrible tag, 'Shaw's translator', was indelibly affixed to Siegfried Trebitsch, type-casting him in a role from which he was unable to escape, and leaving him in a perpetual struggle to assert his own identity as an original author. In an epilogue to his edition of Shaw's letters to Trebitsch, Weiss tells the story of the translator's passing:

> In 1956, having arranged to sell Shaw's letters, which he had guarded as a treasure, Trebitsch went to his bank, retrieved the heavy bundle of correspondence, and suffered a heart attack. He was in his eighty-eighth year. On 3 June, Siegfried Trebitsch – felled by the hand of his dead friend – died . . . . (Weiss 1986: 471)

This is the stuff that plays are made of: the Viennese author and translator suffers a fate not unlike that of his own character, Professor Bruno Haldenstedt, who dies of a heart attack in the opening moments of *Jitta's Atonement*, leaving a weighty manuscript behind for posterity.

On 4 June 1956, *The Times* of London published an obituary that generously saluted Trebitsch for his efforts as both a writer and translator, although beneath the headline 'Dr Siegfried Trebitsch' is a subhead that characterizes him as 'Shaw's Translator', a role for which he is said to have earned a 'vicarious, reflected fame'. Trebitsch's original work is politely assessed: 'attractive, if not very profound, society novels' produced early in his career, and then a life's work which, while not impressive, is deserving of 'respect, even admiration' given the 'enormous spiritual and material work accomplished simultaneously in the service of the greater man'. The eulogistic column ends with an evaluation of Trebitsch's translations that is far more positive than opinions expressed by critics or, for that matter, by Shaw himself during their long association with one another:

> His translation of Shaw's dramatic work was, indubitably, one of the most voluminous, most difficult and most ambitious tasks of its kind ever undertaken by a single writer; and, as indubitably, one of the most perfectly accomplished transfers of thought and form from one language into another, without loss of the author's very particular characteristics.

Significantly, however, the greater man upstages his translator even in death. Halfway down the single-column obituary a second subheading has been inserted – 'Shaw as Translator'. Under that heading, the article refers to Shaw's own efforts as a translator and names *Jitta's Atonement*: one play during a lifetime extending over ninety-four years, a single translation compared to the monumental body of translations done by the man, about whom, after all, the obit has been written.

Figure 2 Alice Toklas (left) and Gertrude Stein (right) at home at 27, rue de Fleurus. Above Stein's head is the portrait by Cézanne, which, along with Flaubert's *Trois Contes*, inspired her to write *Three Lives*. Photograph by Man Ray, taken in 1922, now held by the National Portrait Gallery, Smithsonian Institution. © Man Ray Trust / SODRAC (2017).

Gertrude Stein and the Making of Translations

I have lived in France the best and longest part of my life and I love France and the French but after all I am an American, and it always does come back to that I was born there, and one's native land is one's native land you cannot get away from it.

–Gertrude Stein, *Wars I Have Seen*

'America is my country and Paris is my hometown': A life in translation

Penned by someone who spent more than half her life among expatriate writers and artists in her beloved Paris, these words signal the double affiliation of a writer living abroad.[1] They evoke a striking case of hybrid identity. Stein was a Jewish lesbian American in Paris; she was a writer preoccupied with ambivalent relationships – with her sexual and religious identities, her audiences, her mother tongue, and her homeland. These ambiguities play out not only in her original writing but also in her alleged, aborted, and actual translations.

Gertrude Stein was born on 3 February 1874, in Allegheny (now part of Pittsburgh), Pennsylvania and raised in Oakland, California. She spent a year living in Paris as a child and moved back to the city in 1903 at the age of twenty-nine, joining her brother Leo, who had settled there shortly before. She lived with him at what later became a famous address – 27, rue de Fleurus, in the 6ᵉ *arrondissement* – until the arrival of Alice Toklas a few years later. By the time she died in 1946, in Neuilly-sur-Seine, a suburb of Paris, she had lived most of her adult life in Paris. With the exception of her 'barnstorming' tour of the United States in 1934–1935, she never returned home.[2]

Stein had a sustained and passionate, though conflicted, attachment to Paris, to France, to the French language, and to all things French; translation runs through her life and lifework not only as an occasional literary activity but also as a theme and, to some extent, a fiction. This chapter will examine Stein's self-imposed exile in Paris, the context in which these paradoxical elements converge, and the ways in which she not only embarked upon translation but also expressed – or suppressed – her authority and authorial voice in translation.

Stein was a prolific author: twenty-five books were published in her lifetime, and another twenty-five were published after her death. She tried her hand at most literary genres: poetry, novels, plays, opera libretti, children's stories, essays, and unique pieces she called 'portraits'. Interwoven with such original works were several translation projects. Early in her career, she translated Flaubert's *Trois Contes* (or perhaps only began to do so before turning to her own writing). Later, she undertook a translation of or 'meditation on' a cycle of poems by surrealist poet Georges Hugnet. The last instance was the aborted and unpublished translation of speeches by Vichy leader Maréchal Philippe Henri Pétain. She attempted some other translations from French or original writing in French; she was also known to have done some self-translation, providing her translators with a crib from which they could produce suitable French versions of her work. While each instance of translation, or each engagement with the act of translating, is problematic in that a certain degree of 'non-translation' or resistance is involved, each one is also instructive.

Exiles and expatriates

The so-called 'Lost Generation' has captured the American imagination, having been abundantly portrayed and immortalized in both fiction and nonfiction, as well as in the cinema – in Woody Allen's 2011 film *Midnight in Paris*, for example.[3] Stein was one of its most prominent representatives, but she actually preceded and outlasted that group, many of whom arrived in Paris as the First World War was ending, then returned home as the Great Depression began. Paul Auster, as chapter three will show, would also embrace this 'enduring literary myth' of American writers learning their *métier* in a Parisian garret; Gertrude Stein tops his list of examples. Stein did settle in Paris early, as a matter of fact, and even claimed to have 'created' the twentieth century, but she was actually part of a longer tradition, which merits closer scrutiny.

The term 'exile' is generally associated with banishment, expulsion, and dislocation. The American artists and writers who found their way to Paris were not driven by famine, poverty, persecution, or war. While they could more properly be considered 'expatriates', the truth is that they branded themselves as 'exiles'.

Ezra Pound, notably, claimed 'world citizenship' for himself (1909; quoted in Dennis 2000: 89) and founded a short-lived magazine called *The Exile*. In 1934, Malcolm Cowley, a magazine editor and minor figure in the Lost Generation, published a book called *Exile's Return*, showing the movement of authors out of America after the First World War and then back again after the 1929 financial crisis. In his 1947 memoir, *Paris Was Our Mistress*, Samuel Putnam observed that Paris was 'a good deal nearer than New York or Chicago to being the literary capital of the United States' (5); he, too, used the term 'exile' to refer to the many American writers who flocked to Paris, where they lived not out of necessity, but willingly (31).[4]

There was a long-established pattern of Americans travelling to Paris, as David McCullough shows. In the nineteenth century, James Fenimore Cooper and Henry James, among others, found inspiration in Paris. Other well-known Americans included Samuel F.B. Morse, better known now for his Morse code, who left home to study painting at the Louvre, and poet Oliver Wendell Holmes, Jr, who went to Paris to study medicine. Many of them had little knowledge of French culture or the French language, but they were captivated by French art and architecture (McCullough 2011). In the 1830s, Americans in Paris numbered less than a thousand – a mere fraction compared to the English, Germans, or Italians. This number rose significantly one century later, although Americans were still a minority among foreigners, and members of the Lost Generation were not alone in the community of expats.[5]

Regardless of whether they settled on the Left or Right Bank, most expatriates came to Paris for the freedom it afforded. Self-imposed exile to Paris allowed an escape from repressive institutions or restrictive social and cultural practices at home. Some Americans came to Paris to enjoy 'prosaic freedoms': to drink and to avoid paying taxes (Green 2014: 5). France was a place where African-Americans could flee the racial segregation they were subjected to in the United States. Others came to avoid the Puritanical culture of home, which constrained their ability to enjoy sexual freedoms.

Both Leo and Gertrude were drawn by these freedoms. They were also influenced by Henry James's view of the intellectual benefits of travelling abroad. James was an early transatlantic writer, who had spent the last three decades of his life as an expatriate in Europe. Gertrude Stein, known to be a prodigious reader, paradoxically claimed to experience few influences. She took great pains to dismiss the notion that she was in any way 'influenced' by James, although he is the subject of one of the four portraits that comprise *Four in America*, completed in 1933 around the time of *The Autobiography of Alice B. Toklas*. And she does admit that he was her 'forerunner' (in the 1946 'Transatlantic Interview', for example, in Stein 1971b). In the *Autobiography*, Alice says that she herself was a 'great admirer of Henry James', and that she had thought of turning his novel, *The Awkward Age*, into a play (4); however, it was Henry's brother, William James, Gertrude's professor at Radcliffe, who had made a 'lasting impression' on Gertrude.[6]

Before the publication of the *Autobiography*, Gertrude Stein spoke to Putnam about her 'place in literature':

> My place in literature? Twentieth-century literature *is* Gertrude Stein. There was Henry James, of course –
>
> Yes, there was Henry James –
>
> He was my precursor, you might say; but everything really begins with my *Three Lives*. (Putnam 1947: 138)

Whether she liked to admit it or not, Gertrude Stein followed a certain tradition of American expatriate writing. For Henry James and others like him, distance from home provided an opportunity not only to escape America but also to enter into a dialectal relationship with identity. Stein, too, insisted that creative individuals needed another civilization in addition to their own. 'Writers have to have two countries, the one where they belong and the one in which they live really', she writes in the 1940 publication that is widely referred to as her 'love letter to France' (*Paris France*, 2). She also felt that a writer should have more than one occupation, which in her case involved looking at paintings and collecting them. Paris satisfied both these needs (Brinnin 1959: 47). France – in contrast to inhospitable America – was a place where she was free to fashion her self and her lifestyle, and to experiment with her craft. She reiterated this attraction toward the end of her life: 'and so there is the Paris France from 1900 to 1939, where everybody had to be to be free' (*Paris France*, 37). At the same time, she emphasizes her own role in spearheading the modernist movement: 'Paris was where the twentieth century was ... the place that suited those of us that were to create the twentieth century and literature' (11–12).[7]

> Of course they all came to France a great many to paint pictures and naturally they could not do that at home, or write they could not do that at home either, they could be dentists at home because she knew all about that even before the war, Americans were a practical people and dentistry was practical. (*Paris France*, 19)

In benefiting from the freedom to live and write as she pleased, she resembles other expatriate women in Paris, many of them lesbian like her, such as Sylvia Beach and Adrienne Monnier, Natalie Barney, H.D. and Nancy Cunard. Far removed from a patriarchal American literary heritage, she could 'put aside her American fathers', as Benstock suggests, 'assuming the authority invested in the male in order to explore the troublesome interior world of her femaleness'; she could 'deny her predecessors' in order to address her 'anxiety of authorship' (1986: 192). Stein, like other prominent women of the Left Bank, was committed to turning her exile to advantage and 'charting new territory' (Sloboda 2008: 4–9).

An additional factor that may have influenced Stein, albeit in subtler, less overt ways, was her Jewishness. Citing such writers and thinkers as Freud, Benjamin, Adorno, Celan, and Kafka, Gluzman has pointed to a 'three-way correlation between modernism, exile, and Jewishness'. Regarded as the 'paradigmatic diaspora people', Jews have 'celebrated' exile, presenting it as a 'vehicle for individuality, freedom, and resistance' (1998: 231–2). Gertrude Stein participated in this celebration of expatriation, in the 'exuberance and unending self-discovery' evoked by Edward Said with respect to what he calls 'exilic displacement', affecting even those who are not actual migrants but rather metaphorical exiles in the sense that they are outsiders within their own society (1996: 62–3). That said, her first years in Paris may have been less joyous than she retrospectively claimed, as Leon Katz suggests.[8]

> The picture that she herself offers in her autobiographies of an eager, not to say bouncing, enthusiast for Parisian art, for friends, for her new life, was written from the happily distant perspective of the Nineteen Thirties when she associated nothing of her life in Paris with unhappiness ... times such as these were lost to her in a mist of self-congratulation, daily pleasures and indeed of a newly reinforced egomania that had begun to overtake her after she finished *The Making of Americans* and recognized frankly and with a kind of astonished joy the overwhelming scope of her achievements. (Katz 1963: 53)

Stein arrived at her brother's place, intending to stay only a short time, after having abandoned her medical studies (Katz 1963: 52). Depressed following an unhappy love affair, but with vague hopes of becoming a writer, she read prodigiously and took notes. It was not until she completed *Three Lives* in 1909 and then *The Making of Americans* in 1911, that she began to gain confidence – and audacity. 'Slowly I was knowing that I was a genius', she recalled much later in *Everybody's Autobiography* (76). She began to see herself not merely as a participant but as a leading figure in the trend which later emerged as modernism. For Stein and those who gathered at 27, rue de Fleurus to view the avant-garde paintings that she and her brother had hung, exile to Paris, expatriation and cosmopolitanism were viewed as the path to increased freedom and heightened creative powers, which all came to be linked to a fresh sensibility and the new aesthetics of modernism.

The language(s) of exile: 'parsing her perverse English in Paris'

While Gertrude Stein's double affiliation may well be considered more of a 'liberating privilege' than the 'tormenting lack' that afflicted many others (Gluzman 1998: 247), it is also true that questions of identity, as well as issues of language, remain problematic in her writing, manifesting themselves in her paradoxical engagement with the task of translating.

Stein had occasion to rub shoulders with modernists who were preoccupied to varying degrees with dichotomies of mother tongue/foreign tongue, or homeland/ foreign country. She would have encountered many people who were quite content to speak English while sipping wine on the *café-terrasses* of Montparnasse. Others, on the other hand – many of them not only writers but also translators and self-translators – embraced wholeheartedly the culture and language of their adopted country. Multilingualism was a key element of modernism and the movement's most visible proponents emphasized the productive aspects of cosmopolitanism. Ezra Pound, for instance, relied on the translation of foreign works as a source of inspiration and newness. James Joyce was a polyglot who merged several languages in his unique brand of English and, like his famous character Stephen Dedalus, left home for Paris in a journey of (self) discovery.

While modernism produced what Kellman calls a 'literature of exile' associated with a 'translingual imagination', many writers – Stein included – did *not* cross linguistic boundaries:

> some of modernism's most influential champions have stubbornly clung to their native languages thousands of miles from where it is spoken. Consider Gertrude Stein parsing her perverse English in Paris, Witold Gombrowicz and Czesław Miłosz composing in their Polish in Buenos Aires and Berkeley, respectively … heroic figures of the artist who maintains literary loyalty to the native language from the native land. (Kellman 2000: 6)

Long before Salman Rushdie (1991: 17) employed the expression 'translated men', metaphorically, to describe his condition as a migrant, Gertrude Stein was herself living a life in translation. Yet she struck a characteristically ambivalent pose: she remained resolutely unilingual while maintaining a love affair with France and French – the country, the people, and the language.

'I talk French badly and write it worse'

In addition to what she has reported in her autobiographical writing, various accounts of Stein's life confirm her love of France. The earliest testimonial is a memoir published in 1948, two years after her death, by W.G. Rogers, the American 'doughboy' whom she met during the First World War and affectionately called 'the Kiddie':

> She adopted the city as her permanent home several years after leaving Johns Hopkins; she wrote *Paris France* as a heartfelt tribute, and her inscription in my French copy of the book, which was printed in 1941, reads in part: 'All about our dear France'. The place crept into the Stein blood, for brother Leo lived with her there in the early years, and so did brother Michael, and Michael's son settled in Paris. (Rogers 1971: 45)

Linda Wagner-Martin (1995) evokes Gertrude's affection for the French people, which in her view took the place of any definitive political stance or allegiance, even in wartime. Never conventionally political, Gertrude and Alice responded to situations as the human beings they were: the French people who were their friends were those they helped. Soon after the Second World War was declared, they hosted 'mysterious evening gatherings' at their country home in Bilignin (238).[9]

Despite Stein's enthusiasm for Paris and France, she spoke little French and showed little interest in modern French writers. She is said to have 'lived within her own walls' (Josephson 1972: xxiii) and, according to biographer Elizabeth Sprigge, did not join 'the vehement gatherings of foreign writers and artists on the *terrasses* of the Rotonde and the Dôme'; nor did she and Toklas frequent the restaurants of the *quartier latin* or the literary salons of Paris (Sprigge 1957: 148). The self-portrait Stein presents in the *Autobiography* (28) of being 'in the heart of an art movement of which the outside world at that time knew nothing', is debunked by Katz, who says that far from being 'on the horizon of current French art', she lived in a 'foreign oasis' of mainly English-speaking relatives and acquaintances (1963: 98). She remained 'adamant about her loyalty to her homeland' (Sloboda 2008: 74), as evidenced in her 1945 memoir, 'I love France and the French but after all I am an American' (*Wars I Have Seen*, 132). While she appreciated the pleasures and liberties that Paris afforded, she remained 'very much of an *American*' according to Carl Van Vechten's introduction to the 1933 New York edition of *Three Lives* (1933a: ix).[10]

This stance was not uncommon. Several other Americans spent time in Paris with little contact with their French counterparts as illustrated by a similar comment from fellow expatriate Virgil Thomson: 'It was all right to be a foreigner working in France, but not a pseudo-Gallic clinger-on. I had not gone to France to save French music, but merely to improve my own' (Thomson 1967: 116).[11]

As a prelude to investigating Stein's involvement in translation, it is useful to try to determine how much French she actually knew, and to assess the extent to which she was able, or willing, to speak, read, and write in French. As can be expected, there are conflicting reports, including from Stein herself.

Speaking: 'I talked it all right, but I never read it'

Stein addresses the issue of language in *Everybody's Autobiography* (1937), her second autobiographical work, which recaps the major events of her life and her impressions of her American tour. Recalling a conversation with Mary Pickford, she writes: 'She said she wished she knew more French and I said I talked it all right but I never read it I did not care about it as a written language' (7). Some of those who knew her well have said that she spoke fluently, with a slight accent, while others are more critical of her command of French.

Writing about Stein and her wartime years in the Bugey region, a French observer remarked that her French was 'approximatif' (Saint-Pierre 2009: 22). In the memoirs she wrote much later, Alice recalls that while Gertrude knew French, 'She did not like to read or speak anything but English, although she knew German and French' (Toklas 1963: 28). Gertrude deliberately avoided speaking French, unlike Alice, who transacted the business of the household in French and made an effort to learn the language, arranging to take French lessons from Picasso's companion Fernande (Toklas 1963: 32).

In the countryside later in life, however, Gertrude is reported to have walked long distances, conversing with the neighbours in French. She appeared to be 'proud of her Americanized French, which she did not use much in Paris'. This endeared her to the local people, who were 'pleased that she had chosen to live among them, and didn't care about who she was and what she did' (Wagner-Martin 1995: 191). This has been corroborated by Joan Chapman, who was a young woman when Gertrude was still alive: 'Gertrude spoke French fluently and with great ease. She had a slight accent. Her voice was light and feminine. She loved to communicate and talked to everybody asking questions and making remarks. People loved her'.[12]

Reading: 'they are not books to me unless they are translated into English'

In her writing, Stein frequently underlines the importance of the French language and culture during her childhood. This is recapitulated in *Paris France*, in which she claims to have learned to speak French when she was very young.[13] Gertrude's father had taken his family – wife and young children included – to Europe. After spending some time in Vienna, the family moved to Paris for one year when Gertrude was four years old. Her mother kept diaries in which she recorded the activities and rich cultural life of her children.[14] When the family returned to the United States, they settled in California, where there were many French families. Young Gertrude saw French plays (Sarah Bernhardt came) and French paintings (Sprigge 1957: 15; and *Paris France*). From a young age, she was a voracious reader, but she consumed English literature mainly. Even when she read French authors, like Jules Verne, who was very popular in the United States at the time, she did so in translation. As she says in *Paris France* (3), as well as in *Everybody's Autobiography* (146), 'we seemed to have Jules Verne in everything except in French of course I only read him in English'. In a 1939 piece entitled 'My Debt to Books', she writes:

> So many books have been important to me, it is like the man who said about automobiles when someone asked him is that mark a good one, all automobiles are good … of course only English, I cannot read any foreign language. I cannot lose myself in them, and so they are not books to me unless they are translated into English.[15]

The *Autobiography* reports that there were no French books or newspapers on Stein's desk. This is corroborated in a letter written by Alice Toklas to a student at Princeton University.[16] During the war years in the countryside, she did look at local newspapers, but, in general, French was not for reading, but rather for speaking.

Writing: 'it is … not at all natural to write french, English is what I write'

With a few exceptions, Stein did not write in French either, unlike her compatriot Edith Wharton, who was very fluent and who composed *Ethan*

Frome, a novel set in New England, in French before translating it into English (Sloboda 2008: 74). And when she did use French, on occasion, it was far from fluent. Her friendship with Pablo Picasso lasted a lifetime; they conversed and exchanged letters and postcards in French: 'I talk French badly and write it worse but so does Pablo he says we write and talk our French but that is a later story' (*Everybody's Autobiography*, 14). The quality of her French is apparent in a random sample taken from a letter to Picasso dated 1922: 'Nous menons un vie tres simple nous et le petit Ford [her automobile]. Je travaille beaucoup, j'ecrit beaucoup de lettres et je nettoy le moteur' (Madeline 2005: 270); needless to say, Picasso's responses were equally error-ridden.

The few pieces she did write in French needed extensive editorial work to make them suitable for publication. She was not at ease, for example, when she wrote *Picasso* in 1938: 'I have just written a french book in french about Picasso and it was a frightful struggle it is not natural not at all natural to write french, English is what I write, I kind of feel the English language' (Letter from Stein to William P. Sears, Jr, dated 10 December 1937; quoted in Wagner-Martin 1995: 234). The fact that the essay on Picasso was written in French was considered a 'significant departure from Stein's usual habit'; the manuscript was revised by her friends, art dealer Daniel-Henry Kahnweiler and Baronne Pierlot (Burns 1970: 117). It was then translated into English and adapted for publication by Toklas, who was thus 'assuming the voice of the companion who had earlier '*translated her*' by purporting to tell her life story' (Sloboda 2008: 161 n. 11; emphasis added).

Her friend Virgil Thomson sums it up: 'Though she read and spoke French comfortably, Gertrude did not aspire to write in it, beyond the necessities of social correspondence. And she had never used her literary powers for translating works she admired' (1967: 185). He does mention exceptions: a short scenario in French about how she acquired a poodle, *Deux sœurs qui ne sont pas sœurs*, written at the request of Hugnet, and then, as a 'concession to French' (185), her translation of Hugnet's poems, to which we will return below.

'Living with so very many people and being all alone with english and myself'

The *Autobiography* paints the picture of a cosmopolitan group of people coming and going from the Stein home in Paris. When Toklas looks back in her own memoir, *What Is Remembered*, she, too, evokes a multilingual, multi-ethnic entourage: 'Pierre Roché, who spoke a smattering of several languages including Hungarian; Hans Purrmann, a German painter devoted to Matisse' (1963: 31). Toklas also notes the foreigners who came to Matisse's school: Czechs, Hungarians, an Italian, a Russian and 'quantities of Germans' (1963: 43). Stein emphasizes the benefits of being with so many people who knew *no* English.

> One of the things that I have liked all these years is to be surrounded by people who know no english.... No, I like living with so very many people and being all alone with english and myself. (*Autobiography*, 70)

And yet, living 'within her own walls', she remained relatively isolated from the French community around her. She did not entirely embrace the lively life of the Left Bank, teeming with intellectuals and artists of diverse backgrounds. She also seemed to reject the spoken French she heard around her:

> Picasso and I were talking the other day. I always said I never minded living in France. I write with my eyes, not with my ears or mouth. I hate lecturing, because you begin to hear yourself talk, because sooner or later you hear your voice, and you do not hear what you say. You just hear what they hear you say. As a matter of fact, as a writer I write entirely with my eyes. The words as seen by my eyes are the important words, and the ears and mouth do not count. ('Transatlantic Interview' in Stein 1971b: 31)

Stein's denial of the importance of her 'ears and mouth' is disingenuous, however. In the words of Dydo, 'nothing could be further from the truth'. So much of Stein's work is based on wordplay, on puns that are 'both visual and auditory' and not, in fact, limited to English (Dydo 2003: 221, n. 14). As she experimented with new forms of writing, as she explored the complexities of the English language, the presence of French around her allowed her to take a fresh approach to her own language, and may also have inspired new formulations.

These ambivalent, often conflicting, reflections on language can be linked to Stein's 'aesthetic of struggle' (Katz 1963: 2), which she herself mentions when she draws a parallel between Picasso's move to cubism, Matisse's 'new school of color', and her composition of 'Melanctha', the second story of *Three Lives* (*Autobiography*, 54). In the case of Stein grappling with language in her foreign 'home town', it can be instructive to apply the notion of a 'shadow language', in the words of Eric Ormsby: 'a concealed or tacit foreign language which exerts a strong and sometimes fruitful pressure on the native tongue of a poet'. In contrast to Joyce who made a more overt and deliberate use of foreign tongues, Stein benefited more subtly from the subterranean presence of French, which contributes, perhaps, to bringing forth what is 'strongest, most resonant' in her English work (Ormsby 2003: 22–5).

These various preoccupations or anxieties, associated with language and homeland, are closely tied to the place of translation within Stein's body of work. A key consideration in the case studies that follow will be the way in which her linguistic isolation and 'denial' of her literary predecessors (Benstock 1986: 192) is reflected her stance vis-à-vis the (male) authors she translates.

'She had begun ... as an exercise in literature to translate Flaubert's Trois Contes'

Given her less than fluent command of French and, even more importantly, her almost stubborn refusal to embrace the French language, it is no wonder that Stein is not well known as a translator. Nor was she a polyglot like other members of the avant-garde expatriate community. And yet, surprisingly, translation is present in her work as both a trope and an actual practice.

It is widely known that *The Autobiography of Alice B. Toklas*, composed in 1932 and published in 1933, is not actually an autobiography of Gertrude's companion, Alice, but rather the story of her own life and times told in Alice's voice. It was the book that finally made Stein famous after decades of writing. In it, she becomes her own Boswell, or, as she says in the concluding paragraph, her own Defoe:

> About six weeks ago Gertrude Stein said, it does not look to me as if you were ever going to write that autobiography. You know what I'm going to do. I am going to write it for you. I am going to write it as simply as Defoe did the autobiography of Robinson Crusoe. And she has and this is it. (*Autobiography*, 252)

An obvious fiction, or literary hoax, the book delighted its audiences because of its sprightly account of exciting times in Paris, France. It abounds in tales of brilliant people who enriched the lives of Gertrude and Alice, along with an inventory of Gertrude's achievements and qualities. Slipped in among the anecdotes are several references to French translations of Stein's work, as well as a pithy account of how her first published novel, *Three Lives*, came about:

> [The Cézanne portrait] was an important purchase because in looking and looking at this picture Gertrude Stein wrote Three Lives.

> She had begun not long before as an exercise in literature to translate Flaubert's Trois Contes and then she had this Cézanne and she looked at it and under its stimulus she wrote Three Lives. (*Autobiography*, 34)

The *Autobiography* cannot be fully trusted: it is not always easy to discriminate between what actually happened and what Stein is making up, or at least exaggerating. When not directly under attack by its detractors (Jolas 1935), the *Autobiography* has been depicted as a 'rousing good yarn' (Rogers 1971: 22), and readers have been cautioned: 'it is always advisable to check [its] testimony... against other evidence' (Bridgman 1971: 35). We do know, however, that the purchase of the Cézanne painting was real and that she was particularly attached to it throughout her life.[17]

This much is also true: she did have a copy of *Trois Contes* in her library. However, the book does not look well used or marked up – except for a sketch of several people (Gertrude and a triangle of three individuals?) on a blank page at the end, which was presumably drawn by Stein. Leo was an avid reader of Flaubert and probably urged her to try translating the French master. Yet, in the abundant archival material left to Yale University, in the notebooks she filled as she wrote *Three Lives* in 1905–1906, there is nothing resembling even the beginnings of a translation.[18]

Katz, among others, reports how the Stein papers were acquired. In 1936, Thornton Wilder suggested that she send her unpublished manuscripts to the United States for safekeeping in case war broke out on French soil. All manner of papers were packed pell mell into a trunk and shipped to Yale: manuscripts, correspondence and even 'scraps of paper that Gertrude never threw away, budget lists... old forgotten bills' (1963: i). In the course of his doctoral research, Katz observed that some of the pages of the extant notebooks, including those pertaining to *Three Lives*, had been excised (1963: 71–2, n. 2). Despite the considerable volume of material, therefore, it is also possible that a fragmentary translation – if one ever existed – was lost or discarded along with the sliced-out pages.

What did Stein mean when she wrote in the *Autobiography* that the book she had written three decades earlier was composed after she 'had begun... to translate Flaubert's Trois Contes'? Citing biographers Sprigge (1957) and Brinnin (1959), Katz says that this story of translating Flaubert 'has been repeated many times', but, in his view, the presumed translation might have amounted to no more than a single paragraph, after which she launched into writing her own stories (1963: 71). Nonetheless, the story of the Flaubert translation has been taken more or less at face value. Retold over time, it has now become enshrined as a 'fact' in the oft-recounted life and times of Gertrude Stein. An entry on modernism in *The Columbia History of the American Novel*, for example, affirms both the act of translation itself and its association with the lasting influence of Flaubert on modernist writing.

> Inspired by Gustave Flaubert, whose story 'Un Coeur Simple' she had translated to improve her French, Stein told the stories of these exploited women in severely unadorned and stripped prose that would make Flaubert's style the enduring standard of the language of modernist fiction. (Norris 1991: 312–13)

Getting at the 'true story' is a matter of sleuthing and speculation: did she really translate Flaubert and, if so, how far did she get and why did she do it? How does this act of translation fit within her literary trajectory? To what extent did Flaubert influence her writing and *Three Lives*, in particular? How was this story told over the course of her life, and to what purpose?

'Everything I have done has been influenced by Flaubert and Cézanne'

Stein critics and biographers have spilled much ink exploring the different ways in which Flaubert influenced Stein's writing, composition, and themes. They have given credence, to varying degrees, to Stein's belated tale of having translated Flaubert's *Trois Contes*. Biographer Elizabeth Sprigge expresses 'surprise' at the alleged translation and frames the Flaubert anecdote in this way:

> She was now giving words much attention, and after finishing *Q.E.D.* began as an exercise to translate Flaubert's *Trois Contes*. In general French literature did not interest her; what little she read was in translation ... French was a speaking language and English the writing one ... So this translation is surprising, except that Leo had been reading Flaubert, and Gertrude was still his disciple.
>   Before she had gone far she found that she wanted to write again herself. The heroine of *Un Cœur simple* recalled one of her own servants and she was eager to portray some such strong simple character. So, with Flaubert in the forefront of her mind and William James at the back of it, Cézanne before her eyes and Baltimore in memory, she began to write *Three Lives*.
>   Any literary influence came less from Flaubert than from other reading.... (Sprigge 1957: 54)

The task of translation to which Stein refers briefly in the *Autobiography* has also been inflated, described as a 'germinal' labour, a 'unique undertaking for her', 'upon which she now quietly worked through the length of every night'

(Brinnin 1959: 56). In her 2006 critical edition of *Three Lives* (and *Q.E.D.*), editor Marianne DeKoven states quite simply that Stein 'was translating Flaubert' when she began *Three Lives* (327); among the various 'authoritative texts' – both old and more recent – that DeKoven includes, are several that repeat the story and then make elaborate comparisons between Stein and Flaubert.[19]

It seems fairly certain that it was Leo who encouraged his sister to attempt a translation, either to improve her French, as has been suggested, or else to divert her attention from some of the painfully introspective writing she had been occupied with since arriving in Paris (Bridgman 1971: 47). Whether or not Stein translated Flaubert – and, if she did, she did not get far at all – she seems to have done what generations of writers had done before her in imitating an established model. In fact, she appears to have borrowed the structure from Flaubert, and even his title: 'Trois Contes' became 'Three Histories', and eventually 'Three Lives'.[20]

One of the three stories in the book, 'The Good Anna', resembles Flaubert's 'Un cœur simple' in depicting a woman servant. (Stein based her portrait on her own housekeeper in Baltimore, Lena Lebender.) She even makes use of a symbolic parrot, as does Flaubert, although Anna is less attached to her parrot than Flaubert's character Félicité: 'Anna never really loved the parrot and so she gave it to the Drehten girls to keep' (*Three Lives*, ed. DeKoven, 44). Beyond these elements, however, which may have given *Three Lives* its 'impetus', Flaubert was 'of minimal significance for Gertrude Stein' (Bridgman 1971: 47). Stein's originality, in fact, was 'absolutely underived' according to Mabel Foote Weeks, whom she had enlisted to help find a publisher. 'It would be a fruitless search to try to find your master in those pages'.[21]

Genealogy of a story

Of more significance than what actually transpired at the time – an incomplete translation in which Stein may or may not have been invested – is her narration of the composition of *Three Lives*. Over time, it evolved into the kind of 'delightful story' she refers to, also in the *Autobiography*, when evoking another translation (ad)venture involving the poems of Georges Hugnet, which we will examine later. Writers are frequently prone to creatively fashioning an image, or a myth, of themselves as writers – Meizoz (2007) uses the terms '*posture de l'auteur*' and '*mise en scène*'. Autobiography is a genre that lends itself to this kind of 'self-fashioning' (Greenblatt 1980). Stein wrote a number of essays focusing specifically on the art of writing; she also describes her writerly self in *The Autobiography of Alice B Toklas*, as well as in more 'authentic' self-definitional texts such as *Everybody's Autobiography*, *Wars I Have Seen*, and the obscure 'Stanzas in Meditation', a 'real' autobiography she was writing as the fictional *Autobiography* was being put together. But it's the popular *Autobiography*, in particular, that 'creates many fictions', as Dydo has said (1985: 20, n. 12).[22]

The staging of Flaubert, as well as the idea of translation itself, becomes clearer if interpreted in this context of fictionalization. The notion of 'influence' was always problematic for Stein, as Katz points out in his introduction to her very early work *Fernhurst* (which predates *Three Lives* and was later integrated into *The Making of Americans*). Despite being a prodigious reader, having devoured most of English literature from the fifteenth to the nineteenth centuries while she was in London in 1902–1903, she was not in search of models. In the words of Katz, which echo those of Weeks, 'she was influenced by few writers – and even by these, in only small ways – as one understands 'influence' of ideas and styles' (Katz 1973: xxi).

As she fashioned her authorial self, Stein was concerned with the idea of original authorship, with portraying herself as a genius – both father and mother to her work, and even as the mother of twentieth-century literature. Yet, beginning with her early efforts to find a publisher for *Three Lives*, and continuing well along in her literary career, Stein did not enjoy a wide readership. Publishers were reluctant to take her on, and when her works did appear in print, reviewers often mocked her experimental style of writing. When looking back on her development in the *Autobiography*, some thirty years after she had started writing, she invokes the names of two authorities, one in literature and the other in art, Flaubert and Cézanne. By this time, Flaubert, the perfect writer who had dispassionately sought *le mot juste*, had been dead for more than a half century and was widely regarded as a model in French letters. 'For anyone then seriously concerned with literature, the respectful mention of Flaubert was mandatory. He was a tutelary presence', Bridgman writes (1971: 47). Flaubert, therefore, figures in Stein's discourse, amid her claims to originality.

The genealogy of *Three Lives* is one of the leitmotifs in Stein's writing, and the theme of Flaubert's influence – important, although minimal – is an enduring one. In interviews she granted journalists as she arrived in America to begin her lecture tour in 1934, she reaffirmed her 'affection' for Ernest Hemingway, and specifically alluded to the influence of Shakespeare, Trollope, and Flaubert (Rogers 1971: 123). In the last year of her life, Stein reiterated this motif:

'Everything I have done has been influenced by Flaubert and Cézanne and this gave me a new feeling about composition', although the emphasis is more on Cézanne than on Flaubert ('Transatlantic Interview' in Stein 1971b: 15).

Alice Toklas retold the Flaubert story, after Gertrude's death, in response to a query from a graduate student who had evidently asked about influences on Stein. In Alice's version, interestingly, Gertrude merely 'started to translate', and not all of *Trois Contes*, at that, but rather a single story, 'Un cœur simple', which she soon gave up to '*write* a story'. Although she does mention Flaubert in her letter, she does so none too emphatically, the 'real' influence having been that of William James.

> She was as American as Four in America. She hadn't for years – many many years read French at all. Literally – not even the newspapers (until the occupation when she read the local one). Her first real influence was William James – he formed her mind – directed her path – before she was thirty – but left her free. She didn't read Flaubert until nearly ten years after. It was when she started to translate Un Cœur Simple that she decided rather than do that she would write a story. She always from her childhood was rereading all of Jules Vernes [*sic*] and Alexandre Dumas in translation. She read all of Anthony Trollope over and over again. All this for the simple pleasure it gave her. She would certainly not have considered that it had any influence. (Alice B. Toklas, Letter of 16 November 1947)[23]

Alice recalls in her own memoirs, written long after her companion's death, that she had been reading Flaubert's letters in French when travelling to France in 1907 (Toklas 1963: 23). When she mentioned this to Gertrude, she adds, Gertrude had inquired whether the Flaubert letters had been 'translated into English' (Toklas 1963: 28). This might suggest a link to Stein's own efforts to translate Flaubert just a few years earlier in preparation for writing *Three Lives*; however, it is also possible that Alice, in turn, is using the idea of translating Flaubert, as Gertrude had in 'her' *Autobiography*, to prop herself up and give herself greater credibility. Or, that Alice is retrospectively trying to 'one-up' Gertrude by claiming to have read Flaubert in the original.

In the conjoined reference to Flaubert and Cézanne, Stein – an American writer – is using Flaubert to anchor herself to the French literary tradition. By invoking the Cézanne painting, which she now owns and can look at over and over again, she affirms her links to the French avant-garde art movement. She derives her authority from this double association, seeking the *gloire* she craves and feels she deserves after having been ignored and even scorned. At the same time, she refuses to unreservedly acknowledge her literary forebears. We have Stein's spin on the influence of Henry James, whom she simply categorizes as her 'forerunner' as opposed to conceding that *she* might have followed in *his* footsteps. She similarly casts the influence of Flaubert as both incidental and fleeting, dismissing it as a mere moment of translation, which as a subsidiary art, in her mind, would not jeopardize or detract from her own originality, or undermine her authorship/authority.

It is interesting to note how someone as close to her as Van Vechten downplays the literary influences and emphasizes the role of Cézanne. In his introduction to *Three Lives*, he proclaims the book to be a masterpiece, which he finds astonishing considering it is her first book (it was actually her first 'published' book rather than her first, as explained below). He draws a parallel between her stylistic innovations and the artistic movement of the times, but makes a point of saying that he doubts Stein even read Flaubert:

> Reasonably enough, when one considers her subsequent association with painters, the book is imbued with the influence of Cézanne more than with that of any literary forerunner. The plans and distorted lines of that great painter are definitely to be discovered in Miss Stein's sturdy prose. The subject matter, two servant girls and an unhappy Negro girl, is similar to the subject matter of the realists, Zola and Flaubert (Un Cœur Simple instantly rises to mind) but so different is the treatment that any question of influence may be immediately dismissed. Indeed, it seems doubtful if Miss Stein had read Zola or Flaubert before she wrote the book....If we cannot look back of Miss Stein and find a literary ancestor, it is easy to look forward: a vast sea of writers seem to be swimming in the inspiration derived from this prose. (Van Vechten in Stein 1933: ix–x)

Stein's literary experimentation has been tied to her support of artistic innovation: 'Gertrude did for the English language what the French painters did for French painting' (Raffel 1971: 137). Gertrude Stein, along with her brothers and sister-in-law, played an important role in collecting works of art and promoting representatives of the avant-garde art movement in Paris. The Steins supported artists and bought their pictures at a time when no one else did. In preparation for the New York Armory Show in 1913, American painters went abroad and consulted them. However, the actual influence of Cézanne has also been called into question. Thomson, for one, says he doubts the 'validity, or at any rate the depth, of such a statement' (1967: 172). Thus, Flaubert and Cézanne form a pair of 'stimuli' that may well be more imagined than grounded in reality.

French connections

One of the influences that Stein does not mention overtly is that of George Sand, although Sand was one of the many 'Georges' in her life, which also included the male George Washington and Georges Hugnet and the female George Eliot. Upon arriving in Paris in 1903, Stein would have become familiar with Sand's reputation for sexual activities and literary exploits. As she took her regular walks through the Jardins du Luxembourg, a park located close to home, she would have had occasion to pass the statue of the French novelist. According to Wagner-Martin, the lives of Sand and Stein 'dovetailed' and Stein most likely admired Flaubert's 'Un cœur simple', knowing that it had been written for Sand (Wagner-Martin 1995: 163–4).[24]

Stein listed in her early notebooks the names of authors and books she was reading, including the memoirs of George Sand (Katz 1963: 13–14). It is quite possible, therefore, that she was aware of the connection between George Sand and Gustave Flaubert. She may have heard, as well, that Flaubert had written 'Un cœur simple' to please Sand, although that piece of information may not have been available in Sand's memoirs.[25]

Gertrude Stein tried out a pseudonym when drafting *Three Lives*, the only time she contemplated doing so, and the name she chose was a nod to George Sand. The title on the first notebook of *Three Lives* (then called 'Three Histories') reads: 'The life and death of the good Anna by *Jane Sands*'[26] She soon gave up the idea of using a name other than her own, and in fact disapproved of pseudonyms out of a 'sense of authorial integrity' (Dydo 2003: 459, n. 70), but the fictional device is significant, as is the epigraph she chose for her book.

Three Lives begins with a quotation in French from Symbolist poet Jules Laforgue: 'Donc je suis un malheureux et ce n'est ni ma faute ni celle de la vie'. In her edition of *Three Lives*, DeKoven provides this translation: 'So I am an unhappy person and this is neither my fault nor life's' (2006: 4, n. 2). This epigraph has mystified scholars and provided fodder for a number of studies. Brinnin mentions the Laforgue quote, taking it at face value (1959: 57). Bridgman says it sounds as if it came from *Moralités légendaires*, but that he has not been able to locate it (Bridgman 1971: 48n). While acknowledging that the exact words quoted by Stein are not to be found in the work of Laforgue, Gutkowski (2003) compares them to the following line from *Moralités légendaires*: 'Eh bien, voilà! Je ne suis qu'une malheureuse, mais j'ai l'âme haut placée, qu'on le sache' (2003: 126) and draws a parallel between *Moralités* and *Three Lives*. Wood makes the most compelling case for falsification: 'it seems a safe assumption that Stein invented the epigraph' (Wood 2006: 303, n. 3), yet he devotes his article to an examination of Stein's tribute, or 'bow', to Laforgue through the 'paradoxical, suggestively ambivalent content of the fictional epigraph', which falls within the tradition of Romantic irony. He also cites a number of biographers who have taken Laforgue's influence for granted (2006: 303–5).[27]

This is not to dispute the remarkable impact of Jules Laforgue on the course of both French and English poetry. The chain of influence extends from Mallarmé to modernist poets like Pound, Joyce, and Eliot. Having arrived in Paris only two years before she began writing *Three Lives*, after spending time in London reading a prodigious amount of English prose, Stein was unlikely to have been well versed in Laforgue's work itself, although she was probably aware of his reputation.

The choice of author to quote can be more significant than the text of the epigraph itself, as Gérard Genette points out. An epigraph is a phrase, or quotation, used to introduce a piece of writing, generally linking that work to a particular individual, literary tradition or context. The epigraph was frequently used by gothic novelists such as Radcliffe, Lewis and Maturin (a genre Stein would have been familiar with as she ploughed through several centuries of English narrative). Genette specifically mentions Walter Scott, whose epigraphs are 'generally attributed to a real author, which does not automatically guarantee their accuracy or authenticity' (1997: 147). In the context of Stein's first published, and hence first public, novel, the Laforgue 'quotation' is significant in that it serves as a sign of 'prestigious filiation':

> The epigraph in itself is a signal (intended as a *sign*) of culture, a password of intellectuality. While the author awaits hypothetical newspaper reviews, literary prizes, and other official recognitions, the epigraph is already, a bit, his consecration. With it, he chooses his peers and thus his place in the pantheon. (Genette 1997: 160; emphasis in the original)

These two tributes – to George Sand through the pseudonym and to Jules Laforgue via the epigraph – were integral to the original composition of *Three Lives*. They are not unrelated to the act (real or alleged) of translation. It is possible that Stein translated Flaubert to hone her writing skills, as an 'exercise' or, as in the case of the Cézanne painting, as a 'stimulus'. The idea of translation as an exercise is interesting in itself; it would be taken up later by Paul Auster, who follows a well-established tradition. For example, Shelley, who translated Plato's *Symposium*, Dante and others, is said to have regarded translation as a 'propaedeutic, a poetic exercise which helped to ignite his creative faculties' (Webb 1976: 48).[28]

On the other hand, there are likely more profound reasons behind Stein's efforts – however incidental – to frame the composition of *Three Lives* as a 'translation' when looking back from the vantage point of the 1930s. Translation, generally speaking, had been 'in the air' for some time. Toward the late nineteenth century, intellectuals, writers and artists converged on urban centres, Paris in particular, where they furthered literary and cultural exchange, much of which occurred through translation. The poet Stéphane Mallarmé, for example, who translated the poetry of Edgar Allan Poe, was famous for his Tuesday-night salons, where writer-translators of different nationalities congregated. Much translation occurred both into and from French. This spilled over into the modernist era: Stein's milieu, despite the preponderance of English-speakers around her, was multinational and multilingual, and translation continued to be a fundamental preoccupation.

Also, by the time the Flaubert story found its way into the *Autobiography*, Stein had been translated into French, which had required some degree of collaboration and self-translation on her part. The French version of *The Making of Americans* (*Américains d'Amérique*) is discussed in the *Autobiography*:

> Gertrude Stein in all her life has never been as pleased with anything as she is with the translation that Bernard Faÿ and Madame Seillière are making of this book now. She has just been going over it with Bernard Faÿ and as she says, it is wonderful in english and it is even as wonderful in french. Elliot Paul, when editor of transition once said that he was certain that Gertrude Stein could be a best-seller in France. It seems very likely that his prediction is to be fulfilled. (56)

She writes about translation again in the *Autobiography*, in relation to Faÿ's version of 'Melanctha' and the abridged French edition of *The Making of Americans* he is preparing, with the assistance of the Baronne Seillière (249–50). She owes her growing reputation in France, she realizes, to the work of her translators. Stein is also pleased about a German translation of her portraits by Rönnebeck, which she describes as contributing to her 'international reputation' (101).[29]

By this time, as she recalls in the *Autobiography*, she had already tackled a significant translation project of her own: a long poem by Hugnet, who had published a French edition of *The Making of Americans* and the *Portraits*.

> The first book to appear [in Hugnet's Edition de la Montagne] was sixty pages in french of the Making of Americans. Gertrude Stein and Georges Hugnet *translated them together* and she was happy about it. This was later followed by a volume of Ten Portraits written by Gertrude Stein and illustrated by portraits of the artists of themselves. (*Autobiography*, 230; emphasis added)

On the other hand, Stein also treats the idea of translation disparagingly, as in the following passage about the avant-garde French author H.P. Roché:

> Roché was one of those characters that are always to be found in Paris.... He knew everybody, he really knew them and he could introduce anybody to anybody.... he had gone to the austrian mountains with the austrians, he had gone to Germany with the germans and he had gone to Hungary with hungarians and he had gone to England with the english.... As Picasso always said of him, Roché is very nice but he is only a translation. (*Autobiography*, 44)

Thus, translation figures rather prominently as a theme in the *Autobiography*. Conscious of the importance of translation to her literary reputation, and familiar with the act of translation itself, Stein includes in her fictitious autobiography what could be considered a fictitious translation, a kind of 'pseudotranslation'. Stein uses the device of a purported translation of a well-known work, rather than pseudotranslation in the true sense of the term as an original text disguised as a translation for which there is no source text (Toury 2012: 47ff). There are numerous examples of 'fictitious translations' and literary hoaxes, which likewise blur the boundaries between real and fictional text-worlds (Kaindl 2014). Gertrude Stein, in making explicit use of Daniel Defoe's pseudo-autobiography conceit (*Autobiography*, 252), shows that she is capable of such trickery.

Personal reasons, finally, could account for why Stein's first published book was couched in terms of a translation. I reiterate 'published' because *Three Lives* was, in fact, an adaptation (a kind of translation) of a previous, unpublished novel titled *Q.E.D.* This was an autobiographical narrative about what would have been considered a taboo subject at the time – an unhappy romance involving three young women. In *Three Lives*, the names, gender and race of the characters have been altered, but the book continues to echo Stein's heart-breaking affair. *Q.E.D.*, composed in 1903, did not come to light until the spring of 1932. The *Autobiography* refers briefly to a manuscript about which Stein is 'bashful and hesitant' (84–5). It is described as 'forgotten' – the words 'forgot' or 'forgotten' are used four times in one paragraph – although the manuscript had most likely been concealed. Alice had not known about Stein's love affair or the earlier book, and was apparently not merely jealous, but enraged that Stein had withheld the truth from her. The *Autobiography* is 'Alice's book, written in her voice, her style, and her name ... the only work Gertrude wrote for her' (Letter of 13 November 1948 from Toklas to Van Vechten, quoted by Dydo 1985: 16 and 20, n. 13).[30]

It is conceivable, then, that the 'translation' of Flaubert's *Trois Contes* was a cover, an elaborate construct to deflect attention from the intimate and painful experience on which her early writing was based. In this book written for Alice, she would have needed to downplay the autobiographical origins of *Q.E.D.*, and its successor, *Three Lives*, making it look as if her stories emanated from Flaubert's influence, rather than from her own life experience.

Gertrude Stein, in sum, could well have begun a translation of Flaubert. The translation of a few lines, or a few paragraphs, may have existed and been lost or excised from her notebooks as other material was. This exercise, or at the very least, the *idea* of Flaubert, may have inspired her, resulting in the theme of the good servant and the structure of three stories to form one book, in the same way that staring at the portrait of Madame Cézanne possibly influenced her idea of composition.

On the other hand, there is a fictional dimension to the story. Taken together, these related fictions – an alleged (or pseudo) translation, a pseudonym, and what is perhaps a pseudo-epigraph – two of which are contemporaneous with the composition of *Three Lives*, and the third a later embellishment – all seem designed to give her work credibility by linking it to the French canon. They form part of her efforts – at the time the work was composed, as well as later in life when she was reinventing the experience – to efface an earlier unhappy version of herself and shape the way in which she wanted her work and her identity as an author to be viewed. In light of other forms of self-portraiture such as interviews, correspondence, and so on, it is clear that Stein devoted much of her career to creating the myth of her artistic development. A recognition of both the French female (Sand) and the French male (Laforgue, Flaubert) canon of the time, through so modernist an activity as translation, would have contributed to the image she was attempting to project.

Reimagining Hugnet: How the flowers of friendship faded

By the end of the 1920s, Stein had surrounded herself with a circle of younger men, the 'young generation' she refers to in the *Autobiography* (8). They were expatriates and Frenchmen, writers and artists, who celebrated, promoted, and translated one another, and showered Gertrude with attention. In his memoir, *Confessions of Another Young Man*, Bravig Imbs writes:

> For we were a coterie and most of us young enough to think it very important. We were all going to be great artists and we had all sat with Alice and we had all given our homage to Gertrude, whom Allen considered 'the greatest artist in the world.' (Imbs 1936: 171)[31]

Among that circle of young men was Georges Hugnet (1906–1974), with whom Stein maintained an intense, collaborative relationship over the course of four years in the 1920s. Hugnet first came to Stein thanks to Virgil Thomson, a central figure in her group. This took place in 1926, when Hugnet was just twenty years old. Hugnet and Stein were immediately enchanted with one another. He would soon begin translating her work; later, she would translate his.

Born in Paris, Hugnet had spent his childhood in Buenos Aires before returning to Paris and Saint-Malo, Brittany. He was involved in a number of creative activities such as poetry, publishing, translation, theatre, and cinema. At a fairly young age, he was already well connected to artists and writers such as Picasso, Joan Miró, Man Ray, Tristan Tzara, and Jean Cocteau. He took over a publishing company, Les Éditions de la Montagne, in order to publish his own works and those of his friends. In the 1930s, Hugnet became involved with the Surrealist movement, until he was 'excommunicated' in 1939 by André Breton for refusing to end his friendship with former surrealist Paul Éluard. He was a member of the Resistance during the Second World War, and after the war continued to write while devoting time to collecting and trading in rare books and manuscripts.[32]

Hugnet paid tribute to the older, more experienced Stein in various ways: by composing poetry in her honour, by writing about her, and by translating and publishing her work. In his first book, published in 1928, he wrote these words: 'To Gertrude Stein, whose friendship is for me a refreshing spring' (Dilworth and Holbrook 2010: 69n). In an article published in *transition* in 1928, he observed that American literature, in general, had had little influence on the French, who read English literature in translation only. It was 'quite regrettable', he said, 'that a state of mind and an achievement such as Gertrude Stein's would not be more known in France' (Jolas 1928: 265–6).[33]

Hugnet's first project after taking the helm of the Éditions de la Montagne in the late 1920s was to publish his French translation of selections from

The Making of Americans. Reaction to Stein's 925-page novel had always been mixed, and it continues to be regarded both as a masterpiece and as impossible to read. Completed in 1911, it was not published until 1925, as publishers worried about its readability and profitability. Hugnet issued his book of excerpts in 1929 under the title *Morceaux choisis de la fabrication des Américains. Histoire du progrès d'une famille.* It marked a breakthrough for Stein because her book would be available to the French public in a more readable format. In a letter to Thomson, who had worked with Hugnet on the translation, Stein wrote: 'We are peacefully and completely translating, it goes, I go alone and then Alice goes over me and then we all do it with George [*sic*] and then he goes alone and really it all goes faster than any one would think. I guess we will get it done on time'. The process doesn't look quite as smooth when viewed from the outside. Imbs, for example, reported (with some malice?) that 'Gertrude had the secret of making others wear themselves out for her', adding that Hugnet 'painfully translated excerpts from the "Making of Americans" ... and then published them in a deluxe book which received little attention ...' (1936: 214). Hugnet went on to publish a collection of Stein's 'portraits', which included one of himself. The book was released in 1930 as *Dix Portraits*, with illustrations by prominent modern artists. Again, Hugnet translated these pieces with Thomson's help and Stein's, too. Stein found the *Portraits* 'darn good' (Letter of 16 April 1930 to Thomson, in Dilworth and Holbrook 2010: 150). As she indicates in the *Autobiography*, not long after, she was grateful that these translations into French were giving her some exposure. She owed a debt of gratitude, in short, to Georges Hugnet, who adored her, translated her, and brought her to the attention of a French readership for the first time. As she writes in a letter of 28 February 1928 to Henry McBride, 'young France has discovered me, it reads me it translates me it admires me and it is printing me' (quoted by Dydo 2003: 282).[34]

It is not surprising, therefore, that Stein was not merely willing, but even eager, to reciprocate by translating his sequence or cycle of thirty poems called 'Enfances'. This translation occupied her for approximately two months during the summer of 1930, which she spent, as usual, at her country retreat in Bilignin. While it put an end to the intimate working relationship she had had with the young poet, the act of translating contributed to her own work as a poet: it 'added experience with poetry, especially lines, rhythms, sounds and a sense of voice' (Dydo 2003: 324). Unlike the alleged Flaubert translation, this translation project clearly represented a genuine 'exercise' and preparation for original writing.

'Gertrude Stein offered to translate it for him'

As a result of her efforts at verse translation, Stein articulated a theory regarding Shakespeare's sonnets, which she believed had been commissioned or written for someone else. Her own translations, she felt, bore the same relationship to her true work as the sonnets did to Shakespeare's plays. Stein's contemporaries have recorded the vicissitudes of the Hugnet–Stein relationship, and have painted an intriguing picture of how Stein became engaged in the act of translation. Imbs, for one, writes about having visited her at Bilignin, along with Faÿ, at the time when she was in the throes of translating the young Frenchman's poems. He describes an occasion on which Faÿ read Hugnet's poems in French while a bespectacled Stein read her own translation, upon which Faÿ complimented her. In Imbs's words, 'it was so rare she heard anything complimentary about her writing – and as she esteemed Bernard his praise was all the sweeter'. In Imbs's word, 'this was paying Georges a great honor, for she had never translated any foreign literature before ... the sensation of translating was very strange ... like writing in the mirrored reflection of oneself' (Imbs 1936: 285–6). Stein conceptualized the act of translation in terms of 'mirrors' and 'reflections', common topoi in translational discourse. Interesting theories, indeed, although the mirror she held up to Hugnet's poems refracted more than it reflected.[35]

When she worked with Hugnet on translations of her own work, Stein was in effect doing self-translation, producing a word-for-word translation that was reviewed by Alice, and then reworked by Hugnet. Dydo, in her detailed study of how Stein has translated her own work, has pointed out that it was less important to render the 'sense' than to capture 'the rhythm of conversation, the weight, *débit*, style, color, resonance, and movement of her work'. Only fragments remain, but from these it is apparent that Stein did not write French 'correctly' and that, while Hugnet revised her French, the translated text was 'defamiliarized and strange' (2003: 291–2).

This was Stein's way of exercising very strict control over the letter of her texts. At the time of the self-financed publication of *Three Lives*, Grafton Press had sent a representative to see her in Paris, proposing to edit what he considered to be faulty English; she refused the offer of help and demanded that the manuscript be printed exactly as it was written (Gallup 1953: 42–3; *Autobiography*, 68). In this case, too, she seems determined that the translation replicate her original, that it be literal and faithful on an absolutely elemental level to her text and her wordplay. This would seem to go against the spirit of self-translation, which involves re-creating a work in a new language, in a new context, and for a new audience, often introducing quite significant changes. Instead, Stein, the author, is attempting to hang on to own voice, even in a new key. Stein also exercised control of a different kind over the production of *Dix Portraits*, by selecting the portraits and the order in which they were to appear in the French book. It is interesting to observe how this was perceived by Pierre de Massot, who wrote the preface to the book: in a letter from Hugnet to Thomson he is said to have been in favour of a 'reinvention' of Gertrude Stein instead of the kind of faithful translation Hugnet and Thomson were busy doing (quoted in Dydo 2003: 300).

Once she began translating Hugnet's poetry, on the other hand, *her* translations of *him* were anything but word-for-word. Stein takes the liberty of adapting the text and subverting it for her own purposes. For this reason, subsequent critics – and Thomson, at the time – have often elected to put the word 'translation' in quotation marks. This simple punctuation mark speaks volumes about the end result of this translation project and, perhaps more importantly, the authorial confusion that has arisen over the 'collaboration' between Hugnet and Stein. (There go the inverted commas once more!)

Stein went to the country in early May 1930, obviously intent on doing a good job on this translation. She told Hugnet that she had taken a dictionary to Bilignin: 'one of the biggest English-French French-English dictionaries and that and I and my affection for you will produce something out of my first attempt at translation'. This time it is Stein herself confirming that it is her *first* attempt at translation.

What is clear, from the outset, is that this is no usual translation. When Hugnet learned of the translation, he wrote to his friend Thomson, 'Really I have friends too strong for me'; on receiving Stein's English poems, his reaction was that it was more than a translation. Stein commented to Thomson that it was her 'version' or a 'mirroring of it rather than anything else a reflection of each little poem' (Thomson 1967: 185).[36]

In the following brief excerpt taken from the end of the third poem of the cycle, Stein's English translation of Hugnet's French verse is relatively close, if not 'faithful' (a term that has always been the subject of long and inconclusive debates). Four English lines correspond to the four French ones, although Stein has chosen to make hers rhyme. These lines, however literal (compared to what follows), have been cited as an illustration of the way in which Gertrude's version becomes a feminist stand-in for Hugnet's masculine poem, particularly in light of her replacement of the male sexual organ (*mon sexe*) with the female one (more obliquely expressed by the word 'well').[37]

Rien à cacher	There is very little to hide
je le dis à tous	When there is everything beside
mon sexe a respiré	And there is a well inside
entre leurs mains moites	in hands untied

Two more substantial examples illustrate how Stein moves toward an increasingly free adaptation; they are taken from the first and last poems of 'Enfances'.[38]

1

Enfances aux cent coins de ma mémoire
si ma mémoire est l'œuvre de la passion,
enfances décimées par les nuits
si les nuits ne sont qu'une maladie du sommeil,
je vous poursuis avant de dormir, sans hâte.

In the one hundred small places of myself my youth,
And myself in if it is the use of passion,
In this in it and in the nights alone
If in the next to night which is indeed not well
I follow you without it having slept and went.

30

Enfances aux quatre coins du monde,
dans cette ville où l'on me fit vivre,
parti avec une valise à ma taille, à la mer,
et ignorant le langage des enfants.

…

Enfances, imaginez-vous les honneurs de la forêt
et ce vent palmé qui crée une apologie.

There are a few here now and the rest can follow a cow,
The rest can follow now there are a few here now.
They are all all here now the rest can follow a cow
And mushrooms on a hill and anything else until.

…

And a hope be relieved	And a hope be relieved
By all of it in case	By all of it in case
Of my name.	Of my name
What is my name.	What is my name
That is the game	Georges Hugnet
	By Gertrude Stein[39]

What immediately jumps out when the French and English versions are compared is that they do not correspond even remotely in form. Stein's has longer lines and longer verses. Even in the first poem, which is considered an almost literal rendering (Thomson 1967: 187), or her 'greatest fidelity' after which she 'freely improvised' (Bridgman 1971: 202), Stein makes little effort to preserve Hugnet's imagery, themes and stylistic devices. In the opening line, she does keep the idea of 'one hundred places'; 'enfances' is translated by 'youth'; and 'ma mémoire' is more or less conveyed by 'myself'. But the equivalence between the two poems remains very tenuous. By the end of the sequence of poems, Hugnet's themes are completely discarded. The first line of the first poem, 'Enfances aux cent coins de ma mémoire', which is echoed in the first line of Hugnet's last poem as 'Enfances aux quatre coins du monde', does not reoccur in the last section of Stein's version. The first line of Stein's number 30, 'There are a few here now and the rest can follow a cow' does not refer back to the opening line, but follows on the penultimate poem (number 29), which reads like a love poem to Alice: 'cow' in Steinian language is her code word for orgasm, and evokes the sexual pleasure she gives to her lover.

Rather than translating in the conventional sense, in short, Stein was discovering a new way to write. In one of the lectures she delivered while in America, she described this revelation: 'a very queer thing was happening... I was perplexed at what was happening and I finished the whole thing not translating but carrying out an idea which was already existing' (*Narration*, 52). In so doing, she has censored the author's strong images of death. She has erased Hugnet's accounts of male sexual experience, replacing them with her own lesbian lyricism. She has 'eclipsed' the original in what has been called 'antagonistic rewriting' (Swarbrick and Goldmann 2007: 2).

The resulting translation has been critiqued from different points of view. It has been called, quite simply, a bad translation. 'Gertrude Stein became involved in translation only twice', Posman writes. 'And both times she was a "bad" translator' (Posman 2009).[40] Others have also drawn attention to the inadequacy of her translation: Bridgman, for example, feels that she had an insufficient grasp of French and that she omitted Hugnet's sexual allusions out of 'prudishness' (1971: 202). The Stein version is considered a 'feminist rewriting of a phallocentric original', a 'deconstructive rereading' that destabilizes the terms of the original version (Will 2004: 656). In other words, even before she actually 'broke up' with Hugnet, she had subverted his work, and written on top of ('on') his poems. Thus, she has refused to play the role of secondary author – the listener/reader reinterpreting a text that has been given to her, as a conventional translator might do. In other words, she breaks with the traditional gendered view of what translators should be doing, and asserts her identity as Gertrude Stein, the author of a poem. She even proclaims herself the author of Hugnet himself, as the amended ending denotes: 'What is my name/Georges Hugnet/ By Gertrude Stein'.

History of a dispute

The falling out between Gertrude Stein and Georges Hugnet revolved around a practical matter. The poem was to be published in two versions. It was to appear in the winter 1931 issue (vol. 2, no. 1) of the American periodical, *Pagany*, with English and French text side by side. Hugnet also planned to release a book, illustrated by Picasso, Tchelitchew, Marcoussis, and Kristians Tonny, with his French poem accompanied by Stein's translation. The book was to be published in Paris, in 1930, by Hugnet's Éditions de la Montagne (which had already published the two above-mentioned books by Stein in French translation).

Upon seeing the subscription blank announcing the book, which Hugnet had prepared without consulting her, Stein demurred. She didn't like the layout, which she considered 'disloyal'. She objected to having her name listed in smaller type beneath the author's. She did not wish to be referred to as Hugnet's translator for, in her eyes, they had been 'collaborators'. Hugnet, for his part, wanted to avoid labelling the work a 'collaboration' lest readers think that Stein had written the original and that he had merely translated it, as had been the case for the two previous publications. Stein demanded equal billing and negotiations ensued, with Thomson's intervention. To no avail: Stein, and especially Toklas, were never satisfied with any of the proposed solutions. The following facsimile of the typographical disposition of the names and title is reproduced by Thomson (1967: 193):

GEORGES HUGNET

ENFANCES

SUIVI PAR LA TRADUCTION DE

GERTRUDE STEIN

Stein withdrew from Hugnet's publication project in late 1930. By this time, the winter 1931 issue of *Pagany* was already in press. The only concession Stein could get, when she cabled editor Richard Johns, was to have the title changed to 'Poem Pritten on Pfances of Georges Hugnet', a tongue-in-cheek, if not malicious, title that suggested that instead of being subservient to or 'beneath' Hugnet, she had written something '*on*' his poem. By deforming his title, she was able to assert some degree of authorial control.

In May 1931, Stein published a separate, English-only version, under her own Plain Edition label, entitled 'Before the Flowers of Friendship Faded Friendship Faded' with the subtitle 'Written on a Poem by Georges Hugnet'. The title was allegedly suggested by Alice Toklas, who overheard two French women using a similar expression in a restaurant and translated it for Gertrude. It would appear that Alice played a crucial role not only in publishing the poem but also in sabotaging the friendship altogether, as she had done with her companion's relationships to other admiring young men, including Hemingway.

Hugnet did not publish his own poem in French until after Stein's version had come out. Written in 1929, *Enfances* did not appear in print until 1933.[41]

Gertrude Stein ... consoled herself by telling all about it in a *delightful story*

Like other writers who have doubled as translators at some point in their careers, Stein transforms her experience into a story that recasts the truth in the telling. The story of the translation takes on as much importance as the actual act of translating. Like variations on a theme, translational stories complicate, but give texture to, authorial discourse. The Hugnet episode, like the Flaubert story discussed above, forms part of the narrative structure of the *Autobiography*, a book that from its opening pages seeks to establish Stein's status as a 'genius':

> I may say that only three times in my life have I met a genius and each time a bell within me rang and I was not mistaken. ... The three geniuses of whom I wish to speak are Gertrude Stein, Pablo Picasso and Alfred Whitehead. I have met many important people, I have met several great people but I have only known three first class geniuses and in each case on sight within me something rang. (*Autobiography* 5)

By spinning the tale of the Hugnet collaboration, by mythologizing the process that led from a translation to an original poem, and then – despite some unpleasantness – to a delightful story, Stein is bolstering this picture of herself as a genius.

> In the meantime Georges Hugnet wrote a poem called Enfance. Gertrude Stein offered to *translate* it for him but *instead* she wrote a *poem about it*. This at first

pleased Georges Hugnet too much and then did not please him at all. Gertrude Stein then called the poem Before The Flowers of Friendship Faded Friendship Faded.... Gertrude Stein was very upset and then consoled herself by telling all about it in a *delightful short story* called From Left to Right and which was printed in the London Harper's Bazaar. (*Autobiography*, 231; emphasis added)

In composing the so-called 'delightful' story, actually entitled 'Left to Right', Stein changed the names of the players. Georges Hugnet becomes 'Arthur Williams', Virgil Thomson is 'Generale Erving', and Bravig Imbs, a Dartmouth man, is ironically transformed into 'Frederick Harvard'. The fiction, obviously meant to set the record straight, is described as a 'true story' on the cover of the manuscript notebook and in the story itself. It first appeared in *Harper's Bazaar* (London) in 1931 and was later reprinted in the magazine *Story* in 1933. It has been referred to as 'nasty, pouting... remarkably unpleasant writing and reading' (Dydo 2003: 321). Yet, the story is interesting in itself when viewed from the perspective of writers who translate, illustrating as it does the unique way in which Stein steps out of the (subservient) role of translator to take back her authorial pen. In Stein's account of the facts of the case, Williams (aka Hugnet) proposed that they 'have a book together', but once the announcement came out, it became clear that 'it was his book and it did not say it was my book' ('Left to Right', 17). The story is rather abstract, in Stein's manner, and ends by merely stating: 'We were after that never friends or anything. This is all this true story and it was exciting' ('Left to Right', 20).

New directions, new 'translations'

Whether the Hugnet affair can be considered to have ended well or not (clearly Alice, at least, won the day by banishing yet another potentially dangerous young male from the household and from Gertrude's life as an artist), the experience of translating, or attempting to do so, took Stein in new directions. First of all, as Thomson suggests, translating unlocked the secrets of writing poetry: 'For in her need to catch an English lilt comparable to that of Hugnet's in French, she had caught the cool temperature and running-water sound of her beloved Sonnets' (1967: 186). Secondly, the process of reading, or listening, and then rewriting – all inherent in translating – opened the door to the *Autobiography*, in which she tells her own story in the voice of Alice B. Toklas. Translation is a frequent theme in the *Autobiography*, not just with respect to Flaubert and Hugnet but also with regard to the various efforts by her friends – and also involving herself – to translate her work into French (56 and 249). In the 1946 'Transatlantic Interview', she explicitly equates the *Autobiography* with translation: 'I had done what I saw, what you do in translation or in a narrative. I had recreated the point of view of somebody else' (Stein 1971b: 19). Having been enclosed in her own world of writing for herself, she was now open to addressing others, in what was to become 'audience writing', a form of 'fakery' that resulted in the *Autobiography* (Dydo 2003: 322; Sloboda 2008: 111–13).

Hoax or fakery notwithstanding, this new kind of writing was much more accessible than what she had previously produced and it brought her tremendous fame, adoration and even money – all of which she had coveted for decades. At the same time, the Hugnet translation and the subsequent *Autobiography* precipitated a crisis of authorship, leaving Stein 'unsure of her own voice'. The idea of assuming a public voice, the idea of writing for another audience, instead of for herself, becomes a theme in her next 'autobiography'. In *Everybody's Autobiograpy*, she writes about the American lecture tour. She evokes her anxiety over being in the public eye and her irritation that the public is more interested in who she is than in what she writes. For the first time in her life, she experiences a kind of writer's block. Her identity as an author is as ambiguous and clouded as it was when she was Gertrude Stein, translator of Georges Hugnet.

Autobiography, like translation, is a project that is never finished, involving different perspectives and different voices. In the first *Autobiography*, which has been referred to as 'her, and Alice's, fused autobiography' (Wagner-Martin 1995: 244), she and Alice are both 'co-subjects' and 'co-authors' (Laird 2000: 186). The role of Alice as presumed 'author' in the *Autobiography* continues on in other work having to do with translation. As we have seen, Alice translated Stein's *Picasso* into English. There is also a reference to an article by Marcel Brion, which Gertrude translated and Alice revised (Dydo 2003: 304 and 304, n. 58). Brion's 'Le Contrepoint poétique de Gertrude Stein' compares Stein's method of composition to that of Bach (1930); it was considered to be one of the best pieces on Stein published at the time, but the translation was never published. Throughout their years together, Alice served, strictly speaking, as an *amanuensis*, a secretary who copied out or typed up what Gertrude wrote longhand. But Alice did much more. She was a tireless promoter of Gertrude's work; she was her agent as well as her lover; she established and operated the publishing house, Plain Edition, which brought out work that had been rejected by other presses. While Alice had a *voice* in the *Autobiography*, which Gertrude wrote for her, she actually had a *hand* in writing, translating, and editing occasional pieces (in particular the Pétain notebooks). In translation, therefore, Gertrude doubly relinquishes her voice and authority.

Frénésie: 'Play and beginning translation'

In 1938, Stein 'began' another translation, this one of a three-act play called *Frénésie*. The manuscript survives in authentic, though incomplete, form: she ended up translating scarcely more than two of the twenty-five printed pages. *Frénésie* was authored by Charles de Peyret-Chappuis (1912–1995), a minor French playwright who also worked as a journalist and was later director of the Comédie de Paris. The play was first staged at the Théâtre Charles-de-Rochefort in Paris on 3 February 1938.

In a letter of 31 May 1939 to Stein and Toklas, Thornton Wilder mentions the playwright Peyret-Chappuis. According to one contemporary, French fashion journalist Marie-Louise Bousquet, Stein then began 'chasing after' the playwright and looking for a chance to 'collaborate' with him. The letter also contains an offhand comment questioning Stein's ability to translate the play into 'good English', 'without adding anything of her own' (Burns and Dydo 1996: 229–30).[42]

The opening monologue alone, in which the character Stéphanie talks about what it is like to be 'ugly', would appear to validate Bousquet's opinion of Stein's translation skills. The style is typical of Stein, and quite a bit of her 'own' has indeed been added in. Whereas there are around ten sentences in the original, albeit with some of them trailing off and ending in suspension points, Stein has reduced the entire passage to two very long run-on sentences. The translation skims over some of the details Peyret-Chappuis included. In the original, for example, information is given about the contents of the girls' drawers and even about the type of stitching: 'j'ai compté ses chemises, ses petites culottes, j'ai compris… ses robes étaient brodées; les miennes, garnies d'un simple jour à la machine'. The last part of the sentence would translate as 'her dresses were embroidered; mine were decorated with a simple machine-sewn hemstitch'. Stein simply refers to these items as 'things' and writes, 'she had everything and everything was pretty and she was pretty and everything I had was ugly and I was ugly'. On the whole, the translation is not inaccurate; it is simply an adaptation à la Stein. The translated text does not mirror the original author's style but instead resembles the way in which Stein is accustomed to write, with her characteristically simple language and straightforward vocabulary. The oddly constructed sentences do not conform to the conventional syntactic structures of written English, although they do follow the rhythm of human conversation.

STÉPHANIE – J'ai toujours été laide. J'ai mis un certain temps à m'en apercevoir… Je n'arrivais pas à comprendre pourquoi les autres enfants ne jouaient pas avec moi, pourquoi les amies de ma mère me considéraient avec pitié, m'embrassaient avec dégoût. Un jour – j'avais sept ans – je suis entrée dans la chambre que je partageais avec ma sœur. J'ai ouvert ses tiroirs à linge, les miens; j'ai compté ses chemises, ses petites culottes, j'ai compris… Elle avait dix paires de bas de plus que moi; ses robes étaient brodées; les miennes, garnies d'un simple jour à la machine; seulement, c'était une ravissante petite fille. Cela m'a appris bien des choses, entre autres le prestige de la forme. Je sais, on dit que seul l'esprit compte; qu'une belle âme vaut tous les avantages physiques: ce sont d'aimables idioties. Il vaut mieux avoir l'âme infirme que le corps difforme, c'est moins gênant. On a dû te raconter sur mon compte toutes sortes d'horreurs.

I have always been ugly, just ugly just nothing to look at, it took me sometime to know it, I always knew they did not like me none of them liked me none of the little ones I played with liked me, they never wanted to play with me and my mothers friends when they did kiss me they never kissed me as if they liked to kiss me, they never liked me, they if they kissed me they did it pityingly, yes that was it, and then there was the day I was just seven I went into a bedroom, my sisters and mine, I opened the drawers I looked at her things and I looked at mine, I counted all her things and I compared them with mine, and hers were all nice and mine were all just ugly, hers had underthings in them and she had ten pairs of stockings more than I had she had everything and everything was pretty and she was pretty and everything I had was ugly and I was ugly. Oh dear, I knew then all about it, it is why [it is] being pretty that counts, they tell you that it is what you are that makes you not what you [look] like but that is just said to cheer you on, but everybody knows better, it is much better to have an ugly nature than an ugly body, of course somebody, has told you awful things about me.[43]

Apart from the fact that during the previous decade Stein had been particularly interested in the dramatic genre, there is no indication why she began this translation project, and even less why she abandoned it. Perhaps she became bored with the work (the play is not that interesting, even if the stage performance was successful). Perhaps she saw no opportunity for either publishing or producing the English version. In any case, at that time, in 1938–1939, Stein was occupied with other projects, such as *Doctor Faustus Lights the Lights* and *Paris France*, as well as busy settling herself and Alice into relatively safe quarters in the country, as war broke out around them.

Translating Pétain

When Hitler invaded Poland on 1 September 1939, and Britain and France declared war on Germany two days later, Gertrude Stein and Alice Toklas were still at their country retreat in Bilignin, where they had spent their summers for well over a decade. They obtained a forty-eight-hour military pass enabling them to return to Paris to find their papers and pick up warm clothing.[44] They hastily locked up their art collection, bringing only two paintings with them: Picasso's portrait of Stein and Cézanne's portrait of his wife. They went back to spend the winter in the countryside for the first time ever, and were not to return to Paris for five years. Advised to leave France by the American consul at Lyon and their American friends, Stein and Toklas hesitated, overcome by a 'panic of indecision', until a certain Doctor Chaboux reassured them that their French friends would help them (Mellow 1974: 439).

How Stein and Toklas, as American Jews and lesbians, survived in German-occupied France during the Second World War remains a mystery – although the fact that they were elderly and resided in a part of France that was unoccupied until 1942 is said to have been in their favour. An even greater enigma is how Gertrude Stein came to be the translator of the Vichy leader. Stein's politically conservative stance is well known: she held right-wing views, much like other Anglo-American modernist writers such as Ezra Pound, T.S. Eliot, W.B. Yeats, and Wyndham Lewis. She was also vague about her Jewishness and took an interest in Christian subjects such as the lives of saints. But the degree to which she can be considered to have acted as a 'Vichy propagandist', as some have suggested (Will 2011: 135), is a matter of debate and speculation.

Throughout the war, Stein kept on with her daily writing, albeit at a slower pace. She completed *Paris France* and a wartime diary, published in 1945 as *Wars I Have Seen*, as well as *Mrs. Reynolds* (1989), a novel that featured Hitler and Stalin as thinly disguised characters. She also found the time to embark on a new translation project: an English version of the speeches of Maréchal Pétain, chief of state of Vichy France.[45]

Intended for an American audience, with a laudatory opening text introducing the Maréchal to English readers, these translations have remained unpublished. They are, however, available for consultation in manuscript form at the Stein–Toklas collection held at Yale University. And consulted they have been, particularly of late. The reasons why Stein, in particular, was asked to undertake this translation project are related to a number of factors that will be examined below, but her acceptance of the task and the ultimate outcome are complex and vexing. Given Stein's propensity for life writing and 'self-fashioning', it is strange that the Pétain project is absent from her own records of her work. Unlike the stories of 'translating' Flaubert and Hugnet (with or without inverted commas), the story of this translation has not been told by Stein herself. Although the Pétain translations occupied her, and Alice, for nearly two years during a critical period of their lives, her wartime memoir, *Wars I Have Seen*, never mentions the speeches although it does contain favourable references to Pétain himself. Bernard Faÿ – the Vichy official behind the translation – devotes a chapter to Stein in his own 1966 memoir, *Les Précieux*. He takes credit for having protected the two American Jews and saved their valuable art collection. But he does not refer to the Pétain translations either.

From silence to outcry: The Pétain project comes to light

Although Stein herself was silent on the subject, the work she did on Pétain's speeches has been mentioned by most biographers and scholars over the years. As early as the 1940s, Rogers cited a report in the local newspaper, *Le Bugiste*, which said that Stein had been asked to translate Pétain's messages for her compatriots, and that the arrangements had been made by Gabriel-Louis Jaray, executive director of the Comité France-Amérique. Stein had told Rogers that she wanted to have the introduction published in the *Atlantic Monthly*. He had counselled her to curb her enthusiasm for the project, which he considered 'unwise', although he concedes that Stein was in line with popular opinion and the official US position:

> Miss Stein spoke not only for herself but for many Frenchmen who at least in 1940 and 1941 believed, like our own government and with even more supposed reasons for it, that he had done his best for his country. Nothing came of the proposed translation, and since Miss Stein had undertaken it at a time and in a place where complete information was not available, it might be dismissed by itself as an unfortunate error in judgment. (Rogers 1971: 212–14)[46]

Scholars quietly explored how and why Stein became associated with Faÿ and Pétain, as new movements in literary theory 'inspired a flowering interest' in Stein studies (DeKoven 2006: viii). By the 1990s, her relationship with Pétain began to attract more attention. In the wake of the Paul de Man affair, it came to be viewed as more than a mere 'unfortunate error in judgment'.[47] Graduate student Wanda Van Dusen published Stein's 'Introduction to the Speeches of

Maréchal Pétain', a three-page typed manuscript that had never seen the light of day until Van Dusen uncovered it, with a hand-written comment by Stein's editor at Random House, Bennett Cerf: 'For the records. This disgusting piece was mailed from Belley on Jan. 19, 1942' (Van Dusen 1996: 70). Burns and Dydo also reproduced the introduction (1996: 401–21), accompanied by a meticulous account of the circumstances (carefully sorting out what is known, what is unknown and what can merely be surmised). In the ensuing years, the matter has been the subject of considerable academic detective work, which has increasingly shone the spotlight on Faÿ and his role in Stein's life and lifework. Reactions to the Pétain affair have ranged from simple curiosity or even sympathy, to shock and outrage.[48]

The debate took on new proportions and gained further visibility in 2011–2012, at the time of an exhibition entitled 'The Steins Collect. Matisse, Picasso and the Parisian Avant-Garde'. Works of art collected by Gertrude, her brothers Leo and Michael, and sister-in-law Sarah – which had been purchased, sold off, and divided among the Steins over time – were reunited in a show that highlighted the Steins' contribution to avant-garde art. Held in San Francisco, Paris and New York, the exhibition raised questions about Gertrude Stein's past in Vichy France. Public outcry, coverage in the mass media, and intervention from politicians such as Manhattan Borough President Scott Stringer and New York State Assemblyman Dov Hikind induced curators at New York's Metropolitan Museum to add supplementary information (Galvin 2016: 287). The exhibition was almost over, when, toward May 2012, a short statement was posted on the wall about Stein's translation of Pétain, with a reference to Barbara Will's (then) recent book, *Unlikely Collaboration* which dealt with Stein's relationship to Faÿ.[49]

The controversy spread to a wider audience, with pieces appearing in such publications as *The New York Review of Books*, where a review by Michael Kimmelman erroneously states that Stein translated speeches in which Pétain outlines Vichy's anti-Semitic measures. Former Harvard law professor Alan Dershowitz (2012) comments in *The Huffington Post* on Stein's 'ignoble role in the Nazi occupation of France' in a piece pointedly entitled 'Suppressing Ugly Truth for Beautiful Art', and Greenhouse (2012), writing in *The New Yorker*, decries Stein's translation of a hundred and eighty pages of explicitly anti-Semitic tirades.[50]

At the same time, others have attempted to put matters into perspective. Will's 2011 book presents an engaging and exhaustive analysis of the issues and their complexities, with an emphasis on the role of Faÿ. Burns had in 1987 co-signed a letter in *The Nation* with Dydo, refuting an allegation connected to an FBI file that Stein had Nazi connections. They observed then that not all commentators are in full possession of the facts, and they continued to provide background information. In addition to his 1996 essay with Dydo, Burns contributed to the dossier in *Jacket2* intended to 'set the record straight' (Bernstein 2012).[51] In a piece published in the Jewish magazine *Tikkun* and also included in the *Jacket2* dossier, Renate Stendhal (2012) similarly argues that 'campaigning by Stein detractors like Dov Hikind and Alan Dershowitz, labelling her a Nazi, a Hitler fan, a fascist, a collaborator, is symptomatic of the ignorance or willful besmirching that keeps the urban legend of Stein alive'.

Translation is of course central to this case, but an aspect that merits further consideration is the agency of Faÿ, Stein's friend, acolyte, French translator and promoter.

The Faÿ Factor

Bernard Faÿ (1893–1978) was an historian of Franco–American relations. He had earned a Master's degree in modern languages from Harvard, before going on to do his doctorate at the Sorbonne. His published works included biographies of American luminaries Benjamin Franklin and George Washington, and he was short-listed for a Pulitzer Prize.[52] In 1940, he was appointed director of the Bibliothèque Nationale. As an expert on Freemasonry, he was responsible for documenting the presence of Freemasons in France under the Vichy Regime, which led to the imprisonment and death of a great many of them. In 1946, he was convicted for collaboration with the Nazis, condemned for what was called *indignité nationale* ('national unworthiness') and sentenced to life imprisonment at hard labour. In 1951, he escaped to Switzerland, where he lived, and taught history, until he was pardoned and able to return to France in 1958.

Stein met Faÿ in the mid-1920s and, before long, they were close friends. Their friendship was cemented by shared interests and mutual needs. They had in common their homosexual orientation, although, as Will points out (2011: 30), subtle 'erotic courants' flowed between them, as they did between Stein and some of her other male admirers. But there was also a strong intellectual bond between them. Stein attended the lectures that Faÿ gave when he was appointed to the inaugural chair in American civilization at the prestigious Collège de France in 1932, a chair that was revoked in 1946 (Will 2011: 178 and 255 n. 146). As Imbs reports: 'Gertrude saw that Bernard was headed straight for the College de France and was a popular lecturer in America and so would do her a lot of good, while Bernard was stimulated by Gertrude's mind and appreciated her original outlook on American history' (1936: 207).

When Imbs translated Faÿ's biographies of Franklin and Washington, Stein went over the English versions; according to Faÿ, she taught him to 'think and dream in English' (Faÿ 1966: 154). But he had a lot to offer her, too. Faÿ was well connected, and as his star rose, he cultivated people of influence in the world of politics and culture. He was instrumental in bringing her work to the attention of the French public. Hemingway, who helped to get Stein's *Making of Americans* serialized in Ford Madox Ford's *The Transatlantic Review*, points out how preoccupied Stein was with 'publication and official acceptance' (2010: 17). It was Faÿ who gave her the opportunity to see more of her work in print.

Translation was critical to their relationship. Stein had initially invited the French writer René Crevel to translate *Three Lives*, but he fell ill with tuberculosis. In 1930, Faÿ, with the help of his student Grace-Ives de Longevialle, translated 'Melanctha'. Subsequently, he contributed to a new translation of *The Making of Americans*. While Hugnet had published fragments not long before, Faÿ's was a more substantive, albeit abridged, version of 260 pages, rendered in elegant French that could nonetheless be considered true to the Steinian original. *Américains d'Amérique*, translated in collaboration with Baronne J. Seillière, was published in 1933 with a foreword by Faÿ, in which Stein is heralded as 'l'un d'entre nous' or 'one of us' (Stein 1971a: 11). This is high praise indeed from someone of his standing. The following year, in 1934, he also translated the *Autobiography*; following the book's success in the United States, he drew on his extensive contacts in American academia to help organize Stein's lecture tour.

As Stein's 'agent', as it were, Faÿ was even more effective than Hugnet, given the greater degree of respect he commanded. His translations of her work, as well as the other means he deployed on her behalf, combined with his own stature as a well-regarded intellectual with political clout, made it possible for him to consolidate Stein's reputation both in France and in her own country. The agency of Faÿ, in addition to his significant intellectual capital, were critical to Stein's trajectory. In *Les Précieux*, Faÿ recalls Stein's enthusiastic reaction upon receiving the translation of *The Making of Americans*.

> J'ai lu chaque mot de la traduction. C'est parfaitement beau; j'en suis complètement et absolument heureuse et contente, plus heureuse même que je ne puis dire, et je peux dire vraiment que je suis heureuse. Mon cher Bernard,

je vous dois beaucoup, notre amitié fut un tournant dans ma vie, cela m'a rendu le cœur léger et sûr de moi après une longue vie de doute. (Faÿ 1966: 155)

I have read every word of the translation. It is perfectly beautiful; I am completely and absolutely happy and content, even happier than I can say, and I can really say that I am happy. My dear Bernard, I owe you a great deal, our friendship was a turning point in my life, it made me light-hearted once more and restored my self-confidence after a long life of doubt. (My translation)

'Ainsi se répandit la gloire de Miss Stein' (this is how Miss Stein became a celebrity), Faÿ concludes (1966: 156). Although prone to self-congratulation in this autobiographical work written late in life, Faÿ is not exaggerating Stein's own sentiments, as expressed in the *Autobiography*, where, as we have seen, she specifically refers to his translations.

Stein's sense of gratitude and loyalty may have accounted, in part, for her later decision to embark on the translation of the Pétain speeches. Conversely, Faÿ needed Stein and her capital as an American celebrity. The fame that she had finally earned as an American writer would have struck Faÿ as particularly useful. Asking a famous American writer to translate Pétain's speeches, preceded by a glowing introduction, would have seemed a brilliant strategy for seeking the approval of Americans for Pétain and the Vichy Regime at a time when the United States was not yet in the war.

Faÿ was close to Pétain. During the war, he acted as the 'eyes and ears for the Marshal in Paris', spending one week a month in Vichy as his advisor (Letter of 13 September 1941 to Stein in Gallup 1953: 356; Burns 2012). By most accounts, the translation project was undertaken at Faÿ's suggestion, most likely with the direct approval of Pétain himself. Stein began to translate the speeches in 1941. The introduction was completed after the attack on Pearl Harbour (to which she refers: 'the action of Japan has made us realise the grief and the terror of war') and sent to her publisher in January 1942. She continued translating even after the persecution and deportation of Jews had begun. But she stopped in 1943, when her friend Paul Genin and the *sous-prefet* of Belley, Maurice Sivan, told her that the project would draw too much attention to her at a time when she was already at risk (Burns 2012). But her loyalty to Faÿ, and in some ways to Pétain, outlasted the translation.

The texts

Stein's Pétain translations were never completed and never published. What she did finish is contained in three handwritten notebooks, totalling some

180 pages. In addition, there is both a holograph version and typed copy of her introduction, along with a few typed pages of some of the speeches. The notebooks more or less follow the order in which the speeches appear in the published edition of Pétain's speeches that she was working from, where they are classified thematically, although she omitted some speeches, for reasons that remain unclear. Curiously, the third notebook ends in mid-sentence about midway through Pétain's Christmas address of 1940 (speech xxxviii). This was unlike Stein, some critics have said, maintaining that she usually finished what she was working on. It is also at odds with what her copy of the original book looks like. Stein had the 1941 Lardanchet edition in her personal library. In contrast to her copy of Flaubert's *Trois Contes*, discussed earlier, this book looks as if it has been worked on. She highlighted the occasional difficult sentence, and marked off sections as she completed them. It also looks like she read through the whole book, because pages are marked up and dog-eared all the way to the end. It has been suggested that she might have started a new notebook, in which the sentence or even the entire Christmas speech were completed, but, if so, that notebook has never been found. On the other hand, the other instances of starting translations and leaving them unfinished would suggest that the Pétain situation is less unusual than some would think.

The cover of the first notebook has a picture of a skier and the words 'le ski' on a pink background. This gives it a strangely carefree appearance that seems incongruous with the speeches themselves and the events they reflect, especially seen with hindsight. It has been said that Stein's choice of notebooks was never gratuitous: is she trying to signal her determination to maintain some kind of 'normalcy' despite the frightening times?

Stein composed an introduction to the translations, which she sent to Random House before the translations were actually completed. Unlike a more conventional translator's note or preface, this text is not used as a platform to discuss methodological or technical issues directly related to the act of translation. Instead, Stein uses this space to glorify her author. She compares Pétain to George Washington, riding in on a white horse, 'first in the hearts of his countrymen' (Stein 1996: 1). Her *skopos*, to use the terminology of Hans Vermeer (2000), goes far beyond a simple desire to communicate the content of the text to a new audience: it is clear that the translation, and the related paratext, were intended to make an American audience more favourably disposed to the Vichy Regime.

While Stein's links to Vichy authorities have generated discussion, only a few studies have attempted to assess Stein's translation strategies and to examine the language in which she chose to re-express Pétain's messages. While quite painstakingly reviewing the context of the translation, Will takes a somewhat cursory look at the actual mechanics of translation. She calls the translation 'stupefyingly literal', 'incongruous, even inept', resembling the work of a 'bungling student' (Will 2011: 139), which she finds odd given Stein's previous 'translations' of Flaubert and Hugnet. As a translator who is 'in thrall to the aura of a great man', Stein is party to a 'collaboration undertaken under coercion' and has no choice but to adopt a strictly literal approach (Will 2004 and 2011). This position echoes that of Sarah Posman (2009), who alludes to the translations of Pétain's *Paroles* as 'docile and strangely French' and wonders whether Stein's 'franglais' should be taken as an extremely faithful translation or, either consciously or unconsciously, as a subversive one ('rebelle'). In any case, Posman concludes, it is impossible to tell since Stein herself gave no clues.

In his contribution to the *Jacket2* dossier, Václav Paris (2013) lists all the speeches translated by Stein, providing the equivalent number and date of Pétain's speeches. He offers reasons why Stein might have translated some speeches and not others, and applies a corrective lens to Will's analysis. In her recently released study, Rachel Galvin (2016) goes even farther, aiming to 'unsettle prevalent readings that depict Stein as intellectually and creatively subservient to Pétain' (261). The translation, she finds, 'reveals a carefully crafted poetics that fits within the general idiosyncratic style, or Steinese, of her published work' (269). The 'translational disobedience' and 'Steining' of the speeches are deliberate translation decisions, she says, instances of Stein's interlanguage between French and English (274 and 284). Thus, the translations bear Stein's 'own distinct signature' and should be placed within the 'stylistic spectrum of her other writing' (286).

As absorbing and compelling as these studies are, the work of Stein the translator remains as baffling as it is inconsistent. This translation cannot be dismissed as either inept or literal compared to the Flaubert translation, which likely did not exist, or to the translation of Hugnet, whose poem she merely intended to mirror rather than 'translate'. (None of the above commentators has questioned the authenticity of the two previous forays into translation.) The Pétain document is, in fact, literal in places, to the point of being incorrect, but at other times it is fine.

The manuscript notebooks reveal a great deal of effort on the part of Stein. In drafting other works, Stein's handwriting is generally confident and smooth, with relatively few self-revisions. As Hemingway points out in *A Moveable Feast*, she 'disliked the drudgery of revision' (2010: 17). In the introduction to the translation, there are few changes, in contrast to the translations themselves, where the writing is tortuous and laboured, with many deletions and corrections. The manuscripts also give clues as to the very close collaboration of Alice Toklas, who hitherto played the role of 'amanuensis'. Often Alice suggests correct alternatives to Gertrude's attempts, although at other times, she brings the text closer to the French and hence makes it sound awkward. What accounts for this laborious method? Can it be attributed to an inadequate knowledge of French or difficulty grappling with the complexities of translation? Secondly, why is Alice so visible in this project? She has intervened in previous translations, undoubtedly because of her grasp of French. In this case, she is coming close to becoming a co-author.[53]

The following excerpt is taken from speech VIII, dated 23 June 1940.

FRANÇAIS!

Le gouvernement et le peuple français ont entendu hier, avec une stupeur attristée, les paroles de M. Churchill.

Nous comprenons l'angoisse qui les dicte. M. Churchill redoute pour son pays les maux qui accablent le nôtre depuis un mois.

Il n'est pourtant pas de circonstances où les Français puissent souffrir, sans protester, les leçons d'un ministre étranger. M. Churchill est juge des intérêts de son pays: il ne l'est pas des intérêts du nôtre. Il l'est encore moins de l'honneur français.

Notre drapeau reste sans tâche. Notre armée s'est bravement et loyalement battue. Inférieure en armes et en nombre, elle a dû demander que cesse le combat. Elle l'a fait, je l'affirme, dans l'indépendance et dans la dignité.

[11 lines omitted]

M. Churchill croit-il que les Français refusent à la France entière l'amour et la foi qu'ils accordent à la plus petite parcelle de leurs champs?

Ils regardent bien en face leur présent et leur avenir.

Pour le présent, ils sont certains de montrer plus de grandeur en avouant leur défaite qu'en lui opposant des propos vains et des projets illusoires.

Pour l'avenir, ils savent que leur destin est dans leur courage et leur persévérance.

(Pétain 1941: 45–6)

1 People of France
2   The government and the people of France heard yesterday with stupification
3 and sadness the words of Mr. Churchill.
4   We understand the anxiety which prompted them. Mr. Churchill fears for his
5 country the evils which in one month have overwhelmed ours.
6   There are nevertheless no circumstances under which the French people can

7   permit without protest the admonitions of a foreign minister. Mr. Churchill is the
8   judge of the best interests of his country, he is not of the interests of ours.
9   He is even less of French honor.
10   Our flag remains unstained. Our army has fought bravely and lyally. Inferior
11   in arms and in numbers it was necessary to ask that fighting should cease. This has
12   been done I maintain with independence and dignity.

[…]

13   Does Mr. Churchill think that the French people do not give to the whole of
14   France the love and faith that they give to the smallest parcel of their soil.
15   They look their present and their future in the face.
16   For the present they are certain to show more greatness in their
17   defeat than in duping themselves with vain propositions and illusory projects.
18   As for the future they know that their destiny lies in their courage and their
19   perseverance. (From the Stein typescript)[54]

The English version of this address, which Pétain gave in response to a speech by Churchill, illustrates how Stein translated, as well as the way in which Toklas assisted her. Except for the beginning of the first notebook, Stein writes her translation on the right hand (recto) page and leaves the opposite page (verso) blank for Toklas to make comments. Toklas goes through and makes annotations in red pencil directly on Stein's version; she sometimes suggests alternatives on the verso, which Stein accepts or rejects. In some cases, Toklas proposes a version that is more correct; however, in an effort to be closer to the French, she sometimes errs on the side of literal and hence unidiomatic English.

In lines 2 and 3, Stein corrects herself. In the manuscript she has first written 'with a saddened stupifaction' for the French 'avec une stupeur attristée'; she strikes this out and replaces it with the less literal 'stupification and sadness'. However, 'stupifaction', which should strictly speaking read 'stupefaction' in English, could be considered a 'false friend' in that it does not have the same connotation as 'stupeur' in French, which means 'astonishment' or 'consternation' as opposed to the 'stupor' or 'insensibility' suggested by Stein's word choice. In line 4, there is hesitation around her translation for the French 'angoisse': in the notebook, Stein has struck out a word that may be 'horror' and replaced it with 'anxiety'. On the opposite page, Toklas has proposed 'anguish' and 'mental agony', which have been crossed out. This is a case where Stein has not accepted one of the alternatives offered by Toklas. The sentence beginning 'Mr. Churchill fears' (lines 4–5) follows the French syntax very closely, although

Stein has moved 'in one month', originally at the end as it is in the French, to a different position in the sentence.

The paragraph referring to Churchill as a judge of the interests of his country (lines 6–9) begins with a slight mistranslation in Stein's first draft, then corrected by Toklas. Stein first writes: 'It is nevertheless not under these circumstances that the French people …', which Toklas amends, rightly so, to read: 'There are nevertheless no circumstances under which …'. Stein replaces the verb 'allow' with 'permit' resulting in the Steinian alliteration 'permit without protest'. The last two sentences (lines 8–9), on the other hand, may well sound somewhat Steinian, but they are hard to follow.

The paragraph beginning 'Our flag' (lines 10–12) seems to have presented particular difficulties for the pair of translators. The first two sentences (line 10) are smoothly and correctly translated (except that 'loyally' is incorrectly written 'lyally'); the formulation 'remains unstained' has a sonority to it that an alternative word choice – for example, 'remains unblemished' – would not have had. However, the last two (lines 11–12) have gone through numerous transformations, with so many strikeouts and edits that they are rewritten on the opposite page. It is interesting that, in the manuscript, Toklas has suggested translating '*elle* a dû demander' as '*she* …' before settling on 'it', which refers of course to 'armée' and not to any female person. In line 13, Toklas has suggested using the verb 'give' as a translation for 'accordent' instead of the very literal 'accord' that Stein had initially put.

Line 15, 'They look their present and their future in the face', has come out sounding relatively idiomatic, but in draft form it began as the word-for-word (and nonsensical) 'They look well in the face their present and their future' as a translation for 'Ils regardent bien en face leur présent et leur avenir'. In the subsequent paragraph (lines 16–17), there is an interesting intervention, likely deliberate, on the part of Toklas. In the draft notebook, Stein's version reads: 'For In For the present they certainly are certain to word? show more greatness in acknowledging their defeat than in duping themselves with vain propositions and illusory projects'. There is hesitation over simple expressions like 'for the present' and 'are certain' but the rest of the sentence is translated effortlessly and accurately. In the typescript, however, there is a gap between 'in' and 'defeat'. In transcribing the speech, or perhaps editing her typescript, Toklas has erased the word 'acknowledging'. Pétain himself refers to the idea of admitting defeat ('en avouant leur défaite') but perhaps Toklas decided it was unwise to allude to the idea of voluntary capitulation given the controversy, by this time, around the armistice (see Galvin 2016: 277).

What conclusions can be drawn from an examination of the Pétain manuscripts? Since Stein herself has not commented on her intentions, as she does so freely on other occasions, it is difficult to say conclusively whether she had any method at all. She certainly does her best to remain close to the French text – justifiably, as this type of discourse requires a greater degree of fidelity than poetry, for example. Like translators of legal texts, or sacred ones (if we buy the idea of hero worship), Gertrude and Alice are striving for accuracy. In some cases, there is evidence of 'ineptitude' or inexperience, at the very least. In others, Stein and her collaborator cum editor are doing a fair job. The introduction reveals an admiration for the author she is translating. She is perhaps in awe of him, as she is of great men, and heroes generally, including female saints, but was this enough to influence her translation strategies?

What is certain is that this project represented hard work for both Stein and Toklas, who seemed to agonize over the slightest choice of word, even as they got nearer the end, more so than in other Stein manuscripts. She may have been experiencing unease at the loss of her own voice, as she shares authorship with Toklas and is overshadowed by the authority of Pétain. As Stein became increasingly aware of the way in which the country was moving, she felt a sense of personal danger that she may or may not have associated with Pétain. She soldiered on as a translator, but it is not completely surprising that she left it unfinished. She had abandoned *Frénésie*, too, not necessarily in mid-sentence, but in the middle of a scene.

Survival, liberation, afterlife

We come back to the question of what motivated Stein to take on this curious project. What motivates any translator? In particular, what motivates a writer, who has his or her 'own' work to produce, to devote creative energy to transposing the work of another writer? Stein was asked to take this on because of her stature as an American writer, but her acceptance of the task, as a Jew in Nazi-occupied France, remains a mystery.

It has been said that the Pétain project was motivated more by friendship than it was by ideology (Posman 2009). The friend in question was Bernard Faÿ, one of the few with whom Stein remained close throughout her life (*Autobiography*, 248). Their relationship, however, was also grounded in shared intellectual interests – discussions of American literature and history – and common political views. Complicating their relations and tipping the balance of power, as it were, was Stein's gratitude to Faÿ for the crucial role he had played in translating her work and securing her success as a writer. Of course, the ties that bound Stein and Faÿ have wider implications, as Will has amply demonstrated in her meticulous studies of their relationship, in which she highlights the political overtones of the term 'friendship' in the interwar years (2008 and 2011).

Beyond her loyalty to Faÿ, which might account for why she agreed to translate Pétain's speeches, Stein evinced a genuine admiration for the elderly Marshal. In this she was not alone. A hero of the First World War, Pétain was widely regarded as someone who could save France from the dangers posed by Germany, particularly the devastating loss of young men the country had seen in the earlier conflict. Support for Pétain extended even beyond France, as evidenced by the sympathetic *New Yorker* profile written by journalist Janet Flanner as late as 1944.[55]

In his introduction to the French edition of Pétain's speeches, Jaray depicts Pétain in both military and religious terms. The Maréchal is described not simply as a military leader, but also as 'l'homme providentiel' (vi), 'l'homme du destin' (xx) (a man of providence, a man of destiny). Jaray concludes with a juxtaposition of attributes that seem ironic in retrospect:

> Le Maréchal apparaît donc à l'historien comme l'inspirateur d'un monde nouveau, humain, chrétien et tolérant …
> Sur le fond d'un drame qui se prolonge, sa figure apparaît comme une annonciatrice de temps nouveaux. (Pétain 1941: xxi)

> Historians will thus regard the Marshal as having inspired a new world, a world that is human, Christian and tolerant …
> Against the backdrop of a crisis that continues to unfold, his presence heralds the coming of a new age. (My translation)

Faÿ would have conveyed the tenor of these views in presenting the project to Stein, and, if so, he would not have failed to captivate her. She admired great men, saints, and other figures of authority. She was fascinated with the dynamics of power and ambition, because of her preoccupation with her own genius and place in the literary hierarchy. As she writes in *Everybody's Autobiography*, at a time when she had finally become famous, 'In America everybody is [a celebrity] but some are more than others. I was more than others' (168).

Beyond an admiration for Pétain the hero, beyond her identification with him, Stein – like many of those on the right – was nostalgic for pre-revolutionary

France. Initially, at least, Stein quite publicly 'presented herself as sympathetic to the regime' (Will 2011: 135). The degree to which her political views were both extreme and well known is reflected in Picasso's outrage, often quoted by critics (although with his most insulting comments omitted): 'That pig! A real fascist, what's more. She always had a weakness for Franco. Imagine! For Pétain, too. She wrote speeches for Pétain. Can you imagine it? An American. A Jewess, what's more. And she's fat as a pig' (Lord 1994: 15).

Stein may well have been in awe of the Vichy chief of state, but she was neither safe nor welcome in Vichy France. Two 'Statuts des Juifs' were enacted, in October 1940 and June 1941, which excluded Jews from public life, established an anti-Jewish ministry, and eventually led to the deportation of Jews to concentration camps. Stein was on the *Liste Otto* of banned writers but was evidently missing, as was Toklas, from any official Vichy census of Jews (Will 2011: 125). To some extent, Stein was naïve in her certainty that all would turn out well, yet at the same time her anxiety and fears bubble to the surface in her wartime writing. In *Wars I Have Seen*, she reports having been warned by the *sous-préfet* to leave the country to avoid being sent to a concentration camp and says repeatedly that she 'felt funny' (50–51). Stein and Toklas did not leave. They had earned the trust of the local people, and hence were supported by them, as the doctor had promised. As Imbs testified: 'when I was walking from Belley to her place and asking my way, everyone knew of *les mademoiselles américaines* and often advanced the information that they were very nice and very esteemed in the region. Gertrude always had this gift of imposing the respect among the common people' (1936: 284).

Still, more was required. There is evidence that they were helped by people in high places. Faÿ claims that he discussed the two American Jewish women with the Maréchal, who then dictated a letter to the *sous-préfet* of Belley instructing him to watch out for them and to ensure that they were supplied with sufficient fuel and food (1966: 162). Faÿ's role in protecting Stein and Toklas and in saving their art collection was also used in his defence when he was on trial for collaboration after the war (Burns 2012).

It is possible, then, that the Pétain translation project was the key to the survival of Stein and Toklas. Consciously or not, she negotiated their safety by agreeing to translate Pétain's speeches and to promote him in an introduction that was very probably seen and approved, if not by Pétain himself, then by his private secretary, Dr. Bernard Ménétrel, with whom Faÿ met to discuss, among other things, the Stein project (Burns 2012). Stein remained positive, although conflicted, about both Faÿ and Pétain until the end of her life. As she says about Pétain in *Wars I Have Seen*: 'so many points of view about him, so very many. I had lots of them. I was almost French in having so many' (53). Stein also wrote in support of Faÿ when he was on trial after the war (although her endorsement was less than enthusiastic).

In an ironic turn of events, Stein became a celebrity anew, and recovered her voice, once she was 'liberated'. Having lived in France for the better part of her life, she now revelled in the fact that, after all, she was an American. She befriended GIs; she mothered them and she mentored them. She celebrated the liberation in a radio broadcast to Americans, proclaiming to her countrymen that: 'this native land business gets you all right' (Mellow 1974: 456). She found her way into *Life* and other mainstream American magazines, heralded as 'America's most famous literary expatriate'.[56]

Paradox endures in the Steinian world. Stein was not wholeheartedly engaged in the Vichy propaganda machine; she was supportive of the Maquis and also contributed to periodicals that published the work of banned Jewish writers as well as homosexual ones.[57] As Wagner-Martin writes, citing Stein, 'life at war was filled with contradictions' (1995: 247–8), but, in truth, her entire life was filled with contradictions. Stein was double in multiple ways, forever blurring the lines in her politics, in her identities, and in her stance and voice as an author/translator.

When Gertrude Stein died in 1946 of cervical cancer, she left behind a grieving widow and a bereft friend. In a letter of condolences to Alice Toklas, Faÿ writes how much he 'admired and loved Gertrude' and 'enjoyed her so much, so genuinely, so thoroughly' (Letter of 1 August 1946, in Gallup 1953: 402–3). Toklas and Faÿ were united by a bond of loyalty, mutual rescue and survival, although theirs is also a story of betrayal and duplicity. In 1950–1951, Alice Toklas sold two works by Picasso to help fund Faÿ's escape from prison (Burns 2011: 261). Faÿ later assisted her in converting to Catholicism, which she did because she believed that by abandoning the Jewish faith she would have a better opportunity for an afterlife, and thereby for joining her departed companion after her own death.

Did Stein ever act out of a true translation 'drive' (*pulsion de traduire*), to borrow a concept from Berman (1992)? The motivation for the Pétain translation, and its nature as an actual act of translation, have been the subject of conjecture: the word that is most consistently used with respect to this chapter in Stein's *œuvre* is 'speculative'. Perhaps we can do no more than speculate.

The legacy of Gertrude Stein

Despite the current renaissance in Stein studies, her readers continue to be divided between 'inspiration' and 'bafflement', as the editor's note to her article in *Life* suggests. Her efforts as a translator could be judged unsuccessful on two counts. First of all, her aborted attempts have not resulted in the circulation of any cultural product. Further, her agency as a translator moulded by the historical events around her has cast her in a negative light, 'at a steep price to her historical legacy' (Karlin 2011). Nonetheless, analysis of her engagement with the idea and process of translation, regardless of the actual outcome, yields fruitful insights into the complexities of both the writer and her body of work. Translation enters into her efforts to construct a myth of herself as a writer; its use as a trope reflects both the hybrid voice she adopted and the hybrid space she inhabited.

Translation was many things to Gertrude Stein: an 'exercise' or pre-text for original writing (Flaubert); a 'meditation on' someone else's work (Hugnet); a pretext, pretence and means of survival (Pétain). Like Paul Valéry, who compared the influence of Edgar Allan Poe to that of a Wagnerian leitmotif, Siegfried's horn call, Gertrude Stein harnessed (hijacked?) the idea of translation, both real and fictionalized.

As we have seen, Stein 'translated herself' in the metaphorical sense, and lived her life in translation, deliberately setting out to forge a new self in a new place, to create the persona of a writer and sexually free being in a perpetual state of foreignness and ambiguity. An assimilated Jew, like Toklas, she spoke little about her Jewishness, yet was later in a precarious position under the German occupation precisely because of it. Yet, she and Alice did not return to the United States, as they were urged to do, because they did not want to live as 'refugees' there. Instead, they stayed on in a state of exile, in the truer sense of the word, living in fear, uncertainty at best, as war was waged around them and Jews were deported to death camps. It was in this context, ironically, that Stein undertook the only 'real' translation of her life. She claimed to have translated Flaubert, she rewrote, or reimagined, Hugnet's poetry, but this was the first time that she applied herself to translation *per se*. The Pétain work is more laboured, even plodding, than when she is writing her original material, perhaps because her very survival is at risk.

Exiled and ambivalent about her identity in life, Gertrude Stein remains exiled in death: she died at the American hospital in a Paris suburb, in July 1946, but was not buried until October (Jewish burials take place within days, not months).

Prayers were read in the American Cathedral, an Episcopalian Church. Her grave lies in Père Lachaise Cemetery alongside those of famous French artists and celebrated expatriate ones such as Oscar Wilde and Frederick Chopin. Alice Toklas died as a Roman Catholic and is buried with Gertrude, although she insisted that her name be inscribed on the back of Stein's tombstone.

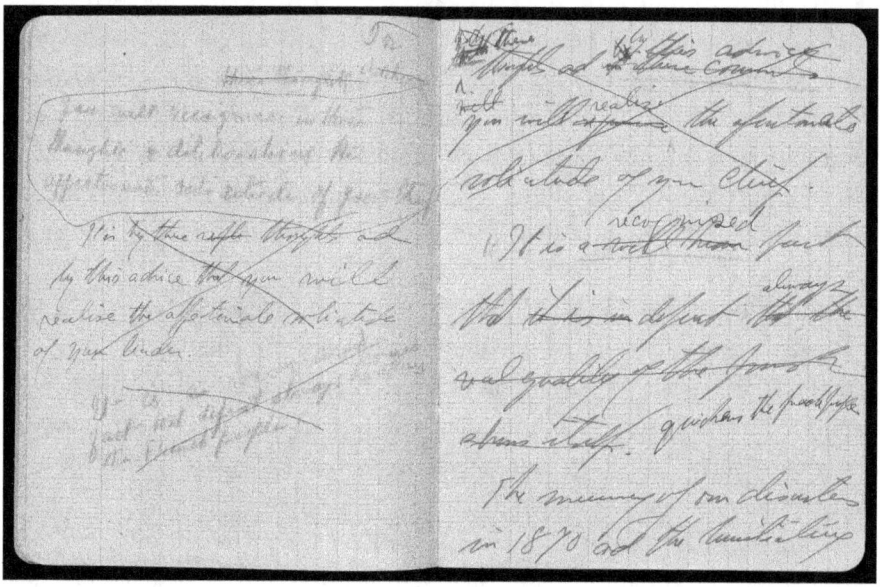

Figure 3 Excerpt from the first notebook of Gertrude Stein's translation of Pétain's *Paroles aux Français*, showing her handwriting and self-edits with Alice Toklas's corrections and suggestions. Used with the permission of the Yale University Library, Beinecke Rare Book and Manuscript Library, Yale Collection of American Literature, Gertrude Stein and Alice B. Toklas Papers, YCAL MSS 76 (Box 64, folder 1138).

Figure 4 Photograph of Paul Auster, by Lotte Hansen.

Paul Auster: The Writer and His Double

Dostoevsky, Heraclitus, Dante, Virgil, Homer, Cervantes, Kafka, Kierkegaard, Tolstoy, Hölderlin, and scores of other poets and writers who have marked me forever – I, an American, whose only foreign language is French – have all been revealed to me, read by me, digested by me, in translation. Translators are the shadow heroes of literature, the often forgotten instruments that make it possible for different cultures to talk to one another, who have enabled us to understand that we all, from every part of the world, live in one world.

I would like to offer a salute and a declaration of thanks to all these men and women, these translators, who toil so selflessly to keep literature alive for everyone.

–Paul Auster[1]

Another American in Paris

Paul Auster, like Bernard Shaw and Gertrude Stein, is a writer of remarkable breadth and scope. His astonishing output includes fiction, poetry, screenplays, and essays. His work has been translated into over forty languages. Over the course of his career, he has penned more than fifteen novels and several important memoirs. In addition, he has produced a considerable body of work as a translator and editor of translations, and he has written about translation. A 'literary decathlete', in sum, 'at ease in any genre'.[2]

Born on 3 February 1947 in Newark, New Jersey, Paul Auster resides with his wife, author Siri Hustvedt, in the writerly neighbourhood of Park Slope in Brooklyn, New York. His years studying literature at Columbia University were punctuated with stints overseas, in a self-imposed 'exile' in France much akin to that of his compatriot Gertrude Stein several decades earlier. In the early part of his career, he wrote poetry, he translated, he eked out a living. He appears to have abandoned both poetry and translation once he launched his writing career with the memoir *The Invention of Solitude*, followed closely by his first works of fiction. As we shall see, however, the situation is more complex, and the sequence of his work is not as cut and dried as it appears to be. Even after he seems to have substituted original writing for translation, translators and translation continued to inhabit his imagination. His fiction is 'translational' in that translation, translators, and related themes are woven into the fabric of his creative work.

This chapter looks at how Auster came to embrace the French language and things French in the first place, at what he translated, at his translation methods and at his conceptualization of translation in a variety of texts and paratexts. A final section examines several works of Auster's fiction in which the thread of translation is intertwined with other themes, in the form of characters who translate and who embody or grapple with related issues of language, displacement, identity, and authorship.

Auster has shared details of his life in autobiographical works, ranging from his first major publication *The Invention of Solitude*, written after his father's death and published in 1982, to his two later memoirs *Winter Journal* (2012) and *Report from the Interior* (2013). His intellectual journey, from New Jersey to New York, to France and back, has been recounted in these works of nonfiction, in a number of published interviews, as well as in a personal interview with the author.[3]

Auster attended public schools in Newark, where he had exceptionally good teachers who gave him a good grounding in French. He left for Europe after he finished high school, not even waiting to attend his graduation ceremony. Those were the days when you could get by on five dollars a day, he says, in *Hand to Mouth: A Chronicle of Early Failure* (in *Collected Prose*, 164) and during our conversation. During that summer, between high school and college, he spent time in Paris, where he hung out with people who did not speak English. By the time he enrolled at Columbia in the fall of 1965, his French had improved so dramatically that he was exempt from taking French language and was allowed to register in a literature class. He signed up for a course in nineteenth-century French poetry with Donald Frame, a noted translator of Rabelais and biographer and translator of Montaigne. That early exposure to French poetry was critical to Auster's development because it provided him with a double introduction, to reading and translating:

> I hadn't read French poetry at that point. I was just a boy. It was a great revelation and I think that in order to help myself understand the poems that we were

reading I made little efforts at translating them, just to get my feet on the ground. Not with any eye to doing anything polished or publishable, but simply out of a desire to penetrate the material better. (PA-int)

Another enduring influence was an uncle by marriage. Allen Mandelbaum (1926–2011) was a distinguished translator of Italian and classical poetry, widely recognized as the world's leading translator of Dante's *Divine Comedy*, for which he was honoured by the City of Florence and the Italian government. He knew ancient Greek, Latin, Hebrew, Arabic, and the major European languages. Not only did he translate classics such as Homer's *Odyssey* and Ovid's *Metamorphoses*, he was also known for his translations of modern Italian poets Giuseppe Ungaretti and Salvatore Quasimodo. Mandelbaum did his master's and PhD degrees at Columbia University; he taught English and comparative literature at the City University of New York and later at Wake Forest University in North Carolina. He was also a published poet in his own right. Auster continues to pay homage to him.[4]

And he was probably, I would say, at this late moment in my life, the most brilliant literary intelligence I've ever encountered. He was one of these boy wonders. He was a great influence and he was also the person who read my early efforts as a poet. He was my counsellor, advisor, reader, teacher. All private. One on one. He was of great importance to me. (PA-int)

A fictional uncle makes an appearance as early as the 1989 novel *Moon Palace*, a kind of *bildungsroman* in which Uncle Victor leaves one thousand four hundred and ninety-two books to his nephew Marco. 'A propitious number', Uncle Victor says to his nephew, 'since it evokes the memory of Columbus's discovery of America, and the college you're going to was named after Columbus' (*Moon Palace*, 13). Marco learns a lot by reading these books, which also allow him to survive financially, as he sells them off, bit by bit, to a used-book dealer.

The true story of the uncle's library is recounted in several places.[5] When the uncle and his wife went to live in Italy for several years, they left their substantial collection of books in the attic of Auster's family home, a household that otherwise had few books. These books opened a 'whole new world'. When asked about his trajectory as a translator, Auster still goes back to the story of his uncle, who 'directly inspired' him to try his hand at translating. Translating, he opines, is perhaps unusual for young writers these days, although there is a long tradition of it (PA-int).

Passionate about what he uncovered in his uncle's treasure trove of world literature, motivated to study at Columbia, perhaps because his uncle had gone there, and inspired by the French literature he discovered as a student, Auster went back to Paris in 1967 for his junior year abroad. The Paris experience, which he has amply documented, was quite simply a 'disaster' – principally in the bureaucratic sense because he was unable to sign up for courses he was interested in (given by Roland Barthes, for example). Auster wanted to quit school altogether, but the alternative would have been to go home and risk being drafted at a time when the United States was still at war in Vietnam. His stay in Paris, on the other hand, allowed him to acquire books of poetry, which he began translating 'for the fun of it'. He occupied himself by reading and writing, writing poems and translating poems (*Hand to Mouth*; PA-int).

He came back to New York and, in the end, did not serve in the military thanks to a high lottery number. He went on to graduate with a BA and MA in English from Columbia University, in 1969 and 1970, respectively. During his later years at Columbia, he took on freelance work, including translations 'tossed his way' because of his knowledge of French, and found that he was 'developing a taste for the kind of literary hackwork that would keep me going until I was thirty' (*Hand to Mouth*, 183).

After working at odd jobs, for example on an oil tanker, he went back to Paris in February 1971. The reasons are set out in autobiographical pieces and works of fiction: he knew French, there was a sense of 'unfinished business' about his earlier stay there, he was trying to figure out who he was, and he wanted to write. In 1973, he moved to Provence, where he and Lydia Davis lived together and worked as caretakers of a farmhouse. He and Davis, now an accomplished writer-translator known for her very short stories and translations of *Madame Bovary* and *Swann's Way*, had met as undergraduates. They married after returning to the United States in 1974, and had one son together, Daniel.

It was never Auster's intention to remain in France and become an expatriate (*Hand to Mouth*, 195). Still, he benefited from those years by becoming well acquainted with French cultural life and honing his writing skills. Translation was very much part of the work he did during the 1970s, partly as a solution to the financial problems he had at the time. Money and associated problems are very present in Auster's autobiographical writings as well as in his fiction. As the very title of the above-quoted essay suggests, he was just scraping by, living in grinding poverty. His problems persisted until he received a small inheritance from his father, about which he says: 'It was vital; it just gave me a little space.

I was living with a fifty-ton piano on my back. The thing about money is that if you don't have it, you think about it. And the good thing about having money is that you don't have to think about it all the time' (PA-int).

Many of his translations, first in Paris, and then later, when he was back in New York, were serious: art books, op-ed pieces by Sartre and Foucault for *The New York Times*, and poetry. Other assignments were less literary in nature, such as translating the new North Vietnamese constitution (from French to English). Some, such as translating an 'exceptionally tedious document from the French Embassy about the reorganization of its staff' (*Hand to Mouth*, 183), were just a chore. He translated books with Lydia Davis, but they were 'undistinguished works that ranged in quality from not very good to downright bad. The money was bad as well' (*Hand to Mouth*, 220). Even when occupied with tasks that might have been relatively interesting, such as writing entries for a catalogue of art publications, he was tasked with the more demeaning job of making tuna fish sandwiches for lunch (*Hand to Mouth*, 213). Looking back on this time, Auster calls the work 'grim', 'gruesome', and the material translated quite simply 'junk': 'I could have made more money flipping hamburgers than translating those books' (PA-int).

While continuing to translate, mainly for money, Auster published a number of critical essays and two collections of his own poetry, *Unearth* (1974) and *Wall Writing* (1976). A confluence of circumstances toward the end of the 1970s – the breakup of his marriage, for example – led to what he calls 'trouble' and then a new direction.

> By the late 70s I was in all kinds of trouble, emotionally, artistically, and just couldn't write anymore. And I was stuck for about a year. And when I started writing again, it was prose. And I've just been doing that ever since, but it was somehow a return to the very beginning rather than a complete break. (PA-int)

The inheritance, along with some grants, allowed him to devote more time to original writing, and to leave the world of freelance translating behind. Toward the early 1980s, when he began publishing prose – nonfiction and fiction – he appeared to have abandoned both poetry and translation to take up fiction. But, as he explains, it's more complicated than that. The novels did not come out of nowhere: quite the opposite, he had accumulated about 800–1000 pages of manuscripts, which he had written at a much younger age and on which his later novels were based. He also continued with translation for a while, well into the 1980s, publishing several collections in book form until, at the suggestion of Jacques Dupin, he did his last commercial translation, a book of Joan Miró's writings.[6]

From 1986 to 1990, Auster taught creative writing at Princeton University. Teaching comes up as a fall-back occupation in his novels: in *Leviathan*, for example, Peter Aaron applies for a community college job with a paltry salary at the same time as he is getting by on translation (60). Teaching seems to be nothing more than a way to earn money, and college professors are depicted as 'edgy' and 'high-strung' (*The Book of Illusions*, 73). Evidently not drawn to teaching in general, he seems to have enjoyed teaching translation, which he did as part of his duties as Princeton. He gave workshops on poetry translation. Students picked one poet to translate during the semester, as long as it was a 'good poet, a great poet'. The experience was obviously gratifying: 'It was very enjoyable. I got some great work, I must say. Tremendous work' (PA-int).

From a little anthology to a massive one

Auster's compilation of translated poetry stands out among his many successes, culminating in his scholarly edition of French verse. His talents as an anthologist date back to his school days, when his interest in reading, and then translating, French poetry was first kindled. In 1967, he purchased a small anthology of contemporary French poets at the college bookstore. This 'thin book' contained the work of exciting young postwar poets such as Yves Bonnefoy, Jacques Dupin, André du Bouchet, and Philippe Jaccottet. He began with Dupin, whose books he tracked down when he went to Paris for his junior year abroad. He 'just started translating for the fun of it', he says, and 'one thing led to another and eventually these things were published'.

Back home after the year abroad, he began to translate the Surrealists. This resulted in his first book, entitled *A Little Anthology of Surrealist Poems*, produced while he was still an undergraduate at Columbia. It was published in 1972, in mimeographed form, by a small publishing house called 'Siamese Banana Press'. The book, dedicated to Lydia Davis, is a compilation of Auster's English translations of ten Surrealist poets (on rectos only, without French originals on the versos). The cover is illustrated by George Schneeman, an artist known for his collaboration with poets. Along with the names of the poets (André Breton, Paul Éluard, René Char, Benjamin Péret, Antonin Artaud, Tristan Tzara, Philippe Soupault, Robert Desnos, Louis Aragon, and Hans Arp), Schneeman has drawn a rowboat on the cover. In it, he has placed a headless boatman reminiscent of Charon, the *passeur*, who ferried the souls of the dead across the River Styx, often used as a metaphor for translation, in the etymological sense of 'carrying across'. It shows Auster's engagement, even at that early stage in his life, with the kind of intercultural mediation carried out by translators. The anthology was reprinted in 2002, with a preface in which Auster tells the story of this early exercise in translation. As he explains, his first attempts at translation coincide with the tumult of the Vietnam War, and the riots and sit-ins at Columbia. In that context, the discovery of the Surrealists provided a model of 'poets dreaming of revolution, of how to change the world'.

> Translation, then, was more than just a literary exercise. It was a first step toward breaking free of the shackles of myself, of overcoming my own ignorance. *You must change your life.* Perhaps. Back then, it was more a question of searching for a life, of trying to invent a life I could believe in.... (Preface to *A Little Anthology of Surrealist Poems*, in *Collected Prose*, 459; emphasis and ellipsis in original)

In 1982, Auster published his best-selling anthology, *The Random House Book of Twentieth-Century French Poetry*, which contains a large number of French poems as well as a substantial commentary on translation and the historical links between English and French language and literature. This book has been immensely popular since it came out; it can be considered, if not Auster's crowning achievement in the realm of translation, then certainly one of his major accomplishments.

What appears on the title page is revealing (as Genette would suggest, these choices are not innocent): the title is accompanied by the qualification 'with Translations by American and British *poets*' and followed by the words '*Edited* by Paul Auster' (*Random House Book* 1982a: v; emphasis added). In the context of this monumental project, Auster is at once a translator, editor, and anthologist, which involves – as he describes it in his introduction – being a 'matchmaker' between the poets and translators (XLVIII).

Auster uses the paratextual space afforded by the introduction to conceptualize translation in general and discuss the way in which he has put the anthology together. His essay is stunningly insightful on a number of levels. First, he examines the shared linguistic and cultural heritage of England and France, beginning with a quotation from Wallace Stevens that emphasizes their interdependence: 'French and English constitute a single language'. He cites examples of early English writers, like Chaucer, Wyatt, and Spenser, whose work is constructed, in part, through translation from French or through imitation of French models. The influence of French continues through to modern literature, when the English emulated the poetry of Baudelaire and then the French symbolists. Pound and Eliot, giants of American literature, were also inspired by French literature. Auster discusses the cross-fertilization of European and American modernism, as illustrated by the 1913 Armory Show, and reflected in magazines such as *The Little Review*, which originated in Chicago yet ended in Paris, and which published authors from both sides of the Atlantic. Finally, he enumerates the many American writers who found their way to Paris, beginning with Gertrude Stein in the early twentieth century. This path, of course, was taken by Auster himself, whose conclusion with respect to the American-in-Paris experience is that it 'has so thoroughly saturated American consciousness that the image of the starving young writer serving his apprenticeship in Paris has become one of our enduring literary myths' (xxvii–xxx).

Translation was at the heart of that literary exchange during what Auster calls 'the most fruitful period in our literature'. American and British poets have consistently translated their French counterparts, and many of the major contemporary poets writing in the English language have tried their hand at translating French verse. The reason Auster gives is key to understanding these poets and to understanding him as well: translation is seen 'not simply as a literary exercise', but also 'an act of discovery and passion'. This wealth of translations gives Auster a deep pool of gifted translators, and this is what makes his anthology so rich, offering as it does French poetry alongside translations that have been 're-imagined and re-presented' by English-language poets (xxx–xxxi).

Having traced the 'symbiosis' between the English and French traditions, Auster goes on to highlight the differences between them. He takes as his example that most illustrious of self-translators, Samuel Beckett, who was intimately acquainted with the 'capacities and limitations' of the two languages. While imposing constraints on literary language and norms, the French Academy has given poets traditions they can react against. French poets such as the Dadaists and Surrealists have consequently become more 'rebellious' than British or American ones. Pound and Eliot, on the other hand, have sought to create tradition by turning to the Old World. What Auster highlights particularly about twentieth-century French poetry is its diversity; 'various, tumultuous and contradictory', its creators – Apollinaire, Milosz, Segalen, Tzara, and Jabès, to name a few – originate from outside the Hexagon. Hence the 'trap' of trying to frame a restricted number of poets in a single anthology, which becomes, in Auster's words, a 'kind of cultural dinner, a smattering of national dishes served up on a platter for popular consumption'. To avoid drowning out the voices of individual poets through this kind of totalizing approach, he prefers to regard the anthology as a 'threshold opening on to a new space' (XXXII–XXXIV).

In the third of four sections, Auster gives us a brief survey of the French poets he has selected, depicting the characteristics of their poetry, their personal circumstances and the role they have played in initiating literary movements or tendencies. He paints a detailed and nuanced picture of the ebb and flow of French poetry from the early twentieth century, through two world wars, and up to more recent times, into 'uncharted territory' where boundaries between formal categories break down. In the last section, finally, Auster shares with us some of the technical challenges he dealt with during the two years he spent putting the collection together. The enterprise is viewed as a form of literary life-saving. Whenever possible, he has used existing English translations, which he did by hunting around – with great pleasure – in magazines and out-of-print books, 'rescuing a number of superb translations from the obscurity of library shelves and microfilm rooms' and printing some translations that had existed only in manuscript form (XLVIII).

Auster plays multiple roles: translator, editor, anthologist, and commissioner.[7] When he felt that the existing translations were inadequate or when they simply did not exist, he commissioned new ones, acting like a 'matchmaker' and trying to 'arrange the marriage with care'. He claims not to have followed a consistent 'policy' with respect to translation method, although he considers the majority of the versions to be 'faithful to the originals'. He sets out the following translation strategy:

> Translating poetry is at best an art of approximation, and there are no fixed rules to follow in deciding what works or does not. It is largely a matter of instinct, of ear, of common sense. Whenever I was faced with a choice between literalness and poetry, I did not hesitate to choose poetry. It seemed more important to me to give those readers who have no French a true sense of each poem *as a poem* than to strive for word-for-word exactness. The experience of a poem resides not only in each of its words, but in the interactions among those words – the music, the silences, the shapes – and if a reader is not somehow given the chance to enter the totality of that experience, he will remain cut off from the spirit of the original. It is for this reason, it seems to me, that poems should be translated by poets. (XLVIII)

Here, Auster joins the age-old tradition of distinguishing literal and free translation. Yet, in the classical debate that places word-for-word translation at one end of a continuum and sense-for-sense translation at the other (*non verbum e verbo sed sensum de sensu*), Auster changes the terms somewhat. The opposite of a word-for-word rendition is 'poetry', for he believes that the true 'sense' of a poem resides not in the meaning of the words themselves, but in the relations between the words through what he calls 'the music, the silences, the shapes'.

Back matter in the anthology consists of biographical notes for each of the poets, who are listed alphabetically; an acknowledegments section that gives the sources of originals and translations; and an index of translators. Some information is lacking – for example, the date of publication of each of the original poems (Brooks 1983) – but taken as a whole the collection is a valuable work of scholarship. The line-up of translators is impressive; it reads like a who's-who of American and British writers (with an overrepresentation of Americans?): Wallace Stevens, John Dos Passos, Lawrence Ferlinghetti, T.S. Eliot, Samuel Beckett, Ezra Pound, Richard Wilbur, to name a few. Others, while authors in their own right, are well known for their translations: Michael Hamburger, translator of Hölderin, Celan and other German poets; Helen Weaver, translator of Antonin Artaud; Jackson Mathews, translator and editor of Paul Valéry. Lydia Davis is a contributor and Auster's uncle, Allen Mandelbaum, too, makes a cameo appearance, with the translation of a single poem, 'Flame Point', by Jules Supervielle.

The *Random House Book* is a bilingual collection featuring the work of forty-eight poets. The French text is on the left-hand page, and its corresponding English version on the right side. As Hoyt Rogers (2015) says, in relation to the translation of *Openwork* discussed below, a bilingual edition 'opens the door for point-by-point criticism of the translation', but at the same time it can 'inspire readers to pursue the poet's text on their own' and even encourage them to explore the language in which the poetry was originally written. Eighty-four translators contributed to the anthology. Auster did over forty poems of varying lengths himself, re-using many of his previously published translations, going as far back as his first book. However, not all the poets collected in the *Little Anthology* have found their way into the Random House book: for example, Hans (Jean) Arp is excluded (as Auster indicates in his footnote on page XLVII). Of those who are in, not all the poems are translated by Auster. For example, Paul Éluard's 'L'Amoureuse/Lady Love' and 'Seconde Nature V/Second Nature V' are translated by Samuel Beckett rather than Auster (*Random House Book*, 201 and 203), and the translation of Tristan Tzara's 'La Mort de Guillaume Apollinaire/Death of Guillaume Apollinaire' is by Lee Harwood (167). Auster makes minor changes, and some more substantial ones, to translations he first did in the 1960s. In Philippe Soupault's 'Le Nageur/The Swimmer', for example, his translation of the line 'Et les vagues visages perdus chuchotent' (*Random House Book,* 226) was 'And a lost blear face murmurs' (*Little Anthology,* n.p.); in the *Random House* version, this becomes 'And lost vague faces whisper' (227). The following example is taken from his translation of 'L'Homme approximatif' by Tristan Tzara, 'Approximate Man' (the definite article in the earlier title, 'The Approximate Man' is dropped):

FRENCH
quel est ce langage qui nous fouette nous sursautons dans la lumière
nos nerfs sont des fouets entre les mains du temps
et le doute vient avec une seule aile incolore
se vissant se comprimant s'écrasant en nous
comme le papier froissé de l'emballage défait
cadeau d'un autre âge aux glissements des poissons d'amertume

(Random House Book, 170)

ENGLISH 1
what is this language that whips us as we summersault into the light
our nerves are whips in the hands of time
and doubt comes with a single colorless wing
screwing compressing crushing in us
crumpled like unfolded wrapping paper
gift of another age from the slivering of the fish of bitterness

(Little Anthology)

ENGLISH 2
what is this language that whips us as we tumble into the light
our nerves are whips in the hands of time
and doubt comes with a single colorless wing
twisting tightening shriveling inside us
like the crumpled paper of an unpacked box
gift from another age to the slithering fish of bitterness

(Random House Book, 171)

Some changes have been made from one version to another. The choice of 'tumble' instead of 'somersault' represents a slight alteration, but it adds a touch of alliteration with the repetition of 't'. The replacement of 'screwing compressing crushing in us/crumpled like unfolded wrapping paper' with 'twisting tightening shriveling inside us/like the crumpled paper of an unpacked box' brings the new translation more in line with the sense and form of the original text. The new version has a musicality that is closer to that of the French verse, which has internal rhymes (viss*ant*-comprim*ant*-écras*ant* and papier-froissé-dé*fait*). This is a good example of the way in which Auster is able to translate literally *and* make poetry at the same time.

The anthology also draws on Auster's translations from the 1970s: translations of Dupin, published in 1974 as *Fits and Starts: Selected Poems of Jacques Dupin*, and of du Bouchet, published in 1976 as *The Uninhabited*. They are reprinted virtually as they were in the first published editions. An exception, in the case of du Bouchet, is the compression of du Bouchet's characteristic blank spaces. In compiling the book for Random House, Auster was struggling with constraints of space, and had to resort to using a typographical mark consisting of two parallel lines (_____) to signify the spaces that had appeared both in the original and in his previous translations. There are a number of other poets whose translations Auster had previously published not in book form but in periodicals; Auster's translation of 'Brain-Cry' by Jean Daive, for instance, appears in a 1975 issue of *TriQuarterly*, the literary magazine of Northwestern University (Zulauf and Cifelli 1978: 32).

The *Random House Book* showcases Auster's productivity as a translator of poetry, mainly during his Paris years and those immediately following his stay there; it is also a testament to his considerable achievement as an editor and anthologist. In the past decades, the production of anthologies and similar collections has been investigated by translation scholars, who view anthologizing as a form of rewriting comparable to translating. Anthologies, particularly when they involve translations, have implications for intercultural relations and for the formation of cultural identities; they contribute to the circulation of national and international literary canons. Anthologists collect texts and put them 'on display', as it were, like artefacts in a museum, thereby contributing to the shaping of tastes (Serruya *et al.* 2013: 1–4).

In this anthology, Auster constructs a certain corpus of 'modern' French poetry, beginning not necessarily with the earliest among them, but with Apollinaire. The choice is logical, as Auster claims, and also appropriate, as one critic has pointed out (Brooks 1983), since the opening poem, 'Zone', bids farewell to an 'ancient world' and ushers in all that is characteristic of the new aesthetics, and also since it is translated by Samuel Beckett, a bilingual writer typifying the polyglot modernism of twentieth-century Parisian exiles. As an epigraph to the section of the introduction in which he explains his choice of Apollinaire, and in which he summarizes the work of the others he has selected for the anthology, Auster uses the opening line of 'Zone': 'In the end you are weary of the ancient world' (*Random House Book,* xxxiv).

Auster is aware that he is liable to be criticized for what he has *not* included, and so explains how he has arrived at his decisions. He had originally planned to feature the work of one hundred poets, and a greater variety of writing. But this, he says, was like 'trying to fit an elephant into a cage designed for a fox'. He gradually trimmed the list down to forty-eight poets. In a footnote, he enumerates the fifty-one he had to leave out. He used the year 1876 as a cut-off point for deciding whether or not to include poets born in the nineteenth century but who continued to write in the twentieth. This allowed him to set aside poets such as Valéry and Claudel, yet keep poets like Fargue, Jacob and Milosz whose work he 'felt was essential to the project' (xlvii). One might question the application of so arbitrary a date; the criterion may have less to do with numbers than with literary style, as he seems to have chosen select older poets who more obviously paved the way for the newness of the twentieth century. Using 1876 as a cut-off date allows him to eliminate someone as *incontournable* as Paul Valéry, for example, who was born in 1871, whereas poems by Valéry's co-editors at the review *Commerce*, Léon-Paul Fargue and Valery Larbaud, born in 1876 and 1881, respectively, manage to find their way into the anthology. Valéry's best work is situated squarely in the twentieth century, even though to Auster it 'seems to belong in spirit to an earlier time' (xlvii). This kind of omission may well 'skew' the anthology, as Brooks (1983) has pointed out, changing its thrust from a 'representation of twentieth-century French poetry' to a collection of *modern* French poetry.

There are other factors at play, too. Beyond these aesthetic, or ideological, considerations, Auster as editor, anthologist and commissioner had to grapple with a set of constraints that have more to do with what André Lefevere, discussing issues of copyright, has called the 'economics of inclusion or exclusion' (2000: 245). Since many of the poems and translations had already been published, Auster was confronted with these same issues. As he says, he didn't make money at all: 'I got a very small advance. And I had to use it all to pay for the permissions. I was actually out of pocket by the time the book came out.... Anything to do with poetry is a labour of love. There's no money in it at all'. In addition, there were tensions regarding the length of the book. At one point, the manuscript had ballooned to 900 pages, and Auster had to negotiate with the publisher, who kept cutting it back, 'whittling it down', to keep costs down. Auster and the publisher were at a 'standoff' until it was taken on by the *New York Review of Books* book club. This allowed the publisher to increase the print run, and in so doing to justify the length (over 680 pages in its final form, including front and back matter). 'That settled the problem', he says. 'But it's always a battle' (PA-int).

Taking stock some thirty years after it was first released, Auster considers this a 'valuable book, a really important thing to do', particularly since it was used in many courses over the years. Which was why it was all the more disappointing for him, as he said during our conversation, that it would soon be out of print. The reason given by Random House was that French is no longer as widely taught at the college level as it once was. When it is, students are less likely to study twentieth-century French poetry – an observation in which I sadly concur.

In compiling these poems, and recovering translations otherwise doomed to extinction, Auster is giving new life to works of literature that might have been lost or forgotten. He has, in fact, ensured their survival by putting them into circulation, or by enabling their authors to step out into a 'new space' (*Random House Book*, 1982: xxxiv). Like translating, putting together an anthology establishes a link with the past, thereby offering 'the possibility of rediscovery and afterlife' (Serruya *et al.* 2013: 4), an act of rescue consistent with what Auster set out to do in publishing his translation of Clastres's *Chronicle*.

Lost and found in translation: The story of Pierre Clastres

At an earlier stage of his career, as we have shown, Auster divided his time between what he has called labours of love – writing poetry and translating poetry – and a wide range of writing assignments that he has called 'grim' but necessary for putting food on the table. Of the disparate and dreary translations he laboured at during that period, one apparent exception was a book of ethnology to which Auster was attracted because of its literary merits.

Pierre Clastres (1934–1977) was known for his contributions to the emerging subdiscipline of political anthropology. Before his promising career was cut short by a tragic car accident at the age of forty-three, he had conducted fieldwork in Paraguay among the Guayaki Indians, a nomadic hunting and foraging people whose name in their own language is *Ache Gatu*. In 1972, he published a somewhat popularized version of his doctoral dissertation under the title *Chronique des Indiens Guayaki*. His book, which came out in the 'Terre humaine' collection of the Librairie Plon publishing house, is at once an ethnographic account and a personal, first-person narrative.[8]

Just how the English translation came about and how it got into print is the subject of a relatively short 'Translator's Note' dated 1997, which Auster published in the 1998 edition of his translation, titled *Chronicle of the Guayaki Indians*. This 'Note', described as a 'foreword' on the book's frontispiece, has attracted considerable attention for a variety of reasons. To begin with, Auster's narrative looks somewhat out of place in a work of this kind, which falls into the category of social sciences. A more 'academic' translation might have been accompanied by other kinds of paratextual elements, such as an introduction situating Clastres in the French ethnological tradition of the 1960s and 1970s rather than emphasizing his literary qualities. Auster does mention that Clastres had been a student of Claude Lévi-Strauss (*Chronicle*, 8), but he goes no further than that. Christine York points out that, in addition to the foreword, there might have been any of the following: an index, a bibliography, a glossary, footnotes (2013: 8), although it is also true that the original French edition does not have much in the way of scholarly apparatus either.[9] Auster also omits the book's original subtitle, 'Ce que savent les Aché, chasseurs nomades du Paraguay' (What the Ache, nomadic hunters of Paraguay, know), which, if translated, might have cast the author in a more positive light.

The 'Translator's Note' is all, then, that the English reader has to go on. Much like Gertrude Stein when she translated Georges Hugnet, Auster has turned the saga of his translation of the *Chronicle* into a 'delightful' story. Written when he already had a number of published novels under his belt, the 'Note' speaks more to his aesthetics of 'chance' than it does to his strategies for translating a substantial work of social science, and says more about the translator than the act of translation itself.

As he explains at the beginning of the 'Note', Jacques Dupin had introduced him to the work of Clastres in 1972. Auster was a 'faithful reader' of the magazine *L'Éphémère*, whose editorial board was made up of Dupin and others, and in which Clastres had published an article entitled 'De l'Un sans le multiple'.[10] Auster was immediately impressed by this 'intelligent, provocative, and tightly argued' piece, and was drawn to Clastres's prose, which 'seemed to combine a poet's temperament with a philosopher's depth of mind' (*Chronicle*, 7). After reading Clastres's article, Auster purchased his book on the Guayaki Indians, a book that was 'nearly impossible not to love' because, rather than turning out a 'dry academic study of "life among the savages" … a report from an alien world', Clastres is asking good questions such as 'what kinds of transactions take place between one culture and another'. He 'writes with the cunning of a good novelist'. Furthermore, he is 'that rare scholar who does not hesitate to write in the first person, and the result is ... a portrait of himself' (*Chronicle*, 8). These are all qualities that would resonate with the writer that Auster was to become.

Still struggling to make a living after moving back home in 1974, Auster grudgingly took on translation assignments that had little value in his eyes. He wanted to translate books that were worthy and the *Chronicle* was at the top of his list. With some difficulty, he finally found a publisher who was interested in his translation of Clastres's book. Auster did the work, which he found 'thoroughly enjoyable', but then money problems, as usual, began to bedevil him. He didn't get paid until he threatened the publisher with physical violence (an episode that finds its way into the novel *Leviathan*). Auster was so broke that he couldn't even afford to make a photocopy of the translation.

Soon a 'small misfortune' became a 'full-blown disaster'. Auster had corrected the proofs (but again, kept no copy) and publication was to take place in the winter of 1977–1978. First, he got the news of Clastres's death in a car crash. He had developed a warm friendship with Clastres through letters they had exchanged, but the two of them had never met. Clastres's premature death was a 'great loss'. Next, the publishing company went bankrupt, and rights were sold to another company. Time went by, and the manuscript was lost: 'it was as if the translation had never existed' and 'the entire project had collapsed into a black hole of oblivion' (*Chronicle*, 10–12).

In 1996, more than twenty years after Auster had first taken on the translation, the manuscript turned up again, unexpectedly. In an extraordinary twist of fate, a friend of a friend, a 'bibliographic detective', had discovered the galley proofs while rummaging through bins at a second-hand bookstore. He turned them over to Auster at a book signing in San Francisco, and the English translation was finally published in 1998. This account, which Auster describes at the outset as 'one of the saddest stories I know' (*Chronicle*, 7), ends in this way:

> Here, then, is my translation of Pierre Clastres's book, *Chronicle of the Guayaki Indians*. No matter that the world described in it has long since vanished, that the tiny group of people the author lived with ... has disappeared from the face of the earth. No matter that the author has vanished as well.... At least there is consolation in the thought that Pierre Clastres's book has survived. (*Chronicle*, 13)

Beyond the 'bleak, miserable' – although no less entertaining – 'saga' (*Chronicle*, 11), Auster has committed a serious error in presenting Clastres's work. When the book was written, several years after he had visited the Ache, Clastres had made the assumption that they would die out, having witnessed a decline in their population from one hundred to around thirty during a five-year period in the 1960s. While they had been persecuted and abused, and their numbers reduced, the surviving Ache, once hunters, took up agriculture instead. They are now employed by a California company in the organic and fair-trade production of the Yerba Mate beverage (York 2013: 10).[11] Clastres was wrong, or at least only half right, and Auster translated blindly without checking on the fate of the Ache, or whether they still existed for that matter.

The reception of *Chronicle* is interesting. As Auster points out, when questioned about the reliability of the story he tells in the 'Note', he received a prize for the translation. (Does a translation prize prove the veracity of the paratextual elements?) The prize is real, corroborated on the publisher's website: *Chronicle of the Guayaki Indians* was awarded the ALTA Prize in nonfiction by the American Literary Translators Association.[12] But the reader has been misled about the fate of the Ache people.

Social science scholars were less congratulatory. When they read Clastres in Auster's English translation around thirty years after Clastres's fieldwork among the Ache, they tended to be negative in their assessments, focusing on the out-of-date approach of the original author. By the time Auster's translation was released in 1998, the field of anthropology had undergone significant change – for one thing, traditional modes of writing about indigenous peoples were questioned. On the basis of the English translation, the American anthropologist Clifford Geertz (2000), for example, described Clastres as a 'romantic pilgrim on a self-testing Quest'.[13] In an earlier review for the *New York Review of Books*, Geertz had already written:

> The book he publishes upon his return he calls, with deliberate, almost anachronistic, pre-modern flatness, as though it were a recently discovered missionary diary from an eighteenth-century Jesuit, *Chronique des indiens Guayaki*. Worshipfully translated by the American novelist Paul Auster ('It is, I believe, nearly impossible not to love this book') – and belatedly published a quarter-century later – the work is, in form at least, old-style ethnographical to a fault. (Geertz 1998: n.p.)

When questioned, Auster maintains that he had not been writing for the scholarly community:

> I figured that any anthropologist is going to know about this book already. It was an old book. It had been out for thirty years by the time it was published here. It just became a different kind of experience. Lost manuscript, dead author, miraculously found when that young man turned up at the Herbst Theatre in

San Francisco. Remarkable, just remarkable. Bankrupt publishers. It was a terrible business. (PA-int)

The end anticipated by Clastres, and then reinforced by Auster in the 'Note', exists, not in reality, but in the fiction constructed around this book. Auster's mistaken conclusion that the Guayaki Indians have long since 'vanished' has been perpetuated by publishers and publicists. The error continues to reside on the numerous websites that still plug the book. The website for MIT Press, a top-ranked academic publisher, still describes the book as 'an encounter with a small, unique, and now vanished Paraguayan tribe'.[14] Another example, cited in part by York (2013: 9), again reinforces the disappearance of the tribe and also the appeal of the translator's story, a mere seven pages out of 350:

> Little was known about the nomadic Guayaki Indians of eastern Paraguay until Clastres, a French ethnographer now deceased, made contact with them. He lived among them in 1963–64 and documented their history and culture. His study is extremely valuable because it documents the experiences of a group of people who no longer exist. Clastres published the French edition of this book in 1972, and it has been translated by novelist Auster, who originally translated this title in the mid-1970s. Auster's trials and tribulations in getting it published are documented in the section entitled 'Translator's Note' and his story alone is worth the price of the book.[15]

In addition to pointing out the erroneous assumption about the vanished people and showing how Auster's translation might have also helped to efface Clastres's reputation as a forward-thinking anthropologist, York critiques the translation *per se*. In her view, some of Auster's translation decisions re-frame the text, tending to 'diminish the politicized voice of Clastres's original, smooth out his anger, and replace it with a romanticized vision of a lost world' (2013: 11).

An example of a shift in meaning is taken from the chapter entitled 'The Grown-ups':

FRENCH:
« Il n'y a pas de grandes personnes » a-t-on pu écrire récemment. Ce propos est paradoxal, d'être tenu dans la civilisation qui *se pense et se pose* comme adulte par excellence, la nôtre. (Clastres 1972: 141; emphasis added)

ENGLISH:
'There are no grown-ups', someone wrote recently. This is a strange remark to make in our civilization, which *prides itself on being* the epitome of adulthood. (Clastres 1998: 141; emphasis added).

While Auster's translation is smooth and elegant, he has added the element of 'pride', absent in the original, which simply states that in our civilization (or culture) we think about ourselves, or conceptualize ourselves, as adults, and assume the posture of adults.

I offer a further example of a lapse in translation, taken from the concluding chapter, aptly called 'The End'.

FRENCH:

Je désire, quant à moi, accorder la préférence au souvenir de la piété ache… Témoigner pour une fidélité exemplaire à un très ancien savoir, qu'en un instant *la sauvage violence du nôtre a dissipé.* (Clastres 1972: 350; emphasis added)

ENGLISH:

For myself, I most of all want to remember the Atchei's piety… To underscore their exemplary faithfulness to a very ancient knowledge that our *own savage violence has squandered* in a single instant. (Clastres 1998: 347–8; emphasis added)

In this brief excerpt, Clastres reverses the old colonializing term 'savage' and applies it not to the Ache, but rather to Europeans' knowledge that has been so violently harnessed to erase ancient knowledge and dominate the peoples with whom they have come into contact. The translator captures the idea of 'savage violence'; he even makes it 'ours', but he fails to apply it to the knowledge of the conqueror, as denoted by the possessive pronoun 'le nôtre'.

But these are perhaps quibbles in the context of a translation that more often than not captures the fine writing style of Pierre Clastres, as in this poetic passage with which the last paragraph of the book begins:

FRENCH:

C'était la nuit. Yva javu, la tempête parlait. Partout, les grondements du tonnerre, la pluie fouettant les huttes de palmes, le vent qui tordait les hautes branches des vieux géants de la forêt. Lorsque Chono laissait, à brefs intervalles, un répit de silence, on entendait le bruit sec du bois brisé par la force de la tourmente. La violente lumière blanche des éclairs arrachait aux ténèbres le campement silencieux, au point d'effacer par instants la clarté des feux dont le vent courbait les flammes. (Clastres 1972: 350)[16]

ENGLISH:

It was night. *Yva javu,* the storm was talking. There was thunder everywhere, the rain was whipping the palm huts, the wind twisted the high branches of the old giants of the forest. When *Chono* left a brief respite of silence, you could hear the dry noise of wood cracking in the gale. The violent whiteness of the lightning tore the silent camp out of darkness, and the flashes were so brilliant that you could no longer see the light of the fires bending in the wind. (Clastres 1998: 348)

Here is an example of a writer who has translated a rather lengthy book (350 pages, think of it!), which to this day he regards as a 'great book, a masterpiece' (PA-int). Yet, along the lines of other storytellers, Auster is more concerned with the writing – writing the translation and writing about translation – than he is about constructing a body of knowledge about a people who may or may not have vanished. This comes as no surprise for someone so interested in 'process', as he says in relation to his notebook fetish (Interview with Michael Wood 2003b, in *Collected Prose,* 571). Like Gertrude Stein before him, Auster has turned his experience as a translator into a story, but one that takes on the quirky twists and turns of a well-crafted Paul Auster yarn – he even throws a 'detective' into the mix. He was undoubtedly happy enough to publish this piece of work he had completed so many years earlier (Auster and the agents who support him engage in veritable literary 'churn', printing and reprinting earlier pieces in multiple forms). But he does not leave it at that; he takes the opportunity to write about the process, and to dramatize the story. York calls it 'self-mythologizing' (2013: 8); it also falls into the long tradition of 'self-fashioning' dating back to at least the Renaissance and extending to postmodern writers. Authors take the platform that paratextual space affords them (Genette 1997) to create their personae as writer/translators – in a way that is different from that of 'normal' translators, who tend to be more preoccupied with justifying or explaining their actual work as translators.[17]

Through this process of self-fashioning, or posturing in Meizoz's (2007) sense of the term, Auster participates in a textual act of memorialization. Auster mourns for an author so tragically taken from him, and from humanity, at so young an age, for a lost people, for a lost manuscript. In actual fact, the 'vanished' world and people in question have not entirely disappeared, and Clastres has not 'vanished' either (his book is still available in paperback in French). The point Auster is trying to make is that there is an afterlife through translation, and especially through his own work as a translator.

There have been other, notable examples in contemporary history. The works of Stefan Zweig, for instance, were burned in Nazi Germany; considered to be the most translated author in the world during his lifetime, Zweig lives on through translation. In this case, Auster is bringing recognition to someone who might otherwise have been effaced from history, albeit to a lesser extent, by translating his work and giving it new life. As evidence of the enduring existence of the *Chronicle* – in its English version, at least – one chapter, 'The Life and Death of a Homosexual', has been reprinted in a collection of travel pieces entitled *The New Granta Book of Travel*. Pierre Clastres is indeed named as the author but, apart from the opening sentence, which says who Clastres was, the editor's introductory paragraph deals entirely with the story of the lost and found translation (Jobey 2011: 119). The lasting nature of the work is associated with its translation, in a vision consistent with the influential views put forth by Walter Benjamin on translation and the afterlife of a text.[18]

It is through Auster's translation, through his story of the translation, that he can dialogue with death and contribute to the afterlife of this particular text (Brodzki 2007: 185). This is not unlike his tribute to Allen Mandelbaum in *Report from the Interior*, published not long after his uncle's death, and not unlike *Openwork*, the subject of our next section, in which he and Hoyt Rogers immortalize André du Bouchet through texts – originals and translations – and copious paratextual material.

Auster is known for presenting strange events as 'true' occurrences. In *The Red Notebook*, for example, he says that, ten years after completing *City of Glass*, he got a phone call from someone wanting to speak to Mr. Quinn, the main protagonist in his first novel. A coincidence, but a 'true story' (*Collected Prose*, 263–4). Like everything else in *The Red Notebook* – like everything else Auster writes – this is possibly a 'joke on the reader'. Commenting on this anecdote, Dennis Barone asks, 'How can a "story" be true?' (1995: 3). So in my interview, I pressed him about the truthfulness of the Clastres story. In reply, he reiterated his account in even greater detail, augmenting it with a further tragic death.

> No, I didn't make any of it up. It's all true. But it's a story. It's a true story. I found out the story of Clastres's death. I hadn't really known what it was. Apparently a group of young French anthropologists of the time, this was late 60s, early 70s, bought little houses in the Luberon in the South of France. Pierre Clastres and his wife Hélène, who was also an anthropologist, had a house. And they were down in the valley and they had friends who lived up in the mountains. They were invited for dinner one night and there was a very narrow perilous bridge over a gorge, I think, on the way. On the way home from the dinner on the mountain he lost control of the car and they fell into the gorge. She survived but she was trapped in the car for two days with her dead husband next to her. So two years go by and the people who lived on the mountain felt so guilty about what had happened. I think maybe Clastres had had too much to drink and shouldn't have been driving the car and so finally his widow sufficiently pulled herself together again to invite the friends from the mountain to come down

to the valley for dinner, which they did. And driving home after the dinner, they too fell off the bridge and were both killed. How do you like that? So, life is really strange, huh?

Translation revisited: *Openwork*

In 2014, Paul Auster and his long-time friend Hoyt Rogers jointly published a selection of writing by French poet André du Bouchet under the title *Openwork. Poetry and Prose*. The book is dedicated to the memory of du Bouchet, who in fact introduced Auster and Rogers to one another in Paris, in 1971.[19]

Rogers, the man behind a significant portion of this edition, is both a translator and a poet in his own right. While less of a literary giant than Auster, perhaps, he has nonetheless published poems, stories, essays, and translations; he is the author of a volume of criticism, *The Poetics of Inconstancy*, and a poetry collection, *Witnesses*. He translates from French, German, Italian and Spanish and is noted, in particular, for his translations of Jorge Luis Borges (*Selected Poems*) and Yves Bonnefoy (*The Curved Planks, Second Simplicity* and the *Digamma*), both of whom – not coincidentally – have been engaged in the theoretical and practical dimensions of translation.[20]

Through their translations and commentary, Rogers and Auster bring their combined talents to bear on drawing the attention of an English-language readership to the work of a lesser-known figure of French poetry. André du Bouchet (1924–2001) is presented as 'one of the greatest innovators of twentieth-century letters', an influential writer who served as 'a model for a whole generation of post-war poets' (Rogers's 'Introduction', OW, xi; Auster's 'Preface', OW, 308–9). What is fascinating about this collaborative enterprise is that it gives us an opportunity to observe writers translating – and promoting – another writer/translator, for du Bouchet, like both of them, is noted for his translations as well as his poetry. Presented not so much as a scholarly edition, or an anthology, but rather as a 'reader', *Openwork* contributes to our appreciation of an undervalued poet, particularly in this bilingual format with French and English texts on opposite pages. In the words of one reviewer (to whose critiques we will return below), 'This collection is both necessary and overdue' (Riley 2015: n.p.).

This was Auster's first translation effort in around thirty years, if one excludes reprints of earlier work. His role, albeit a modest one, involved revising or 'emending' translations done decades earlier, a task that was 'fun to revisit', in his own words (PA-int). Modest or not, this is clearly the work of Paul Auster, the translator, rather than Paul Auster, the novelist. In the words of author and translator Anthony Rudolf, quoted on the back page of the book's dust jacket:

> In this finely edited selection of the poetry and prose of André du Bouchet, *two distinguished translators*, Paul Auster and Hoyt Rogers, enable our eyes and ears to absorb a profoundly authoritative language world of elemental and majestic beauty. Fragmentary, stripped down, elliptical, difficult at times (but never obscure), this language world presents an unmistakable individual in an unmistakable landscape – sometimes violent, always solitary, often displaced. (Back cover of *Openwork*; emphasis added)

The book begins with an essay of some thirty pages entitled 'The Restless Openwork of André du Bouchet', written by Rogers. The first section of 'Early Poems and Notebooks' has been translated by Rogers. The second part, about 125 pages long, is made up of poems from the so-called 'middle period', a time considered to have 'made du Bouchet's name and ... [to have been] the richest period of his writing' (Riley 2015). Auster had translated these poems in the late 1960s and early 1970s; in 1976, he published them in book form as *The Uninhabited*. The translations have been somewhat altered or 'tweaked', as Auster says, for this new edition. Rogers has translated the poems in the third section of the book, called quite simply 'Late Poems'. The volume is book-ended with an appendix, signed 'Paul Auster, Paris, 1973', which remains unchanged since it was first published as a preface to *The Uninhabited*. One would have wished for more new commentary from Auster. This paratext aligns more with the pithy, finely crafted prefaces for which he is known, rather than the more exhaustive and analytical kind of piece he provided for the *Random House* anthology, as discussed above. In keeping with the poetry he is introducing, which he describes as 'generated by a syntax of abrupt, paratactic brevity', his own remarks are equally succinct, simply evoking du Bouchet's unique strengths and influence in an outpouring that is poetic in itself (OW, 308–9). Further back matter consists of bibliographic and biographical information.[21]

The introduction, described by one reviewer as 'the most far-reaching essay on du Bouchet that I have ever read in English' (Taylor 2014), provides information about the poet and sets out a framework for reading his body of work. It is clear, from the outset, that the translators/editors are doing more than simply presenting an English version of selected French poems. To begin with, the introduction sets out to wrench du Bouchet from the shadows, and to give this 'neglected giant of French literature' the place he deserves in the world of letters (OW, xi). Rogers sings the praises of the French poet with an impressively long string of laudatory adjectives:

> Trailblazing poet, maverick philosopher, multifarious critic, trenchant stylist, fearless anthologist, daring editor, prolific diarist, intrepid translator from three languages, tireless explorer of nature and the visual arts, he was an authentic iconoclast who has yet to receive his due, especially in the English-speaking world. This anomaly seems all the more inexplicable, given his dazzling renditions of Shakespeare, Joyce, and Faulkner into French, as well as his lifelong attachment to the classic authors of nineteenth-century America. (OW, xi)

Du Bouchet was born in Paris in 1924. Of Jewish, Russian and American extraction, his family was at risk in Nazi-occupied France. And so, in a move opposite to that of Paul Auster, and Gertrude Stein before him, the family left France to take refuge in the United States. Du Bouchet remained in America from 1940 to 1948, attending Amherst College and then Harvard, where he became acquainted with and captivated by American literature. He was raised in a multilingual environment, which accounts for his linguistic skills. He returned to France in 1948, where he married Tina Jolas (the first of three wives), a future translator and anthropologist (and daughter of Eugene Jolas, cofounder of the literary magazine *transition*).

Not unlike his translators, du Bouchet is a 'cosmopolitan figure' (OW, xi), whose transnational and transatlantic life history thrust him into the world of translation and shaped the texture and topics of his literary output. His relationship to language, in particular, and the tensions between his two main languages, had a lasting influence. As Rogers says, 'His separation from French had created in him a dual consciousness, a distance that encouraged him to approach his own language freshly, testing and stretching its possibilities as only an "outsider" can do. At a deeper level, he had entered the interstices where silence cohabits with speech' (OW, xvii). This portrayal of the bilingual poet grappling with a divided identity echoes the sentiments of Gertrude Stein living among the French, while trying to be alone with English and herself (*Autobiography*, 70). The tense coexistence of speech and silence also foreshadows some of the torment that runs through Auster's fiction. Having been an exile in the United States, du Bouchet returned to France with the feeling of being a 'migrant within his own country of origin'. He 'internalizes exile' and his work is grounded in 'a perpetual motion: cultural and verbal fragments rise and converge only to shatter all over again, in a tireless motion forward' (OW, xxix). The angst of displacement would have resonated with Auster, despite the fact that, unlike du Bouchet, he belongs to the same breed of *willing* exiles as Stein and other members of the Lost Generation.

In the words of Rogers, du Bouchet was a 'poet's poet in the tradition of Mallarmé' (OW, xiii). He wrote poetry as well as essays on literature and art, which he published in leading periodicals, beginning in the United States and continuing once he returned to France. He published some seventy books, which included twenty major translations (OW, xii). He forged close relationships with prominent poets and artists of the day, among them Giacometti, whose airy sketch of the poet – evoking the title of the volume – appears on the book's frontispiece (and jacket). Together with a number of fellow writers, he founded the cultural review *L'Éphémère*.

Du Bouchet's achievements as a translator are highlighted in Rogers's introductory essay and listed in a bibliography at the end of the book. He translated without difficulty from English into his native French. Also, because of his background, he undertook translation from the Russian and German, although he required assistance in these two cases. He translated German poets Friedrich Hölderlin and Paul Celan, as well as Russians Osip Mandelstam and Boris Pasternak. He produced versions of Shakespeare – *La Tempête* (*The Tempest*), *Périclès* (*Pericles*) and other plays – and Faulkner's book of short stories, *Le Gambit du Cavalier* (*Knight's Gambit*). He translated English-language poets as varied as John Donne, Gerard Manley Hopkins, and Laura Riding; in particular, he was one of the first to tackle James Joyce's *Finnegans Wake*, if only in the form of excerpts.[22]

While at first glance the English translations printed in this volume look very similar to Auster's previous versions, a closer examination reveals that there have indeed been quite a few 'tweaks'. It is clear that Auster, the poet/translator, has made some effort to correct, fine-tune and improve previous work. Only in a few cases are the changes not improvements. Despite Auster's claim in his preface to the *Random House Book*, to the effect that when faced with a choice between a literal translation and poetry, he always opts for poetry, he is as 'faithful' in these translations as one can be in translating poetry. He takes an almost word-for-word approach that follows the original text closely, as some of the examples set out below will show, even down to the punctuation and spacing of the words on the page to accurately reflect the 'openness' and silences of du Bouchet. Some of the grammar and sentence structure have been altered in this edition, and there are slight changes in diction. For the most part, these adjustments correct slight misinterpretations or even errors, while in a few other cases his changes seem somewhat less urgent, perhaps even arbitrary.[23]

In the two examples that follow, Auster has changed the wording to correct an error that could be considered a 'false friend', replacing the word 'scorch' as a translation for 'écorche/écorchés'.[24]

'From the Edge of the Scythe III'

FRENCH	Le jour écorche les chevilles.	(OW, 96)
ENGLISH 1	The day scorches the ankles.	(TR, 285)
ENGLISH 2	The day rubs the ankles raw.	(OW, 97)

'The White Motor IV'

FRENCH	…des membres de terre écorchés par une charrue.	(OW, 112)
ENGLISH 1	…limbs of earth, scorched by a plow.	(TR, 293)
ENGLISH 2	…limbs of earth flayed by a plow.	(OW, 113)

An example taken from the poem 'Meteor' shows a change in syntax that restores a more usual word order to the verse:

FRENCH	L'absence qui me tient lieu de souffle recommence à tomber sur les papiers comme de la neige.	(OW, 100)
ENGLISH 1	The absence which takes the place of breath in me begins again like snow to fall upon the papers.	(TR, 287)
ENGLISH 2	The absence that takes the place of breath in me begins to fall like snow on the papers again.	(OW, 101)

The following are examples of grammatical modifications. In the poem for which the original volume was named, 'The Uninhabited', the more formal 'shall' in the first line is changed to 'will' (OW, 163). In 'Postponement', the verb is corrected to better reflect the French subjunctive, and the definite article 'the' is added:

FRENCH	…j'ai couru…jusqu'à ce que le vent plie.	(OW, 186)
ENGLISH 1	…I ran…till wind buckles under.	(TR, 327)
ENGLISH 2	…I ran…till the wind buckled under.	(OW, 187)

The following two short poems, 'Accidents' and 'The White Motor XII' are quoted in their entirety because they are illustrative of Auster's translational style. In addition, they contain a fair number of adjustments. In the first, Auster makes the syntax and wording a little more colloquial and less stilted, and rearranges words on the page somewhat. In the second poem, punctuation has been altered: a comma replaces the period after 'bed'; an em dash replaces the period after 'clearly'. The expression 'above all', missing from the first version, is added to correspond to 'surtout'; 'in its weakness' is replaced by 'when the earth is fragile', which is a more substantive change that brings the English more in line with the meaning of the original French.

'Accidents'

FRENCH
J'ai erré autour de cette lueur.
                Je me suis déchiré, une nouvelle fois,
de l'autre côté de ce mur, comme l'air que tu vois,
                         à cette lueur froide.
De l'autre côté du mur, je vois le même air aveuglant.
                Dans le lointain sans rupture, comme l'étendue
même de la terre entrecoupée que, plus loin, je foule, nul ne
sent la chaleur.

Nous serons lavés de notre visage, comme l'air qui couronne
le mur.   (OW, 102)

ENGLISH 1
I wandered about this glow.
                I was torn again, from the other
side of this wall, like the air you see,
                      in this cold glow. From
the other side of the wall, I see the same blinding air.

                    In the unbreached distance,
like the stretch of broken earth, beyond, I tread, nothing feels
the heat.

We will be washed of our face, like the air that crowns the wall.   (TR, 288)

ENGLISH 2
I wandered around this glow.
                I was torn, once again, from the other
side of this wall, like the air you see,
                    in this cold glow. From the
other side of the wall, I see the same blinding air.

                  In the unbreached distance, like this stretch
of broken earth, up ahead, I walk on, no one feels the heat.

We will be washed of our face, like the air that crowns the wall.   (OW, 103)

'The White Motor II'

FRENCH   En lâchant la porte chaude, la poignée de fer, je me trouve devant
                un bruit qui n'a pas de fin, un tracteur. Je touche le fond d'un lit
                rugueux, je ne commence pas. J'ai toujours vécu. Je vois plus
                nettement les pierres, surtout l'ombre qui sertit, l'ombre rouge
                de la terre sur les doigts quand elle est fragile, sous ses tentures,
                et que la chaleur ne nous a pas cachés. (OW, 130)

ENGLISH 1   In releasing the warm door, the iron knob, I find myself before
                a noise that has no end, a tractor. I touch the base of a gnarled
                bed. I do not begin. I have always lived. I see the stones more
                clearly. The enclosing shadow, the earth's red shadow on my
                fingers, in its weakness, beneath its draping, which the heat has
                not hidden from us. (TR, 301)

ENGLISH 2   In releasing the warm door, the iron knob, I find myself before a
                noise that has no end, a tractor. I touch the base of a gnarled bed,
                I do not begin. I have always lived. I see the stones more clearly
                – above all, the enclosing shadow, the earth's red shadow on my
                fingers when the earth is fragile, beneath its draping, which the
                heat has not hidden from us. (OW, 131)

Openwork was reviewed in *The Fortnightly Review* by poetry editor Peter
Riley (2015). This sparked a debate on the quality of the translation, with Hoyt
Rogers providing a lengthy rebuttal to Riley's article in a subsequent issue of the
online magazine (Rogers 2015). Riley comments on the work of du Bouchet.
Then, in a section of the article entitled 'A postscript concerning translation', he
draws attention to discrepancies between the original and the translation. These
differences, he says, cannot be called mistakes, 'for both translators are French
linguists of the highest degree'. Instead, he considers them 'deliberate shifts and
replacements which relate to a theory of "creative translation" which is common
to modernism everywhere'. He goes on to stress that this form of 'creativity' is
characteristic of poets who translate:

> If you cannot bear not to be a poet then of course you must create your own
> poems instead of translating, which is fine except when you're supposed to be
> helping someone to know what's going on. The translators of du Bouchet make
> a fine job of this, but both are happy to enrich the text by allowing secondary
> senses to accumulate onto the word, which can easily happen when working
> from French to English, neglecting a sparseness which is an important feature
> of the originals. (Riley 2015)

This is no doubt an accurate assessment of some of the modernist poets who have tried their hand at translating, and it could easily have applied to Gertrude Stein's handling of the work of Georges Hugnet, as we saw in the previous chapter. These translations, however, are strikingly close to the originals. They do, in fact, help the reader 'to know what's going on', as evidenced by the examples of 'Accidents' and 'White Motors' quoted above.

In his reply, Rogers points out that both he and Auster had consulted du Bouchet. 'André du Bouchet, who had fully mastered the English language', he says, 'wholeheartedly approved all our English versions of his work completed during his lifetime, and these make up the bulk of the texts in *Openwork*'. At Rogers's request, Auster offered further clarification:

> My translations from *Dans la Chaleur vacante* were made in 1967, when I was a 20-year-old student at Columbia University. After moving to Paris in early 1971, I met André du Bouchet and translated a number of poems from his next major collection *Où le soleil*. A strong friendship and trust developed between us, and because of André's perfect mastery of English, we went over every word and line in every poem together. I'm not saying that all the English versions are literally 'correct', but they represent how du Bouchet felt his poems should read in English. (Rogers 2015)

In response to Riley's categorization of their work as 'creative translation', similar to the approach of other modernists such as Ezra Pound, Rogers describes his own method as a 'fairly dogged imitation of the originals'. But he also quotes David Bellos's 'The Myth of Literal Translation' to show that, in any case, word-for-word translation is simply impossible (Rogers 2015).

There are no winners in this kind of a debate: in responding to his critic, Rogers says that there's no such thing as a perfect translation. As Paul Valéry reminds us, 'A poem is never finished, only abandoned' ('Un poème n'est jamais fini, il est seulement abandonné'). Similarly, a translation of a poem is never finished – infinite revisions are possible until, by surrendering it to the printed (or web) page, its author(s) simply release it.

The translational encounter between the two American poets, Auster and Rogers, and the French poet, Du Bouchet, is significant. Attracted to one another and to a poetics of 'uncertainty, silence and resistance', in Auster's words (OW, 307), they work in close collaboration. Through the affinity that Rogers and Auster feel for du Bouchet, they engage in an act of mediation that reminds us of Baudelaire's mission in translating Edgar Allan Poe for a French audience: they feel a need to 'rectify a glaring omission' by making English-speaking readers aware of the richness of du Bouchet's work (xii). This is a fundamental driver of any translation project.

By revisiting one of his earliest translation projects, by circulating the work of du Bouchet in America, Auster is once again playing the critical role of agent and cultural mediator, a process that allows him, in a sense, to come full circle – *boucler la boucle*, as one might say in the other language.

Ghosts, doubles, and trickery: Paul Auster's transfiction

Roger Phaedo had not spoken to anyone for ten years. He confined himself to his Brooklyn apartment, obsessively translating and retranslating the same short passage from Rousseau's 'Confessions'. A decade earlier, a mobster named Charlie Dark had attacked Phaedo and his wife. Phaedo was beaten to within an inch of his life; Mary was set on fire, and survived just five days in the I.C.U. By day, Phaedo translated; at night, he worked on a novel about Charlie Dark, who was never convicted.

(James Wood 2009)

This clever parody of Auster's fiction is taken from the lead paragraph of a *New Yorker* book review that appeared after the release of the novel *Invisible*. Reviewer James Wood – not particularly enamoured of Auster's fiction, as it turns out – claims to 'check off' the most 'familiar features' of Auster's work. Among them is an aphasic protagonist who is translating a 'visiting text' (Rousseau's *Confessions*, a book that actually makes an appearance in *The Music of Chance*), and who is also writing a novel about a character called Dark (although it's not Charlie, but Henry, Dark who figures in *City of Glass*). While characterized as an 'overtly pugnacious piece' (Hutchisson 2013: xix), Wood's review focuses on elements that permeate Auster's 'transfiction': a translator struggling to become a novelist, and a writer obsessively coming to grips with various kinds of loss.

Translation is becoming a fact of life in today's pluralistic societies and globalized world. Concurrently, translation scholars are turning their attention to the growing presence of the theme of translation in literature and other art forms, such as cinema. The topic of translation and the figure of the translator can serve as narrative devices, reveal aspects of translation theory, and represent problematic personal or social situations such as migration, dislocation and hybridity. It is not uncommon for scholars beyond the borders of translation studies to appropriate the metaphor of translation: in cultural studies, notably, 'cultural translation' has become a common theme (Bhabha 1994). In an oft-quoted observation from his lecture 'Imaginary Homelands', Salman Rushdie (with whom Auster is good friends) famously described himself, and other migrants like him, as 'translated men':

> [T]he word 'translation' comes, etymologically, from the Latin for 'bearing across'. Having been borne across the world, we are translated men. It is normally supposed that something always gets lost in translation; I cling, obstinately, to the notion that something can also be gained. (Rushdie 1991: 17)

As the term 'translation' circulates more broadly, translation researchers are more and more cognizant of its (fruitful) use as a kind of 'master metaphor epitomizing our present *condition humaine*, evoking our search for a sense of self and belonging in a perplexing context of change and difference' (Delabastita and Grutman 2005: 23).[25]

The fictional representation of translators is not new, as Klaus Kaindl says, pointing to twelfth-century German epic poetry containing references to interpreters (2014: 7). Think also of the pioneering novel, *Don Quixote*, which is framed as a translation from the Arabic, by a nameless translator. But it is only in recent times, when the movement of people, knowledge and goods around the world has made translation and intercultural communication indispensable, that translation and its agents have begun to inhabit creative work. The translator is becoming a more prominent figure and translation an ever more present theme, foregrounded in such works as Nobel laureate Ivo Andrić's tale of two interpreters, *The Days of the Consuls*; Brian Friel's play, *Translations*; Jonathan Safran Foer's novel, *Everything Is Illuminated*; Carol Shields's last novel, *Unless*; Eva Hoffman's memoir, *Lost in Translation: Life in a New Language*; Sofia Coppola's film about Americans in Tokyo, *Lost in Translation*; and the Nicole Kidman–Sean Penn thriller *The Interpreter*.[26]

It is not surprising that Auster, as a belated 'American in Paris', for whom translation was both passion and drudgery, would also produce works that are 'translational' in nature. By the time he started publishing works of fiction in the 1980s, his stories were populated with translators. Several of Auster's books are concerned not merely with translation, in the strictest sense of the term, but also with related questions of language, conflicting identities, authorship, movement and dislocation. A hall of mirrors imbued with the leitmotif of 'Frenchness': a sprinkling of French names and expressions, French places (mainly Paris), and even such mundane items as French toast.[27]

After a close look at *City of Glass* (1985), we will also examine the trope of translation in *Moon Palace* (1989), *Leviathan* (1992), and *The Book of Illusions* (2002b). Auster's later novel, *Invisible* (2009) will be analysed in greater detail, to illustrate the extent to which Auster is still preoccupied with translation. In addition, we will provide a few examples of the Frenchness that runs through Auster's work.

City of Glass

Auster's fiction has variously been labelled postmodern detective fiction, 'Kafka goes gumshoe', and a Borgesian labyrinth of writers and doppelgängers – where there are 'doppelgängers even for the doppelgängers' (O'Rourke 2012). *City of Glass,* which was published in 1985 after seventeen rejections, fits all of those descriptions. The first of three novellas that were republished as *The New York Trilogy* in 1987, it weaves together themes of identity, authorship, language, movement, and translation.[28]

The protagonist is Daniel Quinn. His surname, 'Quinn' had been used by Paul Auster as a pseudonym for articles he published in a 'shoddily put together' magazine (*Hand to Mouth,* 184), while his first name is the same as Auster's son; his initials are the same as Don Quixote's. His wife and son are dead and he is alone in the city, separated from his former self. Once a translator, he is now trying his hand at writing mystery stories using the pseudonym 'William Wilson' (taken from an Edgar Allan Poe story of the same name, in which William Wilson has a double named William Wilson). Quinn also doubles as Max Work, a private eye, who is the narrator in his books.

> In the past, Quinn had been more ambitious. As a young man he had published several books of poetry, had written plays, critical essays, and had worked on a number of long translations. But quite abruptly, he had given up all that. A part of him had died ... It was then that he had taken on the name of William Wilson. Quinn was no longer that part of him that could write books, and although in many ways Quinn continued to exist, he no longer existed for anyone but himself. (*City of Glass* in *New York Trilogy,* 11)

The Quinn who previously 'wrote books' that connected him to 'others', like Auster when he translated and mediated between cultures, has ceased to exist. Assuming a new identity, and taking on a new creative genre, Quinn goes on living as William Wilson. A chance phone call, someone calling for a detective named 'Paul Auster', draws him into a new kind of drama as he decides to impersonate the detective. Quinn accepts the assignment intended for this 'Paul Auster', which involves working for Peter Stillman to locate his father, also called Peter Stillman. The younger Stillman had been locked away in a darkened room as a child, as his father experimented with language acquisition. This assignment involves both writing and reading: Quinn buys a new 'red notebook' (a theme that figures in both Auster's fiction and autobiographical essays) in which he records his thoughts on the Stillman case, as well as his reflections on his own identity: 'most important of all: to remember who I am. To remember who I am supposed to be.... My name is Paul Auster. That is not my real name' (65).

Stillman's views on prelapsarian language are written up in a book which Quinn reads, significantly, at the Columbia library. Entitled *The Garden and the Tower: Early Visions of the New World*, the book is in two parts, 'The Myth of Paradise' and 'The Myth of Babel' (50), with different interpretations of the story of Babel. The theme of Babel resurfaces later on as Quinn follows Stillman through the streets of the city. In what initially appears to be a random itinerary, the paths taken by Stillman, when drawn as maps in Quinn's notebook, spell out individual letters (illustrations are provided). When they are unscrambled, Quinn discovers that they spell 'the Tower of Babel'. The iconic tower is, of course, often associated with translation, which has come about precisely because of the multiple languages and diversity of peoples in the world.[29]

Quinn finally meets the character called 'Paul Auster', who may or may not be the double of the 'real' Paul Auster (although the fictional 'Auster' is a writer, as it turns out, not a detective, and, like the 'real' author, he has a son named Daniel and a wife called Siri). What do they talk about? They talk about Cervantes's *Don Quixote*, which they agree is one of their favourite novels. Paul Auster has made the same statement, in real life, as his fictional characters: after reading the new English translation of *Don Quixote* by Edith Grossman, he proclaimed it to be his favourite novel 'of all time', adding that he had read it at least five times (Interview with Carol Burns 2003, in Hutchisson 2013: 131). *Don Quixote* is widely considered to be one of the first novels; it is also a splendid piece of trickery, a superb forgery, in that it is a fictitious translation. In the *City of Glass*, the fictional Auster is writing an essay about *Don Quixote*. He discusses the essay and his theories of authorship with Quinn. He speculates that the story is told by Sancho Panza, and then put into literary Spanish, which is then translated into Arabic. The Arabic manuscript, he concludes, has been translated back into Spanish by Don Quixote himself: 'we shouldn't put it past him ... a man so skilled in the art of disguise' (119).

The doubling of Quinn with the character called 'Paul Auster' blurs the lines between narrator, characters, and the actual author. This is how Auster has explained the presence of the fictional Auster:

> I think it stemmed from a desire to implicate myself in the machinery of the book. I don't mean my autobiographical self, I mean my author self, that mysterious other who lives inside me and puts my name on the covers of books. What I was hoping to do, in effect, was to take my name off the cover and put it inside the story. I wanted to open up the process, to break down walls, to expose the plumbing. There's a strange kind of trickery involved in the writing and reading of novels, after all.... (Interview with Larry McCaffery and Sinda Gregory 1989–90, in *Collected Prose*, 555)

This tradition of 'trickery' has been handed down by other favourite authors of Auster such as Edgar Allan Poe and Jorge Luis Borges. In a talk on Poe, Auster says he has been influenced by 'boys' literature' and 'boy writers'.[30] Poe is the focus of this particular talk, but he also mentions Borges and Pynchon (Auster 2014: 24). In *City of Glass*, there is a 'tip of the hat' to Poe, as he puts it: in the name 'William Wilson' and the Poe novel, *Arthur Gordon Pym*, which Quinn is reading. The tribute continues in other novels: for example, in the name that *Invisible* protagonist Adam Walker chooses for his literary magazine, 'The Stylus', which was a name Poe had given to a similar project (Auster 2014: 4).

Auster also 'tips his hat' to Borges in the opening pages of *City of Glass*, where Auster describes the city of New York as a 'labyrinth of endless steps' in which Quinn loses himself (4). Like Borges, Auster is engaged in a 'subversion of narrative voice and authorial identity' with characters taking on different names and identities, including that of the 'real' author (Green 2014). But the combination of Borges's and Auster's reading of Cervantes helps to shape and give depth to this first novel. Borges regarded Cervantes as the archetypical translator and *Don Quixote* as his greatest accomplishment. Borges's own piece of fiction, 'Pierre Menard, Author of the *Quixote*', as Barnstone has observed, illustrates the 'murky maze of authorship associated with both originality and translation':

> Pierre Menard...has performed the ultimate invisible translation...In actuality we will never find the true author of any text, dead or alive, for, as many have said, there is no work of literature which is not an act of translation from an earlier source. Hence, we will never be able to distinguish fully between the author-creator and a translator-creator. (Barnstone 1993: 87)

Quinn/Auster may well have left translation behind, together with other earlier forms of composition, but the theme of translation continues to haunt the characters, their doubles and their alter-egos throughout this piece of 'original' writing, and through many of the novels that follow as Paul Auster builds his reputation as a writer of fiction.

Moon Palace

In his 1989 novel *Moon Palace*, Auster fictionalizes the influence of his translator uncle, Allen Mandelbaum. Protagonist Marco Stanley Fogg (aka 'M.S.' or manuscript) has a name that calls to mind travellers Marco Polo, Henry Morton Stanley (who found Livingstone) and Jules Verne's Phileas Fogg. He is staying with his friend David Zimmer, a translator. Zimmer has a large translation assignment, 'a tedious document of about a hundred pages concerning the structural reorganization of the French consulate in New York'. Fogg feels that his French is as good as Zimmer's and he offers to take over the translation to repay his friend for his hospitality. While Zimmer is away, Fogg sits at his desk and works on the translation, which has given him a new purpose in life.

> The text was abominable, filled with all kinds of bureaucratic gibberish, but the more trouble it gave me, the more defiantly I stuck to the task, refusing to let go of it until some semblance of meaning began to shine through the clumsy, garbled sentences. The difficulty of the job was what encouraged me. If the translation had been easier, I would not have felt that I was performing an adequate penance for my past mistakes. In some sense, then, the utter uselessness of the project was what gave it is value. I felt like someone who had been sentenced to a term of hard labor on a chain gang. My job was to take a hammer and smash stones into smaller stones ... There was no purpose to this labor. But the fact was that I wasn't interested in results. The labor was an end in itself, and I threw myself into it with all the determination of a model prisoner. (*Moon Palace*, 90)

This passage is of note because translation is perceived as labour – although rather than a labour of love, it is hard labour, a kind of penance. The translator is obliged to translate for money, and merely enough to subsist, and the material is unworthy of him – abominable, gibberish – like some of the hackwork Auster had done as a young man, but the process has value in itself. It builds character and it builds one's resources as a writer. Interestingly, the image of prisoners uselessly breaking up stones persists in later novels such as *The Music of Chance* and *Invisible*. It reflects Auster's view of the mercenary forms of translation as 'grim', but it also concords with the way in which translation for him is also a form of 'discovery', with epistemological value.

To take a break, Fogg goes out to watch children playing at the playground, where he escapes the drudgery of translation:

> I enjoyed the contrast between the dead language of the report I was translating and the furious, hell-bent energy of the toddlers who stormed and squealed around me. I found that it helped to focus my concentration, and on several occasions I even took my work out there and translated while sitting in the midst of that bedlam. (91–2)

He meets his girlfriend, Kitty Wu, in the playground. When she says, 'Hello there, Mr. Writer', he answers, 'I'm not really writing...It's a translation. Something I'm doing to earn a little money' (*Moon Palace*, 92).

Leviathan

As elsewhere in the Auster universe, the story of *Leviathan* (1992) is a 'tangled' one (4): 'every story overlaps with every other story' (57). Auster's seventh novel, *Leviathan* is a tale of two writers, Peter Aaron, the narrator, and his friend Benjamin Sachs. (Note that Aaron has the same initials as Paul Auster, and that Sachs's first name is actually Auster's middle name.)[31] As the novel opens, Sachs is presumed to have blown himself up in a suspicious accident, and Aaron is writing his story, at a place in Vermont, which used to belong to Sachs. When they first meet, Sachs is the more established writer, while Peter, the narrator, has done only a few stories. Peter has just returned from France, where he, too, lived 'hand to mouth' for five years. Sachs describes this as an 'old expatriate adventure', although Peter explains that he picked France because he already spoke French (17). Sachs has already produced a book, which he wrote in prison. He gives a copy of it to Peter and the book plays a role in getting their friendship off the ground (40). They are similar, yet different, competing sides of the same person: as Sachs says, 'we're both sitting in the same place now' (24).

The New Colossus, Sachs's sole novel and one of the 'books within the book', is not a 'thinly veiled' autobiographical story (as many of Auster's are, to some extent at least), but a 'historical novel, meticulously researched', although a 'hodgepodge' of different genres and styles (41–2). Sachs has no job – he works when the spirit moves him (most often late at night) and the rest of the time he prowls the streets of the city 'like some nineteenth-century *flâneur*', a description that might have fit Peter Aaron/Paul Auster in Paris. He walks, goes to museums, galleries, movies, reads books on park benches, goes to baseball games – all to find material for his writing (45). Peter Aaron is not as free as

Sachs, having returned from Paris the previous summer with little money. He has taken a job with a rare-book dealer, a job that involves menial writing tasks, which he combines with his own writing and translation:

> mostly sitting in the back room of the shop writing catalogues and answering letters. I went in every morning at nine and left at one. In the afternoons, I translated at home, working on a history of modern China by a French journalist who had once been stationed in Peking – a slapdash, poorly written book that demanded more effort than it deserved. My hope was to quit the job with the book dealer and start earning my living as a translator, but it still wasn't clear that my plan would work. In the meantime, I was also writing stories and doing occasional book reviews. (46)

Sachs has already made a name for himself, but he gives up on his second novel and writes essays instead. Aaron, on the other hand, is a 'plodder' (54) and ends up translating books full-time. In a situation that mirrors Auster's true life, money troubles force Aaron to choose translation over writing the novel he has been working on for the past three years.

> I wrote as many articles as I could, I took on every translation job I was offered, but still it wasn't enough. Assuming that my novel was dead, that my dreams of becoming a writer were finished, I went out and started hunting for a permanent job. (60)

He begins writing again when he leaves his wife and gets grants to support his creative work. He eventually begins to 'compete' with Sachs in another way – by having a fling with his wife Fanny (whom he has actually been in love with for a long time). As in other Auster books, translation and infidelity are never far apart. But like translation, which is a prelude (or pre-text) to real writing, the affair with Fanny allows Peter to fall in love again and enjoy a genuine relationship when he meets Iris.

Peter's career as a writer flourishes while Sachs's deteriorates. Sachs begins a new book and asks Peter to read the manuscript, although it is only one-third finished. In a merging of the writer and his alter-ego, Peter decides to give his own new novel the same title as Sachs's incomplete one, *Leviathan*, which is of course the title of Auster's book.

There are other subplots that add to the complexity of the novel, involving a woman who creates stories through photography, but translation comes up again in a parallel story, involving yet another character in yet another book within the book. Sachs finds the dissertation of Dimaggio, a man he has killed.

The dissertation, a true story, is about Alexander Berkman, an anarchist who eventually takes refuge in the South of France where he keeps 'body and soul together by doing translations, editing, and ghostwriting' (251). Sachs becomes another kind of ghost as the Phantom of Liberty, bombing replicas of the statue of liberty around the country. After disappearing for a time, he returns to tell his story to Peter Aaron. While living in Sachs's country place in Vermont, sitting at his writing table and breathing the air he once breathed (245), Peter records or 'translates' Sachs's story, but ultimately surrenders the book to the FBI who have been on the trail of his friend turned terrorist.

Sachs's novel bears the same title as a poem by Emma Lazarus, 'The New Colossus', which was inscribed on a plaque and affixed to the Statue of Liberty in 1903. The final verses, in particular, have come to be associated with the waves of immigrants who took refuge in America: 'Give me your tired, your poor/ Your huddled masses yearning to breathe free/ The wretched refuse of your teeming shore./Send these, the homeless, tempest-tost to me,/I lift my lamp beside the golden door!' As Auster has written elsewhere, 'Bartholdi's gigantic effigy' (a gift from France!) was intended as a monument to republicanism, but Lazarus's poem 'reinvented the statue's purpose, turning Liberty into a welcoming mother, a symbol of hope to the outcasts and downtrodden of the world' ('NYC=USA' in *Collected Prose*, 520). It could also be postulated that Auster has reinvented the statue himself, as a new-age Tower of Babel that opens the doors to a multiplicity of languages and cultural difference.[32]

The Book of Illusions

Translation looms large in *The Book of Illusions* (2002), in which David Zimmer, the translator in *Moon Palace*, makes a reappearance. Zimmer, now a professor, is engaged in academic work which is 'connected to books, language, the written word'. He has translated a number of poets, among whom are Lorca and Éluard (a poet Auster translated himself, as seen above). He has also written works of criticism on pro-Fascist writers, including poet-translator Ezra Pound, to whom Auster refers on more than one occasion (*The Book of Illusions*, 13–14). Writing 'out of sorrow' after losing his wife and sons in a plane crash, he has produced a study of the work of Hector Mann, a filmmaker who disappeared without a trace in 1929. While waiting for the Mann book to work its way through the lengthy queue of academic publications, he is looking for another project.

A former classmate, and Columbia professor, commissions a translation of Chateaubriand's *Mémoires d'outre-tombe*. This 2000-page memoir is written from the perspective of someone who has died. This assignment appeals to Zimmer because it allows him to create a distance between himself and his work, although, once again, it is compared to physical labour:

> Much of the work was mechanical, and because I was the servant of the text and not its creator, it demanded a different kind of energy from the one I had put into *The Silent World* [his book about Hector Mann's films]. Translation is a bit like shoveling coal. You scoop it up and toss it into the furnace. Each lump is a word, and each shovelful is another sentence, and if your back is strong enough and you have the stamina to keep at it for eight or ten hours at a stretch, you can keep the fire hot. (70)

Large segments of the memoirs are quoted in English (one presumes that the translation is authentically the work of Zimmer/Auster). These meditations of a dead man are eerily connected to Zimmer's study of the vanished filmmaker. Chateaubriand's attempts to reflect on his life from beyond the grave, similarly, are like those of a translator resurrecting, and remembering, the life and work of an author (who, while not always dead, has in any case preceded the translator, in another time and culture). In one of the excerpts that Auster quotes from the *Mémoires*, Chateaubriand evokes Napoleon in exile, where he spends his time reading Ossian in Casarotti's Italian translation (314). The poems of Ossian have been called a 'textbook case of pseudotranslation', in which author James Macpherson purports to have translated the poetry of the legendary Irish warrior-poet from the Gaelic.[33]

Once the book on Hector Mann comes out, Zimmer receives a letter from Mann's wife inviting him to meet the filmmaker, who appears to be still alive. By this time he is about three-quarters of the way through his translation, which he interrupts to embark upon his journey to meet the man and write his life story. When he meets Hector, the old man tells him that he has read Zimmer's books: 'But you study the works of others. I have read those books, too. Your translations, your writings on the poets' (225). Zimmer does resume the translation work, comparing it to other 'chores' such as taking his truck in for repairs, cleaning the house, and dusting books (297). He completes it and moves away from the place in Vermont where he once lived with his family, and wrote academic books. The move is equated with coming 'back from the dead' (316).

Invisible

Invisible is Auster's fifteenth novel. Published in 2009, about a quarter-century after *City of Glass*, the novel is still concerned with translation both explicitly and implicitly. The story is told in four parts over four decades, beginning in the spring of 1967. Adam Walker, the protagonist, resembles Auster: he is a Columbia student as well as an aspiring poet and critic. He befriends a French professor of political science, Rudolf Born, who offers him money to produce a literary magazine. Adam becomes involved with Born's French girlfriend, Margot. A mugging turns into a fatal stabbing, and Born suddenly returns to Paris. Adam feels 'defeated' by Born and disappointed with himself for failing to do the right thing at the time.

Rudolf Born bears the name of medieval poet Bertran de Born, minus the aristocratic 'de' (he's 'anything but noble', he says (*Invisible*, 4), which is borne out by his later actions). Adam finds a 'clumsy and inept' translation of the poet's work (22). He finds another edition in the library, with the original Provençal and a literal prose version in French on facing pages, and then translates the French prose into English verse. The poem is an authentic one from 1185, which Auster, who does not know Provençal, actually translated from the prose crib (Interview with Nick Obourn 2010, in Hutchisson 2013: 206; PA-int). Adam gives a copy of the poem to Rudolf Born, who treats it as a poem translated *for* him (27); once again, he behaves like Auster, who as a young man translated poets he admired, 'father figures' such as Sartre, Mallarmé and Joubert (Dupre 2007: 11). An elaborate triangle involving Adam, Margot and Born gives rise to conflicting feelings of fidelity, betrayal and deception akin to those experienced in translator/author relations.[34]

In part two, the perspective changes. It is now 2008, with a first-person narrative by Adam Walker's friend Jim. Now a successful writer, Jim receives a manuscript from Adam, who has written about his adventure with Born. Adam is seeking Jim's advice on how to complete the book. A second instalment, about an incestuous affair with his sister Gwyn, is told in the second person – a technique that Auster uses in later memoirs. Jim learns that Adam is seriously ill. Translation plays a role in this section as well. Adam chose to become a lawyer, working among the poor, but only after a stint in London, where he did translations to make ends meet while trying to become a writer:

> I ... spent the next four years toiling in the sewers of Grub Street – cranking out countless freelance book reviews and accepting any translation that came my way, French books mostly, one or two in Italian, regurgitating into

English everything from a dull academic history of the Middle East to an anthropological study of voodoo to crime fiction. (82)

Jim shows up at Adam's house. He finds that Adam has just died, but he is given an envelope containing notes for the next part of the manuscript, entitled 'Fall'. In an interesting switch, Jim becomes Auster as he reaches for a 'Schimmelpenninck', the Dutch cigarillo Auster has been known to smoke (162). 'Fall' is in the third person, telling the story of Adam's earlier trip to Paris, where he is on a junior-year-abroad programme learning French. When he sees Margot again, he speaks to her in French, rather than English, wanting to give her Frenchness back to her (170–1). He sees Born and is introduced to his current fiancée, Hélène, and her daughter Cécile, a brainy though unattractive young woman. Speech and language figure prominently: Hélène is a speech pathologist; Born addresses her by the formal *vous* rather than the more usual, familiar *tu*, in 'the language of counts and countesses' (has he regained his aristocratic status?); references are made to Jakobson and Merleau-Ponty and problems of aphasia and language acquisition, which interest Adam because of his 'engagement with words' (196–7).

Translation is staged, once again, when the erudite Cécile talks about translating Lycophron's poem about Cassandra (199). Walker asks whether it has been translated into English; when Cécile finds a published translation, they both agree that it is terrible because the poetry is missing (213). Born interjects that Adam is a 'poet first, but also a translator of poems. From Provençal, no less. He once gave me a work by my would-be namesake, Bertran de Born... a good poet, and Adam did an excellent translation' (200). When Adam tries to tell Hélène and Cécile about Born's past, he finds himself framed for possession of drugs and deported from France. The end of the story gets more and more sketchy because Adam was ill and has not managed to complete it properly before he died.[35]

In part four of the book, Jim contacts Adam's sister Gwyn. Once she has read her brother's manuscript, she denies what he has written about her as 'pure make-believe' (255). She suggests that Jim complete the unfinished segment and that he change the names to protect the identity of the characters. To find out whether any of Adam's memoir is true, Jim makes his own trip to Paris and tracks down Cécile. What he finds is a plump (childless) fifty-eight-year-old literary scholar. Instead of moving from translating to rewriting and writing (as Jim has done), she merely spends her time studying French writers like Balzac, 'poring over the manuscripts of the dead' (263). This is reminiscent of Auster's rather disdainful remark about archives to which he and his ex-wife

Lydia Davis have left their papers: 'where scholars can pore over manuscripts and take notes for the books they write about other people's books' (*Report from the Interior,* 178). Cécile, however, is in possession of the emblematic 'red notebook', which she uses to compile her findings on the work habits of writers.

The end of the story belongs to Cécile, who has kept a diary. Jim takes possession of her diary, written in French, which he translates and includes as the conclusion to the book. In the diary, Cécile finally finds her own voice, which resembles Auster's (among her reading material are Dupin and du Bouchet, two of the poets Auster has translated). She tells of flying to a Caribbean island, where she meets Rudolf Born, who did not end up marrying her mother, but who proposes marriage to her. He also solicits her help in writing about his double, possibly triple, life in espionage, which he plans to turn into a novel. The very last scene she describes is of black men and women pulverizing stones with hammers and chisels, which reminds us of earlier images of hard labour in Auster's novel.

In addition to specifically mentioning the act of translation itself, the novel is peppered with nearly one hundred references to French, France, or Paris. Adam falls in love with a girl called Patty French, there are allusions to French accents, and the story is replete with language jokes. When Margot prepares dinner, for example, they have the following exchange:

> Rudolf tells me you like lamb, Margot said, so I decided to make a *navarin* – a lamb stew with potatoes and *navets.*
>
> Turnips.
>
> I can never remember that word. It's an ugly word, I think, and it hurts my mouth to say it.
>
> All right, then. We'll banish it from the English language. (33)

Later in the novel, after he meets Cécile, Adam says: 'Dread has become fact. Innocence has turned into guilt, and hope is a word that rhymes with despair' (222). This is a statement that makes sense only if the terms are translated. Hope is *espoir*, and despair is *désespoir*: they rhyme in French, not in English.

The word 'invisible' occurs several times in the novel. Adam tells Jim that he has spent his life working as a lawyer for the poor, the 'spat-upon and the invisible' (83). Jim, for his part, reflects on how he moved from first-person narrative to the third person, a technique he recommends: 'By writing about myself in the first person, I had smothered myself and made myself invisible.... I needed to separate myself from myself ... and began writing it in the third person. *I* became *He*' (89). One can't help thinking of Lawrence Venuti's now-famous book, *The*

Translator's Invisibility (1995), a critique of traditional fluency in translation. Venuti advocates greater intervention on the part of the translator, who is invited to challenge the norms and canons of the receiving culture. Parallels can be drawn between the theme of separation of self that runs through Auster's work – *Invisible*, in this instance – and greater agency on the part of the translator.[36]

Auster has said that *Invisible* is about 'the idea of narrative, and the various shapes it can take, the various voices that it can have, and the various approaches that an author and a reader can have to a story' (Interview with Nick Obourn 2010, in Hutchisson 2013: 204). It is the kind of novel Auster found particularly appealing: 'books that doubled back on themselves, that brought you into the world of the book, even as the book was taking you into the world. The manuscript as hero, so to speak' (Interview with Michael Wood 2003, in *Collected Prose*, 571). Translation, autobiography (diaries, memoires), and fiction are all linked: as the author is shown in a continual drive to shape meaning, the translator is never far off, similarly trying to appropriate and recast someone else's meaning.[37]

These five novels have a particular focus on issues of translating and writing, and language and identity, more generally. While not central to other Auster novels, these themes are not totally absent either. There are passing references to translation in a number of other works, and many to the French language, to France (Paris mainly) and to a range of French people, places and things, as a reminder of Auster's own overseas experience, and, by extension, his life as a translator, and as a 'translated man'. Here are a few examples.

French champagne, French windows, and French kisses …

In the novel *In the Country of Last Things* (1987), translation is not specifically a theme, but 'Frenchness' is. For example, the character Boris tells 'preposterous' stories: 'He would tell me that he had been born in Paris and was the oldest son of Russian émigrés' (146). He refers to a 'tea set that had once belonged to a member of the French court (the duc de Fântomas, I believe) …' (150). This is not only a play on words, 'fântomas' being similar to the French word for ghost, *fantôme*, similar also to 'phantom' as in the 'Phantom of Liberty' in *Leviathan*, but there is no doubt also a connection to *Fantômas*, the character featured in popular detective stories produced in France between 1911 and 1913.[38] Auster uses French directly, with an ironic touch of rhyme: '"*Le chapeau influence le cerveau*," he said lapsing into French. "*Si on protège la tête, la pensée n'est plus bête*"'(154). And, French windows, which would still be present in his fiction twenty years later, are already here: 'He opened the French windows at the back of the house' (176).

The Music of Chance (1990), other than being an allegory for the work of prisoners to which translation is compared in *Moon Palace*, contains no specific allusions to translation. There are French references, on the other hand: 'Should the meal begin with shrimp cocktail or French onion soup?' (154). Also, when the protagonists are told that the bosses are gone, they find out that they have left for Paris, France (164 and 166).

In *Oracle Night* (2003a) we read about the following: 'high-quality imported items: leather-bound pads from Italy, address books from France, delicate rice-paper folders from Japan' (5); 'a jacket she was designing for a book on nineteenth-century French photography' (153); 'this was the second twenty-year-old French-speaking black-woman I had met in two days' (157); 'I made a lightning trip to Paris ... to talk at the funeral of my old friend and translator, Philippe Joubert' (229; Auster had been the translator of *Joseph* Joubert).

The Brooklyn Follies (2005) has the following description of Harry:

> As he saw it, the marriage between the German proper noun and the French modifier would create an arresting, altogether agreeable confusion in the minds of his customers. Some would take the blending of languages to signify a background in Alsace. Others would think he was from a German-Jewish family that had immigrated to France.... No one would ever be certain of Harry's origins.... (40)

When Auster lists his favourite spots, he specifically mentions a French restaurant: '*Saturday evening. May 27, 2000. French restaurant on Smith Street in Brooklyn*' (99). Harry, finally, recalls a former teacher: 'But there was also my French teacher, Mademoiselle Des Forêts, the slender Québécoise with the pretty legs and the bright red lipstick and the liquid brown eyes' (106). Like the French windows with which Auster decorates his novels, the 'French' element pops up in relation to food: 'he set about preparing a couple of pieces of French toast for her' (134).

French champagne is consumed in *Man in the Dark* (2008), where there is much shuttling back and forth to France. We hear about the 'French wife of eighteen years', who is 'now lying in a grave in Cimetière Montparnasse'(102); Sonia, who 'was hardly your typical French girl' (139); 'a French kiss, a French kiss with the French girl who was suddenly the only person who counted anymore' (141); and, inevitably, 'scrambled eggs and bacon, French toast, pancakes, the whole works' (180).

In *Sunset Park* (2010a), translation and French are mentioned to a lesser extent, although Auster recalls the *fatwa* against Rushdie, which resulted in the murder of one of his translators: 'she grew up with the story of Salman Rushdie – the bookstore bombings, the knife in the heart of his Japanese translator' (228).

This overview of some of Auster's fiction has highlighted translation as a form of literary activity, translators as characters, and translation as a structural device or a leitmotif. Interlocking tropes tied to the problematization of translation, they are associated, in today's world, with travel, movement and dislocation. Auster often writes about criss-crossing the city of New York (or Brooklyn) on foot, and also about crossing the ocean to France, more often than not to Paris. These images and references – obsessions, at times – haunt Auster's universe like musical themes, and are accompanied, as well, with serious discussions of language, and of silence, and of the postmodern blurring of the lines between authors and readers, between truth and reality.

In an interesting transfictional and intertextual twist that is very Austerian, a Russian movie has referenced Paul Auster. Entitled *Плюс один*/Plyus odin, or Plus One in English, it was produced in 2008, directed by Oksana Bychkova. The main character is an English-Russian translator who accompanies a puppeteer from the UK to Moscow. She is in the process of translating one of Auster's books.[39]

Acts of discovery, labours of love …

At last count, Auster's work has been translated into over forty languages: nearly every European language, including four different languages in Spain, as well as Asian languages, from Farsi, Turkish, Hebrew and Arabic to Vietnamese, Korean and two different variants of Chinese.

His work is particularly popular in Europe, and he has received awards and distinctions from France and other countries such as the French *Ordre des Arts et des Lettres* (Order of Arts and Letters). He seems pleased by this: 'it's a wonderful vindication of something', he says.

Generally, he does not get too involved in the translations, even when they are in a language he knows (besides French, he reports that he can 'pick his way' through Italian and Spanish). However, he willingly answers questions, which have to do with idioms or the nuances of American life. He doesn't read the translations, nor does he read reviews of the translated works – to see whether there have been comments made about the translations themselves – just as he avoids reading reviews of his work at home. When asked about particular details having to do with French translations of his fiction, he seems indifferent, exhibiting an (almost) blind confidence in the ability of his translators. Overall, he maintains confidence in the value of translators, expressing his assessment of them in the same terms as in the tribute quoted at the beginning of this chapter: 'translators are the very heart of literature because without them, we'd all be confined to our own language' (PA-int).

Translation has meant many things to Paul Auster over the course of his long, prolific and varied career. When recounting his earliest contacts with contemporary French poetry, he calls his translations 'real acts of discovery, labors of love' (Interview with Stephen Rodefer 1985, in Hutchisson 2013: 4) and in the *Random House Book* introduction he again views translation 'not simply as a literary exercise, but as an act of discovery and passion' (xxx). When I spoke to him, nearly thirty years later, his view of translating poetry remained unchanged (PA-int). From its initial value as a didactic tool that helped him to 'penetrate' French poetry and uncover new modes of writing, translation opened the door to becoming a writer. With an interesting reference to Ezra Pound who engaged in translation abundantly and who believed translation was good for young poets, Auster says:

> It was part of my development as a writer to translate and I found it thrilling and altogether helpful not only as a thing in itself but as a way of feeling more comfortable with a pen in my hand looking at a blank page. In a way the pressure's off. You're in the hands of someone who is necessarily more advanced than you, when you're young, and there's a lot you can learn. Certainly translating is the very best way to study anything, a work of literature, be it a poem, novel, or story, and it gives you the liberty to try to do something inventive in your own language, to try to mirror whatever's strong and original in the primary text. (PA-int)

There was also a time in Auster's life, about which he has often written in both fiction and nonfiction, when his 'labours' were more literally laborious. Pressed for cash, like so many of his fictional characters, he took on translations of lesser value and interest as part of the 'hackwork' he did to make ends meet. Translation became drudgery; it was grim, associated as it was, coincidentally, with personal and marital difficulties. There is no doubt that some of those translations were unbearably tedious. At the same time, however, one detects in Auster a certain delight in the difficulties themselves. Both translating and writing take place in prison-like circumstances: locked rooms (*Zimmer* is the

German word for 'room') or isolated cabins (like the room Auster keeps outside the home to work in solitude on a daily basis). The motif of the slogging, toiling writer/translator, doing penance and hard labour to no apparent purpose, is woven throughout his work. And yet, as we have seen in *Moon Palace*, for example, the labour is 'an end in itself' (90), because it develops writerly muscles and paves the way for creation. In this, Auster can be compared to Paul Valéry, who sought out difficulty, who even created his own obstacles, his own 'chains', and who revelled in the labour of artistic creation – for its own sake.[40] In constructing his impressive *œuvre*, Auster has wrapped all of these themes together in an intriguing postmodern labyrinth. Within this maze, links can be made between translation and (auto)biography – genres that contribute to the memorialization of respected figures or works – as well as between translation and movement, or travel, which like biography, are ways of encountering and negotiating otherness. In Auster's world, these are necessary preparations for finding one's own voice and producing one's own book.

'Man has not one and the same life', Chateaubriand wrote. 'He has many lives ...'. These words open *The Book of Illusions*. With this epigraph, Auster signals the importance of excavating and bringing to life these multiple lives and stories, whether the story is about oneself or someone else. In this novel, Zimmer donates insurance money to fund a travel fellowship in his wife's name (17), and spends a lot of time travelling across the United States, as well as to London and Paris, in search of material on Hector Mann, whose biography he is writing. Michel Butor has commented on Romantic writers, Chateaubriand in particular: 'They travel in order to write, they travel while writing, because, for them, travel *is* writing' (1974: 14). We could adapt (or twist?) those words to say: they translate in order to write, they translate while writing, because, for them, translating *is* writing.

Postscript

In January 2017, Paul Auster published his first novel in seven years, *4321*. In this long awaited work of fiction, a mega-*Bildungsroman*, translation is once again featured, for example as protagonist Archie Ferguson follows 'Pound's advice to young poets' and translates French poetry (510). When interviewed some months before the new book came out, Auster evoked the writer's task in terms that are similar to the ones he uses to describe translation: 'It's always difficult. I dedicated myself to this task every day, as I have always done. After a day's work, I was so tired mentally and physically that I literally collapsed onto my bed' (Clément 2016; my translation). Thus, writing is also a chore, a gratifying one for so productive an author, but no less arduous than the translation labours Auster has referred to in works of fiction and nonfiction over the entire course of his career. In many ways, it boils down to what Paul Valéry so perceptively said in one of his essays on translation: all writing is a form of translation.[41]

Epilogue: What Is Translation For?

And wasn't the splendor of translation this very thing – to discover sentences
this beautiful and then have the chance to make someone hear their beauty
who had yet to hear it?

–Idra Novey, Ways to Disappear

Bernard Shaw, Gertrude Stein, and Paul Auster are 'original' writers first and
foremost, but they also craft a vision of translation in acts of textual self-
fashioning. Their position is evident in their approach to the act of translating,
in their articulation of the nature of translation, and in the storytelling itself.
Having profiled these writers and cited myriad words that overflow the
boundaries and breach the threshold of their creative and translated texts, it is
tempting to give the last word to the last among them, Paul Auster. 'Translating
or critical writing... were preoccupations that absorbed me when I was young',
Auster writes. 'Both were about discovering other writers, about learning how
to become a writer myself. My literary apprenticeship, if you will' (Interview
with Michael Wood 2003, in *Collected Prose*, 574).

Suppose we take Auster's point and consider translation as pre-text – or as a
pretext – for something else. Does this perpetuate the stereotype of translation
as a secondary art? Or, on the contrary, by appropriating the idea of translation,
does Auster, along with Stein and Shaw, help to elevate its status? There is
no clear-cut answer to either question, although the projects we have seen
– both real and fictionalized – tend to ensure the prominence of translation
in the literary landscape. Within the framework of modernist paradoxes and
multilayered postmodernism, the practice and theory of translation take on
several shades of meaning, both negative and positive.

Although Shaw was known for comedy, for his exuberant intellect, and for his
commitment to the betterment of humanity, his writings bear the traces of loss –
from the theme of the lost manuscript to his anxiety over his own masterpieces
being snatched from him, combined with a relentless wringing of hands over his
translators' blunders and stupidity, which have inevitably led to shortcomings

in their output. Inextricably tied to his story is the tragic tale of Trebitsch, who gave up his own creative work in order to translate a crazy Irishman, and who later in life concluded that he had accomplished little more than earn a 'terrible' reputation as 'Shaw's translator'.

Because of her writer's ego, Gertrude Stein painted herself into a corner, making it impossible to bring to fruition any of her translation projects; instead, she turned her back on translation to publish her version of someone else's poem, in her own name, under the imprint of her own press. Her translation stories are stories of abandonment, broken friendships, and forgeries. She didn't translate until she was really driven to do so, if not directly under duress, then at least in the dark, ambiguous days of the war, during which her translation project was quite likely undertaken for some other purpose than to endow her culture with a fresh object of beauty.

Paul Auster's fictional world is populated by characters who used to be translators. Translation, for the real-life Auster, and for the people he invents, is hard work; it is mere drudgery, as backbreaking and thankless as the repetitive labour of prisoners on a chain gang. Writers and translators disappear, hand in hand, into the postmodern hole.

This is a bleaker view of translation and of the 'subservient habitus' endorsed by translators themselves (Simeoni 1998). On the other hand, our survey of the work of these three writers has also uncovered extraordinarily constructive affirmations of the art of translation. It is true that they each found reasons to eschew translation. Shaw was not gifted in foreign languages and, after all, had more important work to tend to; Stein didn't want a foreign tongue to interfere with her native English and hinder her experimentation with language; and Auster experienced translation as a form of entrapment and imprisonment.

Nonetheless, these literary titans did, in fact, turn their hands to some form of translating. Furthermore, all three affirmed the value of translation to themselves personally and to cultures generally. The three authors formulated tributes to their translators, and they regarded translation as a kind of tribute in itself. Some were more generous than others, but all three were positive. Consider Shaw's gift of his Nobel Prize money, Stein's praise of her translators in the *Autobiography*, and Auster's salute and thanks to translators cited in the epigraph to Chapter 3 about him. Auster goes the furthest because his translation work was more sustained and his appreciation of translators more wholehearted. And after he gave it up personally, translation arose like a phoenix to inhabit his fictional universe.

These various statements form a collective acknowledgement that translators have contributed to their own success and to the interchange among world literatures. The last word, however, has not yet been uttered. In new works of fiction, translators increasingly step up to take their place on centre stage, and translation continues to bubble up as a theme or literary device. These tendencies continue to attract the attention of translation scholars in the context of what has come to be known as the 'fictional turn'.[1]

'I am you and you are me': Translators and writers in recent works of fiction

Transfictional works by three recent writers illustrate this phenomenon. In their multidimensional stories, Jonathan Safran Foer, Rachel Cantor, and Idra Novey cross languages, genres, and continents. The translators who inhabit these works of fiction all struggle with issues of self-doubt and stare down the spectre of untranslatability. They torture themselves with the inevitability of betrayal, but succeed in overcoming their uncertainty and invisibility by taking control of the narrative, and by writing the story of their translations. The lives of translators and authors are intertwined, reflecting the intimate ways in which a translator must mirror his or her author in order to produce a meaningful translation.[2]

In Foer's first novel, *Everything Is Illuminated* (2002), which was also made into a film by the same name in 2005, one of the two main characters is a translator or, more precisely, an interpreter called Alex or Sasha. His job is to translate for the other protagonist, whom he calls the 'hero' and who has the same name as the author, Jonathan Safran Foer. Jonathan is on a journey to Ukraine to find out about Trachimbrod, the *shtetl* his grandfather came from, where he hopes to find the person who probably saved his grandfather's life. There are shades of Auster here, as Foer inserts himself and his family into the novel, the 'hero' bearing his own name and the translator the name of Foer's son Sasha.

Because of his fractured English, which adds a touch of comedy, Alex is sometimes dismissed by critics as inept or incompetent. His voice is expressed throughout the novel through incorrect usage such as: 'I did *fashion* all of the other corrections you *commanded*', meaning 'I *made* all of the other corrections you *asked* for' (53); 'It was already after the *center of the day*', or 'it was already *afternoon*' (115); and 'If I could *utter* a *proposal* ...', by which he means 'if I could *make* a *suggestion*' (143; emphasis added). Thus the reader becomes a translator as well, having to decipher, every step of the way, the faulty English in which the 'translator' expresses himself. Alex can even be considered fraudulent because of his deliberate non-translation, or mistranslation, of information intended for Jonathan. He sometimes withholds the truth from Jonathan: as he says to himself, 'I present not-truths in order to protect you' (227). At other times, he is open about his interventionist translation: 'Jonathan, this man spoke not so good Ukrainian, but I have made it sound abnormally good in my translation for the story. If it would appease you, I could counterfeit the substandard utterances' (109).

For all his faults, the translator is a crucial mediator. Alex is central to the recovery of the author's heritage. He is key to the act of remembering the grandfather's village, which was eradicated by the Nazis and for which there is but one witness, who tells her story in Ukrainian. As he narrates one thread of the story, he recounts the hero's journey from his own perspective; in another, he writes letters to the hero in which he comments on Jonathan's account of the same events. The personal stories of the two characters are interwoven as Alex grows into a writer, the co-author of Foer's story. Just as the translation is never entirely faithful, both Alex and Jonathan are 'nomadic' with the truth (179). Thus, Foer's novel 'blurs the boundaries between translation and the invention of historical truth, memory and fiction' and the translator is given the 'responsibility for establishing a new relationship to the past' (Strümper-Krobb 2014: 257).

In Rachel Cantor's *Good on Paper* (2016), the protagonist, Shira Greene, has been picked by Nobel laureate Romei to translate his novel, entitled *Vita Nuova*. He has made this choice, apparently, because he has read her translation of Dante's *Vita Nuova* as well as her story about Paul Celan. He faxes her the manuscript a few pages at a time. She observes that the structure of his novel resembles the structure that she herself has used in her paper on Dante, and that increasingly the plot bears a resemblance to events in her own life. In an intriguing twist, translation ceases to be a derivative art; instead, both content and structure of the original are inspired by the translator's work. At one point, Shira counts 'seven images and ideas familiar from my stories' (100); ultimately, the author becomes the thief, stealing from his translator (149). The author 'lures' her into his text, he writes her in, and she becomes a character in his book (274).

The act of translating is accompanied by theoretical reflections on translation. Inspired by Paul Valéry, whose influence Cantor recognizes in her acknowledgements (297), the translator moves 'ever backward, through the labyrinth of an author's ideas and devices … until she arrives, finally, at the moment of creation' (31). Shira's feelings of self-doubt, expressed at various times throughout the book – 'who am I? I'm just the translator!' (149) – are coupled in this way with her efforts to take control, through this kind of theorization, and through the paratext she is working on, a 'Translator's Note', a 'wise and learned piece … to be photocopied and cited by graduate students everywhere' (126).[3]

Translation, in Shira's view, always involves some kind of 'abandonment' because the 'translated one is always betrayed' (49). The translator not only rants about the untranslatability of all texts; she personifies infidelity, even dressing up for Halloween as the *traduttore/traditore*, although just what the costume looks like is left up to our imagination (43). Nevertheless, with translation viewed through the prism of the *Vita Nuova*, we return to the notion of the afterlife of a text, which in its new incarnation outlives the original. As Cantor's narrator concludes, 'Celan's chasm cannot be crossed, there is no true translation, no absolute fidelity. I still think this. And yet, miraculously, it can be, there is, and there is. We experience the new life in glimmers, I think, in moments when we apprehend the *possibility* of new life' (294).

Idra Novey's 2016 novel, *Ways to Disappear*, complements the work of Foer and Cantor in that, seen from the vantage point of a translator, the lines between life and fiction are blurred and translation is staged as central to modern life. Emma Neufeld, an American translator, is the central character. When her author, a famous Brazilian novelist called Beatriz Yagoda, disappears mysteriously after incurring gambling debts, Emma goes to Brazil and, together with the author's children, attempts to find her. Her life becomes entangled with the life of the author.

The book offers a meditation on relations between the translator and her author, between writing and translating. Emma has made regular trips to Rio – 'annual pilgrimages' – to be closer to Beatriz. The trips, which nourish her imagination, are described using the familiar ferryman (*passeur*) image: 'She'd remember a morning in Rio … use that light to illuminate the strange, dark boats of Beatriz's images as she ferried them into English' (9). Like Shira, Emma keeps a journal, which she downplays by saying that it is not writing, just 'boring translator notes' (45). The entries mimic dictionary definitions, but also contain elements of narrative and fragments of her theory of translation. In one such entry, under the headword 'transcribe', the first meaning is given (correctly) as 'to write something anew and fully …'. The second, on the other hand, is more of a commentary: 'To convert a written work in such a way that it alters the expectations of others and/or oneself, often requiring the abandonment of such expectations entirely. **See also:** transform, transgress, translate' (243). Like our other authors, Novey equates translation with abandonment and transgression. She, too, questions the possibility of translation, raising the age-old bogeyman of the '*traduttore, traditore* – that tired, tortured Italian cliché' (97). She is haunted by the idea of being put on trial for her 'crimes' (125).

Beatriz's son, Marcus, with whom Emma is having an affair, asks Emma to read to him from one of his mother's novels, which he has never read. Emma performs a kind of intralingual translation by reading it aloud. It is a book about adultery, also linked to translation, as we have seen, in the case of Shaw's creation of *Jitta*. It is on this occasion that she so eloquently expresses her thoughts on the 'splendour' of translation (132). Her words echo Rossetti's view of translation as bringing 'one more possession of beauty' to a new culture through the magic wrought by the translator, whom he compares to Aladdin in the enchanted vaults (1992: 66).

Novey is both a poet and a translator. She has translated from the Spanish and Portuguese – notably *The Passion according to G.H.*, one of the most celebrated novels of Brazilian writer Clarice Lispector. With *Ways to Disappear*, Novey emerges as a new 'decathlete', writing across different genres, thoughtfully reflecting on the meaning of translation, and infusing new life into the question of what translation is for.

Only time will tell whether they will achieve the stature of a Shaw, a Stein, or an Auster, but writers such as Foer, Cantor, and Novey have helped to enhance the profile of translation. Translators, still subservient perhaps, populate works of literature to a greater extent. Translation – and the idea of translation – endures. It penetrates the discourse of actors in the field of literature who weave it artfully into the fabric of their literary creations. Can any more be expected?

Notes

Introduction

1   This is the premise of Steven Yao's 2002 book, *Translation and the Languages of Modernism*, which underlines Ezra Pound's contribution to modernist approaches to translation.

2   Valéry's comment on Poe is taken from a letter of 13 June 1892, to his friend André Gide, reproduced in *Œuvres*, I, 1957: 1757. He published 'Quelques fragments des Marginalia, traduits et annotés par Paul Valéry' in the journal *Commerce* (1927), using his own byline; although it would appear that while the commentary was his, the translation was not (Woodsworth 2000).

3   Other examples of self-translators abound and have been well documented. See, for example, the work of Rainier Grutman and, in particular, the volume on self-translation edited by Anthony Cordingley (2013). In his contribution to this anthology, Grutman also cites the opposite phenomenon – *non*-self-translators. Canadian writer Mavis Gallant, when interviewed some years ago, said that translating her own work would be out of the question, although she lived in Paris and lived her life in French. Translating her own work would be 'like writing the same thing twice'; when asked whether a translator who is also a writer should translate works of literature, her response was that this would 'not be real translation, but rather "variations on a theme"' (Woodsworth 1988: 52–4).

4   Lefevere, a polyglot literary translator versed in Dutch, French, German, and English, translated works by the medieval Flemish mystic Jan van Ruusbroec, for example. Gideon Toury translated numerous works into Hebrew – those of American novelists such as Ernest Hemingway, John Steinbeck, and Mark Twain, and German ones such as Günter Grass and Heinrich Böll.

5   In addition to Yao's excellent monograph, see Daniel Katz (2007), as well as articles such as 'Polyglot Voices, Hybrid Selves and Foreign Identities: Translation as a Paradigm of Thought for Modernism' by Teresa Caneda (2008).

6   From Daniel Dyer's review of Auster's *The Brooklyn Follies* in the Sunday Forum section of *The Plain Dealer* (Cleveland), published on 15 January 2006.

7   Israel Cohen, in a 1957 article published in Hebrew in *Moznayim* 5 (2), quoted in Delisle and Woodsworth (2012: 54).

8   Gérard Genette distinguishes between a first spatial category, which includes the preface, but also elements such as chapter titles, which he calls 'peritexts', and more

distanced elements that are located 'outside the book' such as letters, diaries, or interviews, which he calls 'epitexts' ('paratext = peritext + epitext', Genette 1997: 5). To simplify matters, I use the broader term 'paratext' to refer to all the various forms of textual devices used by the three authors, which range from titles and author's names to correspondence and recollections written after the fact.

9 For further discussion on Venuti (1995), see Chapter 1. A few studies have appeared recently on the phenomenon of translators' notes; for example, see Sardin (2007) and Toledano Buendía (2013).

10 Gahan is referring to Roland Barthes's now famous essay, 'The Death of the Author' (Barthes 1968).

11 I am grateful to Rainier Grutman for drawing attention to the helpful notion of 'self-fashioning' as well as to the work of Meizoz in the keynote address he presented at the conference on *The Fictions of Translation*, held in Montreal in May 2015 (See Grutman 2018). Looking at the paratexts of self-translators, specifically, he highlights the extent to which they 'allow self-translators to craft their personae as altogether different from that of "regular" translators'.

Chapter 1

1 Born George Bernard Shaw, he insisted on being called simply 'Bernard Shaw'. As of 1890, he adopted the byline 'G.B.S.' for his journalistic writing and his letters are often signed using that abbreviation.

2 Reference books consulted include: Baker and Saldanha (2009), *Routledge Encyclopedia of Translation Studies*; Malmkjær and Windle (2011), *The Oxford Handbook of Translation Studies*; Millán and Bartrina (2013), *The Routledge Handbook of Translation Studies*; and Gambier and van Doorslaer (2014), *Handbook of Translation Studies*. To cite another example, Shaw appears only peripherally in France (2000), *The Oxford Guide to Literature in English Translation*. E. Sylvia Pankhurst, co-translator of the Romanian poet Mihail Eminescu, who was interested in social justice, sent her translations to Shaw, who wrote a preface in which he quipped, 'the translation is astonishing and outrageous: it carried me away' – an observation characterized as 'suitably ambiguous' by the author of the entry (215). In another article on Ibsen, the Norwegian playwright is said to have been so well served by his English translators that 'dramatists from George Bernard Shaw onwards have regarded him as one of their own' (577).

3 Some Shaw scholars, writing notably in the official publication of the International Shaw Society, *SHAW: The Annual (Journal) of Bernard Shaw Studies*, have turned their attention to Shaw's translation of Trebitsch (Gahan 2004; Conolly-Smith 2013, for example). Crawford (2000) has meticulously identified translations of Shaw's

work into several European languages. Shaw's connections to France, including his relations with his French translators, are the subject of a monograph by Pharand (2000); Shaw's adaptation of Trebitsch's play is examined closely by Dukore (1973) and Knoll (1992), as well as Matlaw (1979), who also retranslated the play from the German following the original more closely than Shaw had done.

4   This chapter builds on my earlier essay, 'In the Looking Glass: Bernard Shaw on and in Translation', originally published in 2001 in the journal *Athanor*, and reprinted in 2003 under the same title in *Translation Translation* (Woodsworth 2001, 2003). 'In the Looking Glass' focuses primarily on relations between Shaw and Trebitsch; it contains the complete text of Shaw's 'Translator's Note', his preface to the published translation of Trebitsch's play. Another exception is an article by Hannes Schweiger (2006), tellingly subtitled 'Siegfried Trebitsch als Übersetzer und Vermittler George Bernard Shaws'. In his piece, published in a collection edited by Michaela Wolf, Schweiger emphasizes Trebitsch's role as an intermediary, mediator, or broker ('Vermittler', from 'Mittle', or the 'middle'), examining Shaw and Trebitsch from a Bourdieusian perspective and showing how the habitus of each man influenced translation choices and the way in which the work was received by English and German cultures.

5   Harris's biography, *Bernard Shaw* (1931), subtitled 'An Unauthorized Biography Based on First Hand Information', was completed by the author just before he died. Shaw corrected the proofs and wrote a postscript, calling it the 'oddest' job he ever had to do. Hesketh Pearson's *Bernard Shaw: His Life and Personality* (1942) (released in the United States as *G.B.S. A Full Length Portrait*) was written with Shaw's (at-first-reluctant) assistance:

> Having cautioned me before publication that if a word were said to connect him to the book he would take the most desperate steps to disclaim it, he now spoke openly of the help he had given me; and on seeing my copy of it during a visit, he opened it to write on the flyleaf underneath my signature: 'Also his humble collaborator – G Bernard Shaw'. (Quoted in the introduction by Richard Ingrams, Pearson 2001: xiii)

Other memoirs or biographies have been produced by Langner (1963) and Gibbs (2005); Dan H. Laurence, the eminent Shaw scholar who compiled a four-volume edition of Shaw's correspondence, was overlooked by the Society of Authors, which instead commissioned Michael Holroyd to write a new authorized life of Shaw (4 vols, 1988–1992).

6   The letters exchanged by Shaw and Trebitsch may have numbered as many as 1,000, of which over 600 have survived. Most of the letters are currently held by the Berg Collection of the New York Public Library, to which Trebitsch sold his collection in 1956. In 1986, Samuel A. Weiss published an edited collection of the correspondence between Shaw and Trebitsch, with an introduction closely

examining their relations. In Weiss's 'Bernard Shaw's Further Letters to Siegfried Trebitsch' (2000), he explains the provenance of some supplementary material. In April 1995, Christie's sold thirteen previously unknown letters and cards, but the catalogue provided no information about their content or the identity of the owners. In 1997, these letters, and a fourteenth one, were donated to Colgate University and Weiss was given access to them. He published the letters with copious notes in his 2000 article, commenting, however, that while they provide fresh details, they did not alter in any substantive way the narrative of the 1986 publication (Weiss 2000: 221–2).

7   References to 'divination' are made in the article 'Ein Teufelskerl', where the term is attributed to his translator, Trebitsch, and in his 'Translator's Note', written twenty years later, where he applies it to himself as translator. Both texts are discussed in some detail in this chapter.

8   Based on evidence from Shaw's *Diaries*, Crawford draws the conclusion that German was the foreign language with which Shaw was most familiar (albeit for reading only); he points out that he used exercise books and tutors in an attempt to master the language, although he did not make significant progress (2000: 179–80).

9   Weiss points out that Trebitsch had a horror of the 'convention of birthdays' and incorrectly gave 21 December 1869 as his date of birth, which Shaw repeats in his 'Translator's Note'. The correct date of birth, 22 December 1868, is provided in Weiss's introduction to the collected letters (1986: 5). Writer and art critic Hermann Bahr was the main spokesman for the Young Vienna group; other members included writers such as Stefan Zweig, Arthur Schnitzler, and Hugo von Hofmannsthal. Although Trebitsch claimed affiliation with it, his name does not usually come up in relation to the movement. He is scarcely mentioned in reference books on German literature, for that matter: in *The Oxford Companion to German Literature*, for example, the entry on Trebitsch is limited to a few lines stating his year and place of birth and death, and labelling him a 'minor novelist, best known for his translation of G.B. Shaw's plays' (Garland 1986: 900). Other authors, by comparison, merit several lines or even columns in the encyclopaedic work.

10   Weiss summarizes the way in which Trebitsch met Shaw, taking into account the various versions of the story (1986: 3–17). In 1926, Trebitsch embarked on a lecture tour on the occasion of Shaw's seventieth birthday; his lecture, 'Der deutsche Aufstieg Bernard Shaws' (Shaw's rise to fame in Germany), was published in various forms, including in English as 'How I Discovered Bernard Shaw'. In 1951, Trebitsch published an autobiography, *Chronik eines Lebens*, once Shaw was dead and he was well over eighty years old himself. The references that follow are to the English edition, published in 1953 as *Chronicle of a Life*. Shaw's reports of the incident also varied over time.

11   In evoking 'Schlegel and Tieck', Shaw is alluding to the authoritative German edition of the plays of Shakespeare. The designation 'Schlegel-Tieck' Shakespeare

(1825–1833) is somewhat complicated. The translations of Shakespeare were begun by the German Romantic poet and critic August Wilhelm Schlegel, who was known also for having translated the Bhagavad Gita from the Sanskrit. Ludwig Tieck edited the Shakespeare translations and oversaw their completion by his daughter, Dorothea, and Wolf Heinrich Graf von Baudissin. In his article, 'A Devil of a Fellow', Shaw says that he was not at home at the time of the first meeting, and that he met Trebitsch only on his second visit, when he was invited to lunch. In other versions, there is only one meeting. Shaw merges the two visits into one in the 'Translator's Note'. In fact, a letter from Charlotte Shaw to Trebitsch, dated 17 March 1902, has survived, in which Trebitsch is invited to lunch to discuss the proposition obviously made to Shaw on an earlier occasion (quoted in Weiss 1986: 5).

12 See also Schweiger (2009), where he examines Shaw's role as a 'self-appointed intermediary between Britain and the German-speaking worlds' (277) and provides further information on the ideological debates in which Shaw participated.

13 Unless otherwise indicated, excerpts of Shaw's letters are taken from *Bernard Shaw: Collected Letters*, edited by Dan H. Laurence, published in four volumes between 1965 and 1988.

14 Holroyd says that Shaw bought the house for them (1997: 290); according to Crawford, he provided a mortgage of 30,000 francs (2000: 185); and Pharand uses the term 'loan' to refer to the 30,000 francs (2000:106). In any case, Shaw made sure they had a roof over their heads and a modest lifetime annuity to live on.

15 Pharand's extremely thorough monograph on Shaw and the French covers the translation project in a chapter entitled 'Shaw Frenchified. Augustin and Henriette Hamon *Rewrite* Shaw', the first subsection of which bears the heading 'Beguiling the Anarchist: A *Reluctant* Translator' (Pharand 2000: 101; emphasis added). An early study of Shaw and France was published by Moore (1933), highlighting the influence of Bergson. A further examination of Shaw's relations with the French, including the translation and reception of his work in France, was published in 1956 by Grindea, editor of *Adam International Review*, who had previously mounted an exhibition, 'G.B.S. et la France'.

16 The source that Pharand gives for Hamon's letter to Shaw of 16 November 1905 is Patrick Galliou, 'George Bernard Shaw et Augustin Hamon: les premiers temps d'une correspondance (1893–1913)', vol. 1, 231 (Ph.D. diss. Université Bretagne Occidentale, 1998, 4 vols).

17 The book was translated in 1915 as *The Twentieth Century Molière: Bernard Shaw*.

18 Henderson is quoting a published remark by Vicomte d'Humières, which he has presumably translated from the French; this was also quoted, with slight variations, in Grindea (1956: 3), and subsequently by other biographers and critics.

19 The quotation follows Sanborn's version in the *The New York Times* (1912), except that he writes 'compositor' for 'composer'. The lines were taken from earlier correspondence with Hamon, and then translated and placarded on kiosks in Paris

to advertise the French production of *Mrs Warren*. A note with similar content was also inserted in the play's programme and published in French translation in the Paris cultural publication *Comœdia* on 2 April 1912 (Crawford 2000: 184 and 196, n. 9; also quoted in Grindea 1956: 6).

20 Holroyd describes Sobieniowski as one of the 'exaggerated figures' Shaw took up with, an 'impoverished Polish adventurer', who had blackmailed his lover, Katherine Mansfield (1997: 534).

21 The term 'threshold' is borrowed from Genette (1997). It is used as the title of his seminal book on paratextual materials: the original French version (1987) is called *Seuils*, and the English translation (1997) is entitled *Paratexts. Thresholds of Interpretation*.

22 The article was originally published on 22 February 1903, in *Die Zeit* (Vienna), in a German translation by Siegfried Trebitsch, under the title 'Ein Teufelskerl: Selbstkritik'. The original English text remained in manuscript form until it was published in *SHAW* in 2000. Not to be confused with the present German weekly *Die Zeit*, which was established after the Second World War, this newspaper was a weekly, later a daily, paper that was published in Vienna up until 1919; the editors were Fabians, like Shaw himself. Shaw had already published in *Die Zeit* and was known to its readership, as previously indicated.

23 On 22 January 1903, the *Neues Wiener Tagblatt* published Kellner's critique of Trebitsch's translation of *Candida*. The article was entitled 'Eine verunglückte Übersetzung', as noted earlier. Weiss (1986: 40, n. 1) translates the title as 'Wretched Translation', whereas the editors of the English version of Shaw's article refer to it as 'An Unsuccessful Translation' (Shaw 2000: 250, n. 7). The term 'verunglückte' could also be translated as 'disastrous' – all strong words, in any case.

24 'Translator's Note' (Shaw 1949: 1–7; first edition 1926), hereafter designated in the text as 'Note'. The 'Note' is reprinted in its entirety in my earlier article (2001) and chapter (2003), both referenced in note 2. There are some discrepancies between the published version of the 'Note' and the original 1923 version (reproduced in Mander and Mitchenson 1955: 200–2). There are indications that the 'Note', or at least excerpts of it, was also included in programs for subsequent productions. The 'Note' is also included in *The Complete Prefaces* vol. 2, 548–52. Variations between versions will be discussed where relevant.

25 For more on Shaw's prefaces, see the introduction to *The Complete Prefaces*, edited by Laurence and Leary (vol. 1, vii–xxix). The three-volume collection (1993, 1995 and 1997) contains over 100 prefaces.

26 Trebitsch's play was entitled *Frau Gittas Sühne*. The possessive form, '*Gittas*', is written without an apostrophe in German. Shaw, whose knowledge of German was imperfect, as we have seen, writes '*Gitta's*'. With respect to the 'Translator's Note' and other texts by Shaw, more generally, I reproduce Shaw's idiosyncratic spelling

and punctuation, even when incorrect; when not specifically quoting Shaw, I preserve the original spelling of others.

27 In mentioning the change from 'Gitta' to 'Jitta', Shaw explains that he had to spell her name with a 'J' 'to prevent it being pronounced with a hard G' ('Note', 5). Is Shaw suggesting that the G in German could be either hard or soft, and that he was trying to ensure that it remain soft in English? If so, he is mistaken. There doesn't seem to be any justification for making up the name 'Jitta', which doesn't exist in either language, since the other names in the play are all quite common: Agnes, Edith, Alfred, and so on. When Trebitsch writes about the play *Jitta*, he writes 'Yitta' since the J would be pronounced Y in German.

28 See, for example, an article in which Lefevere defines refraction as 'a rewriting of a text in function of different linguistic, cultural, ideological and poetological constraints', specifically naming translation and the production of plays as two kinds of refraction (Lefevere 1984: 191–2). In translating a play for the stage, these two kinds of refraction come together. Lefevere's 1982 essay on Brecht, reprinted in Venuti (2000), is another example of his work on 'refraction'.

29 The conclusion of the 'Note', in the printed text, enumerates the various productions of *Jitta*: the original, German-language production at the Burgtheater in Vienna, as well as the first London and New York productions. This section is omitted entirely from the version printed in *The Complete Prefaces*.

30 A letter of 17 May 1926, to Trebitsch provides evidence that this revision to the preface was made out of deference to Trebitsch. It was at the request of Trebitsch that Shaw modified the preface to suggest that he was unable to 'do justice' to Trebitsch's original play (Weiss 1986: 270–1).

31 The play had been produced in the original German at the Burgtheater in Vienna for a brief run in 1920; while Trebitsch alleges that it ran at the Burg in 1922 with considerable success (Trebitsch 1953: 183–4), Conolly-Smith points out that *Gitta* had run for only seven nights in Vienna in 1920 and even less in Berlin subsequently (2013: 101).

32 Antoine Berman underlines the importance of the desire to translate (*pulsion de traduire*) that lies behind every translation project (*projet de traduction*), in a conceptual framework that has been adopted and put into circulation by translation scholars since he brought out *L'Épreuve de l'étranger* in 1984 (published in English translation as *The Experience of the Foreign* in 1992).

33 The publication contains 'Maternity', translated by Charlotte Frances Payne-Townsend Shaw, identified as 'Mrs Bernard Shaw'; the two other plays, 'The Three Daughters of M. Dupont' and 'Damaged Goods' were translated by St. John Hankin and John Pollock, respectively. Charlotte Shaw wrote a short foreword and her husband a preface of nearly fifty pages. Subsequent editions also included a new version of 'Maternity' translated by John Pollock to correspond to a revised version

of the original French play. Because of their subject matter – unwed mothers and venereal disease – the plays were censored in England, and production and publication were difficult until Brieux was elected to the Académie française.

34 It is perhaps no accident that Shaw initially misinterpreted the title of Trebitsch's play, calling it 'Frau Gitta's Transgression', confusing *Sühne* (atonement) with *Sünde* (transgression) (Letter of 26 February 1920, Weiss 1986: 212, n. 2; quoted in Gahan 2004: 165, n. 51).

35 The theme of revenge is taken up explicitly by Conolly-Smith, who likens Shaw's 'cheating' on Trebitsch's original text to Jitta's infidelity (2013: 96 ff).

36 It has been suggested that Shaw added his notoriously long stage directions, and prefaces, to make the printed books longer, thereby making them more economically profitable and elevating the status of the theatrical works from mere entertainment to true literature.

37 See Ortrun Zuber-Skerritt's edited collection of articles on transformations that occur in the theatre, *Page to Stage: Theatre as Translation* (1984); the volume includes the earlier Lefevere essay on refraction mentioned in note 28.

38 The terms 'domestication' and 'foreignization' denote translation strategies according to which translators will make a text conform, or not, to the norms of the target culture. Building on Schleiermacher and Berman, Venuti introduced these concepts to translation studies in his 1995 work *The Translator's Invisibility: A History of Translation*. In reintroducing this age-old binarism, Venuti injects an ideological dimension, viewing foreignization as the only ethical choice. Translator/theoreticians have more recently advocated finding a middle ground, or compromise: see Michael Henry Heim, 'To Foreignize or Not to Foreignize' (2013) and David Bellos, 'Fictions of the Foreign' (2013).

39 Gilbert's play, *Pygmalion and Galatea*, was first presented in 1871. *Saint Joan* is obviously based on Shaw's research and his interpretation of the Joan of Arc story, but the play is also said to have been inspired by the parallel story of the exploits of T.H. Lawrence, the so-called 'Lawrence of Arabia', as Weintraub suggests (1996: 162 ff).

40 The reference to 'public' needs explanation. Because of censorship at the time, some theatres were constituted as private clubs. This was the case for the Arts Theatre located in London's West End (theatre district), which opened in 1927 as a members-only club for the performance of unlicensed plays. *Jitta* was never performed in one of the later, commercial theatres of the West End. The play was revived in 1939 on 15 May and 22 May, at the 'Q' Theatre and 'Embassy, Swiss Cottage', respectively, which are both small and independent theatres (Mander and Mitchenson 1955: 200).

41 *Pygmalion* premiered, in Trebitsch's German translation, at the Hofburg Theatre in Vienna on 16 October 1913. It opened at His Majesty's Theatre, in London's West End, on 11 April 1914, and ran for 118 performances (Evans 1997: 223).

42   Lightning Strikes is an off-off-Broadway theatre company, founded in 1990 but
     now apparently defunct, which described itself as an 'award winning not-for-
     profit company of emerging actors, directors, writers and designers' (http://
     www.zoominfo.com/c/Lightning-Strikes-Theatre-Company/36242820, accessed
     23 April 2016). In 2008, Project Shaw was in the third of four years, performing
     all of Shaw's plays at The Players Club. Described as 'New York's most legendary
     private club', this small theatre located at Grammercy Park was founded by
     the Shakespearean actor Edwin Booth, along with Mark Twain and others
     (Broadwayworld.com 2008).

43   Bertha Kalich, known as the 'Jewish Bernhardt', was a star of Yiddish theatre when
     it was in its heyday, but she also performed over a hundred different roles in several
     languages in Eastern Europe as well as the United States. Her association with the
     play undoubtedly gave it some prestige, although Langner was unconvinced of its
     success.

44   The prize recognized a body of work 'marked by both idealism and humanity,
     its stimulating satire often being infused with a singular poetic beauty'. A
     presentation speech was read at the ceremony by Per Hallström, chairman of
     the Nobel Committee of the Swedish Academy. It is of note that, after years of
     struggling with his French translators and receiving less exposure in France
     than in other countries, Shaw is compared to France's most beloved playwright:
     'In France he has been called the Molière of the twentieth century; and there is
     some truth in the parallel'. The claim was first made by Augustin Hamon, who,
     in attempting to promote Shaw, produced an entire book entitled *Le Molière du
     XXe siècle: Bernard Shaw* (translated as *The Twentieth Century Moliere: Bernard
     Shaw*). Sir Arthur Grant Duff, the British ambassador, gave thanks on behalf of
     Bernard Shaw, who was not in attendance, and announced that the prize would
     serve to strengthen cultural ties between Sweden and Great Britain (Nobel
     Prize website, www.nobelprize.org/nobel_prizes/literature/laureates/1925/
     press.html, accessed 5 October 2015). George Bernard Shaw is the only person
     to have won both a Nobel (Literature) and an Oscar (Screenplay); Al Gore is
     alleged to be tied with him, having won the Nobel Peace prize and an Oscar
     (although the award was given for the film 'An Inconvenient Truth', which Gore
     directed, rather than to him personally). The Bernard Shaw prize for translation,
     administered by the Society of Authors on behalf of the George Bernard Shaw
     estate, was instituted in 1991 and has been given out every three years since
     then. The 2015 prize, in the amount of £2000, was presented in 2016 to Thomas
     Teal for his translation of *The Listener* by Tove Jansson. See the websites of the
     Anglo-Swedish Literary Foundation (http://www.swedenabroad.com/en-GB/
     Embassies/London/Contact/Anglo-Swedish-Literary-Foundation/) and the
     Society of Authors (http://www.societyofauthors.org/bernard-shaw-prize,
     accessed 22 April 2016).

Chapter 2

1 This emblematic quip, 'America is my country and Paris is my hometown', is taken from Gertrude Stein's 1936 essay 'An American and France', reproduced in *What are Masterpieces* (1940: 61–70).

2 Gertrude Stein's 'triumphant return' to the United States has been described on the Smithsonian website as a 'barnstorming visit to her native country'. Over a six-month period extending from October 1934 to May 1935, she crisscrossed the country for 191 days, during which she gave seventy-four lectures in thirty-seven cities in twenty-three states (Gambino 2011).

3 The expression 'lost generation' was coined by Stein. It was popularized by Ernest Hemingway, who used it as an epigraph to his 1926 novel *The Sun Also Rises* and explained its origin in his memoir, *A Moveable Feast*, although his version conflicts with Stein's (Mellow 1974: 273–4). The term usually refers to the artists who came of age during the First World War, and then lived in voluntary exile in Paris between the two wars.

4 Putnam, who was founding editor of *The New Review* and a prolific translator (for example, of Cervantes and Rabelais), apparently took on Hugnet's *Enfances*. Stein scholar Ulla Dydo (2003: 303, n. 50) originally noted that Putnam had translated and published the poem after Hugnet and Stein quarrelled. She later concluded that the translation never actually appeared. Posted online by Dydo on 24 March 2006 under the heading 'Plenty More Stein Work': http://epc.buffalo.edu/authors/stein/dydo.html (accessed 6 July 2015).

5 McCullough traces the origin of the expression 'American in Paris' to a book published in 1837 by John Sanderson, who aspired to be 'the Boswell of Paris'; it was released in the United States as *Sketches of Paris: In Familiar Letters to his Friends; by an American in Paris*, and in London under the title *The American in Paris* (McCullough 2011: 58). Nancy L. Green, on the other hand, attributes the designation to a later publication: Albert Sutliffe's *The Americans in Paris* (1887), a sort of 'Who's Who' which lists names, addresses, and visiting days. Sutliffe's book, she says, 'participated in the construction of the community by the very act of publication'. Interestingly, the epigraph to Sutliffe's book is 'willing exiles'. Green writes about the Americans of the Right Bank, who lived in a 'gilded ghetto'; members of a 'transnational elite', they worked in business and diplomacy, although attracted to Paris by the same desire for freedom as those in the artistic community. By the mid-1920s, up to 40,000 Americans lived in Paris, but they still made up only the sixth largest group of foreigners in Paris. Writers and artists comprised less than one-tenth of the total number of Americans in Paris at that time (Green 2014).

6 *The Autobiography of Alice B. Toklas* is hereafter referred to as '*Autobiography*'. I have followed the custom of transcribing quotations from Stein's work exactly

as she wrote them, using her idiosyncratic syntax, spelling, and punctuation: for example, usually no capitalization on proper nouns or adjectives such as 'American' and no italics for titles of books.

7   Mellow attributes the expression 'love letter to France' to American journalist Kate Buss, who used it in a letter she wrote to Stein after reading *Paris France* (Mellow 1974: 438).

8   In 1963, Leon Katz wrote a doctoral dissertation on the genesis of *The Making of Americans*, based on an examination of Stein's notebooks and drafts of the novel, as well as on interviews with Toklas.

9   Bilignin (also spelled Billignin) is a hamlet in the town, or commune, of Belley, situated in a region called Le Bugey, in the administrative *département* of Ain. Stein and Toklas first discovered Belley, in the Rhone Valley, in the mid-1920s. They used to stay at the Hôtel Pernollet at Belley until 1929, when they found a house to rent in Bilignin. When the owner reclaimed his house, they moved to another house in nearby Culoz.

10 Stein met Van Vechten, a writer and portrait photographer, in 1913. She observes that he was 'the first person who published me ... a great believer in me from the very beginning' ('Transatlantic Interview' in Stein 1971b: 30). Van Vechten remained close to her throughout her life, ultimately becoming her literary executor and helping to bring out her unpublished works.

11 Thomson, an American composer, was friends with Stein from 1925 until her death, except for a brief period during which they had a falling out over the Hugnet affair. They collaborated on the opera *Four Saints in Three Acts*, first produced in the United States in 1934. In his autobiography, Thomson takes credit for having been Stein's 'translator, impresario, music setter, and literary agent' (1967: 96).

12 Personal correspondence with Joan Chapman by email (12 June 2014). Ms Chapman is the stepdaughter of Paul Genin, who was Stein's neighbour in the country. The owner of a silk factory in Lyons, Genin was well off. He offered to lend Stein money once the United States had entered the war and she no longer had access to funds she had been receiving from home. Six months later, Stein sold a Cézanne painting and paid Genin back. This anecdote is reported in Burns and Dydo (1996: 418) and alluded to in *Wars I Have Seen* (112).

13 *Paris France* was written in late 1939 and early 1940, and published in June 1940 just after Paris fell to the Germans. It would have been important at that time to demonstrate one's ties to France. Could Stein's professed love affair with France be tinged with opportunism? By the time she published *Wars I Have Seen* in 1945, on the other hand, it would have been more advantageous to emphasize how American she had been all along, since by now the Americans had helped to win the war, and she had become a celebrity for surviving it.

14 In Vienna, for example, they visited monuments and museums, took piano lessons and went skating; in Paris, they walked, shopped, visited the Louvre, and went to

the opera, ballet, and theatre. After her death, Amelia (Keyser) Stein's diaries went to her other daughter, Bertha, who then passed them on to her daughter, Gertrude Stein Raffel. Raffel wrote a biographical essay based on this material (1971). The diaries, dated 1878–1886, are now held by The Bancroft Library. Some of this information is provided online by Dydo at the site referred to previously: http://epc.buffalo.edu/authors/stein/dydo.html.

15 'My Debt to Books' was published jointly with Roda Roda in *Books Abroad* in the summer 1939 edition, as part of a 'symposium on literary influences' that had appeared in the journal since 1936 (Editor's note, 308).

16 Letter dated 16 November 1947 from Alice Toklas to Wm Clifford in response to a letter received November 11 (YCAL MSS 77, Box 12, Folder 190).

17 The portrait was purchased by Gertrude and Leo, and is clearly visible among many other works of art in several of the photos taken of the apartment at rue de Fleurus (Bishop, Debray, and Rabinow 2011: 361–76). Titled 'Madame Cézanne à l'éventail' (The Artist's Wife with a Fan), it was one of about two dozen pictures Cézanne painted of his wife, sometime between 1878 and 1888. It is now held by the Foundation E.G. Bührle Collection in Zurich. See Figure 2.

18 Gustave Flaubert's book was originally published in 1877. The edition held in the Toklas-Stein collection at Yale is the following: *Trois Contes* (Paris: Eugène Fasquelle, 1900; nouvelle édition). The three stories are: *Un cœur simple* (A Simple Heart); *Légende de Saint Julien l'Hospitalier* (Saint Julian the Hospitalier) and *Hérodias* (Hérodias). A bookplate, which reads 'From the Library of GERTRUDE STEIN. Gift of ALICE B. TOKLAS and ALAN D. STEIN' is pasted onto the inside cover. In the 'Transatlantic Interview', conducted in 1946, Stein says that in writing the *Making of Americans,* just before and just after *Three Lives*, she made 'endless diagrams of every human being' (Stein 1971b: 16). Would this piece of doodling in the back of the Flaubert book be one of those diagrams? Otherwise, there is no indication that the book has been pored over as would have been the case had she done a real 'translation'. It is interesting to note, in contrast, that her copy of Pétain's *Paroles aux Français*, to which we return in a subsequent section, has a more used and worn appearance, with markings in ink and red pencil, and some pages folded back. Manuscripts (along with related materials such as photographs and works of arts) are held at Yale University, Gertrude Stein and Alice B. Toklas Papers, Yale Collection of American Literature, Beinecke Rare Book and Manuscript Library, hereafter referred to as 'YCAL'.

19 See, for example, Sutherland's 'anatomy' of *Three Lives* (DeKoven 2006: 263–84; reprinted from his 1951 biography) and Walker's '*Three Lives*: The Realism of the Composition' (DeKoven 2006: 339–58; reprinted from a 1984 study). Walker recognizes that she 'soon abandoned' the translation to write her own story, but says that the title of that story is in 'deliberate homage' to Flaubert's *Trois Contes* (339).

20 Donald Gallup (1948) has documented the history of the publication of *Three Lives*. Stein tried repeatedly to have the work published with the assistance of several of her friends. While prospective publishers were favourable, they had concerns about the book's marketability. Stein ended up having it published in 1909 at her own expense (for $750.38). At the publisher's suggestion, she changed the word 'histories' in the title to 'lives' to avoid confusion with the works of history and genealogy in which the press specialized.

21 Letter to Stein from Mabel Foote Weeks dated 21 April 1907 (quoted in Gallup 1948: 73). Gallup also quotes a positive review, which appeared in the *Kansas City Star* on 18 December 1909, praising the 'originality of its narrative form' (Gallup 1948: 79).

22 The 'Stanzas' are included in Stein (1998a). The timeframe for the composition of the *Autobiography* is a fiction in itself. In *Everybody's Autobiography* (1937: 9), Stein claims to have written it over a six-week period in the fall of 1932, whereas it would appear that she started it as early as the spring of the same year (Dydo 1985: 20, n. 12).

23 Letter of 16 November 1947 to Wm (William) Clifford (cited in note 16). The veracity, or at least reliability, of Toklas has been called into question, however. See Malcolm (2006): 'Ulla Dydo and Edward Burns often spoke of Toklas as a liar'.

24 George Sand was the pseudonym for Amantine Aurore Lucile Dupin, baronne Dudevant (1804–1876). Her literary career began with a few stories she wrote in collaboration with her lover, Jules Sandeau, under the pseudonym 'Jules Sand', a name that led to the pseudonym she used when she began to publish her own work. The statue of George Sand, sculpted by François Sicard, and inaugurated in 1904, still stands at the East entrance of the Gardens, not far from the rue de Fleurus where Stein lived (website of the Senate of France, http://senat.fr/visite/jardin/statues.html, accessed 23 February 2016).

25 In a letter of 29 August 1877 to George Sand's son, Maurice Sand, Flaubert writes: 'I had begun *Un cœur simple* solely on account of her, only to please her. She died while I was in the midst of this work. Thus it is with our dreams' (Sand–Flaubert 1979: 374; 'J'avais commencé *Un cœur simple* à son intention exclusive, uniquement pour lui plaire. Elle est morte, comme j'étais au milieu de mon œuvre. Il en est ainsi de tous nos rêves', Flaubert 2011, n.p.). Flaubert hoped that his story would prove to Sand that he was capable of showing sympathy for his characters, but she died without having read it (Prentki, n.d., http://flaubert.univrouen.fr/etudes/prentkigb.php?imp=1). Alice had read Flaubert's correspondence, but if she discussed the Sand connection with Stein it would not have been until after her arrival in Paris in 1907, by which time *Three Lives* was well under way.

26 YCAL MSS 77, Box 29, Folder 523; emphasis added. She had also considered the alternate pseudonyms 'Jane Sandys' and 'Pauline Manders'.

27 Carl Wood, whose article on Stein's 'homage to Laforgue' is reprinted in the same volume, offers a slightly different English version: 'I'm unhappy of course, and it's neither my fault nor life's' (2006: 303). My preferred translation would be: 'I am an unhappy person, yes, but it is not my fault, nor the fault of life'. All of which is moot, since it would seem that the French quotation has quite simply been fabricated by Gertrude Stein. Wood's article originally appeared in 1975 in *Comparative Literature Studies* 12: 147–58. In his detailed footnote (304, n. 8), he cites Brinnin (1959), Sutherland (2006 [1951]), and Mellow (1974). I did not locate the Laforgue reference either, doing a search on an electronic copy of *Moralités légendaires*.

28 The authenticity of this statement has been challenged by Allan H. Gilbert (1978) in his review of Timothy Webb's book. Gilbert points out that Shelley actually said so little about translation theory that Webb was 'driven to probabilities' (1978: 158). The view of translation as exercise has nevertheless circulated as an idea stemming from Shelley.

29 A letter from Arnold Rönnebeck to Stein, dated 23 April 1941, confirms that he translated the 'Portrait of Mabel Dodge' into German and French (Gallup 1953: 355).

30 *Q.E.D.*, published only after Stein's death under the title *Things as They Are*, was composed on the basis of her correspondence with May Bookstaver, the woman with whom she had been in love. Of the three 'lives', 'Melanctha' is most directly derived from this real-life experience. Once the earlier manuscript was discovered and the truth behind it revealed, Alice insisted that the correspondence with May be destroyed and that all occurrences of the word 'may' – as a verb, as a given name, for example – be stricken from the *Stanzas in Meditation*, which Gertrude was writing at the same time, and replaced with the sometimes nonsensical 'can'. From the spring of 1932 on, Alice and Gertrude continued to quarrel off and on for some years (Dydo 1985; Galvin 2013).

31 Imbs is referring to pianist Allen Tanner, the lover of Russian artist Pavel Tchelitchew, both of whom were among Stein's friends. Imbs was an American writer and musician, whose biographical book on Chatterton was translated by Gertrude Stein's translator, Baronne J. Seillière, as *Vie de Chatterton*. His is one of many memoirs evoking the Lost Generation period (see Monk 2008). Alice put an end to the relationship with Imbs, allegedly because he had been planning to take his wife to the country near Bilignin to have her baby and Gertrude abhorred the idea of childbirth.

32 Website of the Carlton Lake Collection at the Harry Ransom Humanities Research Center, The University of Texas Austin, where the Georges Hugnet papers are held (http://www.lib.utexas.edu/taro/uthrc/00294/hrc-00294.html, accessed 9 March 2016). According to the site, Hugnet and Stein met in 1926, whereas Thomson gives 1927 as the date (1967: 94).

33 'Le Berceau de Gertrude Stein ou le Mystère de la rue de Fleurus/Huit poèmes de Georges Hugnet', accompanied by a musical composition by Virgil Thomson, 'Lady Godiva's Waltzes', was presented by the two young men to Gertrude Stein in April 1928. Hugnet wrote an essay entitled 'La Vie de Gertrude Stein' as an introduction to Louise Langlois's translation of Stein's 'A Saint in Seven', published in the periodical *Orbes* 2 (Spring 1929: 59–61) and later used as the basis for the preface to his *Morceaux choisis*. Translated into English by Basil Kingstone as 'Life of Gertrude Stein', it is reproduced in Dilworth and Holbrook (2010: 309–11). At issue in this essay is Stein's translatability: in her case, 'more than with other writers, translation would be a betrayal' (Dilworth and Holbrook 2010: 310).

34 It is interesting to note Stein's anglicized spelling of Hugnet's given name, without the final 's'. Hugnet's rather odd method of translation is revealed in a letter of December 1928 to Virgil Thomson. Commenting on this letter, the editors observe that an 'interesting Steinian French' has come about through this collaborative translation. They quote Hugnet: 'In this translation what is not "French" is not French because in the text English is not "English"' (Dilworth and Holbrook 2010: 96 and 96 n.; their translation). Hugnet does not appear to know enough English to do the translation on his own, since he needs Thomson's help, as well as the crib Stein has prepared for him.

35 Stein expresses the same views about Shakespearean sonnets in the 'Transatlantic Interview' (Stein 1971b). The comment that she had never translated foreign literature beforehand would seem to confirm that the presumed Flaubert translation was not a wholehearted translation effort.

36 As Hugnet wrote to Stein, 'Ce n'est pas une traduction, c'est autre chose, [in red] c'est mieux. Je fais plus qu'aimer ce reflet, j'en rêve et je l'admire' (quoted by Dydo 2003: 309, who translates this statement as: 'This is not a translation, it is something else, *it is better*', 309, n. 71). Thomson quotes a letter from Stein to Hugnet in which she says, 'la traduction qui est plutôt reflet … C'était pour moi une experience riche et intriguante …' ('The translation is more like a reflection … It was for me a rich and fascinating experience …') (1967: 185–6; Thomson's translation).

37 This helpful example is cited by Posman (2009), who unfortunately goes on to draw conclusions based on her erroneous transcription of the word 'untied' as 'united'.

38 Hugnet's French version, in italics, is followed by Stein's translation. The opening stanzas of the first and last poems of the thirty-poem cycle are quoted, along with the concluding lines of the entire cycle. Stein's translation is reproduced as it appeared in a bilingual version in the magazine *Pagany*.

39 The amended version in the right-hand column was published in the Plain Edition. Alice Toklas had launched this press to disseminate Stein's books, so often rejected by other publishers. The first book to be released was *Lucy Church Amiably* (January 1931). *Before the Flowers of Friendship Faded Friendship Faded* followed in May 1931.

40 My translation of: 'Deux fois seulement, Gertrude Stein se lança dans l'entreprise de
    la traduction. Et les deux fois, elle fut « mauvaise » traductrice'; again, the Flaubert
    translation is not included among her achievements in translation.

41 The events have been recorded by witnesses Thomson, in his memoir *Virgil
    Thomson*, as well as Imbs, in his *Confessions of Another Young Man* (1936:
    298–300). The quarrel has been discussed by biographers such as Sprigge (1957),
    Bridgman (1971), and Mellow (1974), and summed up in meticulous detail by
    Dydo (2003). A letter dated 18 December 1930 shows that Hugnet consulted
    colleagues and publishers before insisting on his 'prior right' (Gallup 1953: 244–5).
    The 'flowers of friendship' anecdote is reported by Bernard Faÿ (1966: 146), as well
    as Toklas (1963: 147); however, Dydo believes Stein had already used the sentence
    in an earlier work, *A Novel of Thank You* (2003: 320, n. 80). Gertrude Stein, of
    course, did not hesitate to tell her side of the story.

42 The letters from Wilder to Stein and Toklas are in the Stein-Toklas collection
    and the letter from Marie-Louise Bousquet in the Thornton Wilder papers, all at
    YCAL. Bousquet was Paris editor of *Harper's Bazaar*. Starting in 1918, she and her
    playwright husband Jacques Bousquet maintained a salon where Picasso, Aldous
    Huxley, and other creative people gathered. Rumoured to be gossipy, her catty
    remarks about Gertrude Stein are not surprising.

43 The French excerpt is taken from Peyret-Chappuis (1938), and the English
    from a holograph manuscript (YCAL, box folder 425; note that the title, in
    Stein's handwriting, is 'Phrenesie', followed by the notation 'Play and beginning
    translation'). The translation, including punctuation, or lack of it, is transcribed
    exactly as it appears in Stein's holograph manuscript, although occasional words
    have been added in brackets when required for the sense. It should be noted that
    there are few hesitations in this manuscript. Stein has made no revisions, in stark
    contrast to the Pétain translation we will look at next.

44 Early accounts mention a thirty-six-hour pass (Mellow 1974: 237; Burns and Dydo
    1987). Biographers also indicate that they did not find their passports, but did put
    their hands on papers documenting their poodle Basket's pedigree – which proved
    to be a good thing because it enabled them to obtain rations for the dog during
    the war.

45 Pétain's *Paroles aux Français. Messages et écrits 1934–1941* was published in Paris
    in 1941 by Lardanchet, under the auspices of the *Comité France-Amérique*, edited
    by journalist and academic Gabriel-Louis Jaray. The *Comité* was founded in 1909
    to improve relations between France and Francophile elites in American states,
    including Quebec. Pétain was the honorary president in 1937–1938; Canadian
    Prime Minister Mackenzie King had also been an honorary president before
    that (Amyot 1999: 202, n. 124; the Canadian government under Mackenzie
    King supported the Pétain régime from 1940 to 1942, and Québécois remained

sympathetic to Pétain for even longer than English Canadians). There is evidence that it was Jaray, executive director of the *Comité* and a friend of Faÿ, who made the arrangements for Stein to translate the Pétain book (Will 2011: 239, n. 4).

46 See also Sprigge (1957), Bridgman (1971), Mellow (1974), and Wagner-Martin (1995).

47 Belgian-born Paul de Man was an influential literary critic in the United States, a member of the Yale School of Deconstruction. After his death in 1983, it was revealed that he had written around two hundred articles for Belgian collaborationist newspapers during the Second World War, some of them considered to be overtly anti-Semitic. Will highlights how 'seemingly progressive or avant-garde' writers and philosophers came to embrace fascist or pro-Nazi ideologies (2011: 13).

48 See, for example, Compagnon (2009), Davis (1998), Galvin (2016), Levine (1999), Malcolm (2007), Van Puymbroeck (2015), Whittier-Ferguson (1999), and Will (2004, 2008, and 2011). Also of note is the *Jacket2* dossier, edited by Bernstein (2012), in particular the articles by Burns, Paris, and Stendhal.

49 Hikind writes about Stein's 'despicable behavior' in http://dovhikind.blogspot. ca/2012/05/hikind-demands-metropolitan-museum-of.html (accessed 4 April 2016). (See also http://observer.com/2012/05/local-politicians-get-met-to-disclose-gertrude-steins-nazi-past/, accessed 4 April 2016.) The nearly 500-page catalogue, *The Steins Collect*, contains several references to Gertrude Stein's relationship to Faÿ; it specifically mentions her translation of Pétain's speeches (Bishop, Debray, and Rabinow 2011: 238, 244–5, 250, n. 26, and 329), and includes a note (265, n. 10) regarding previous studies by Burns and Dydo, Malcolm and Will. The public, of course, could not have been expected to read the voluminous catalogue closely. It is possible that a growing interest in the restitution of Nazi-looted or spoliated artwork, particularly since the adoption of the Washington Conference Principles or Protocols in 1998, has led to a heightened public sensitivity to the matter of Jewish-owned collections that somehow survived the Second World War. Scholars continue to contribute to an increasingly nuanced picture of what must remain, for the time being in any case, a dark and complex period in the history of art collecting in Europe (see Greenberg 2010).

50 Pétain was undoubtedly responsible for some heinous acts of anti-Semitism, but, according to my reading of the speeches, they do not explicitly set out his anti-Jewish policies.

51 Burns delivered the lecture, 'So I Went on Looking at Pictures: Gertrude Stein's Last Decade' on 29 April 2012, in conjunction with the exhibition 'The Steins Collect'. This was later published as 'Gertrude Stein: A complex itinerary, 1940–1944' in the *Jacket2* dossier.

52 Faÿ's 1925 book, *L'Esprit révolutionnaire en France et aux États-Unis à la fin du XVIIIᵉ siècle*, was considered by the Pulitzer Prize committee, but rejected because

it was in a foreign language (Fischer 1994: xxiii–xxiv). It was released in English in 1927.

53   See Figure 3. Timothy Young, archivist and curator at the Beinecke Library (Yale), has put forward the hypothesis that she may have destroyed other manuscripts and kept only those that show her thoughts flowing smoothly onto the page, as a true genius might write. Alternatively, we could conclude that her ideas genuinely flow easily when she is composing in English rather than struggling to find the words to match someone else's words originally written in a foreign language.

54   The draft of this speech was written in the second of three manuscript notebooks, but this is one of the few speeches for which a typed copy exists. Several pages of typescript, some of which are missing, are included in YCAL folder 1141. The typed pages quoted are numbered 13 and 14. The typescript is reproduced as is, with some errors of transcription. Stein incorrectly wrote 20th of June in the notebook, whereas the original speech dates from the 23rd. I have kept the lines exactly as they appear in the typescript and numbered them for ease of reference. Stein's handwriting is difficult to read. When a word is completely illegible, it is marked as 'word?'

55   Janet Flanner, a prominent member of the expatriate community in Paris, wrote a column for *The New Yorker* under the pseudonym 'Genêt'. After returning to the United States in 1944, she produced a series of articles on Pétain, entitled 'La France et le Vieux', reissued as a book, *Pétain: The Old Man of France*. Stein is said to have helped Flanner with her profile, considered to be 'as positive, and as innocuous, as Stein's introduction' (Wagner-Martin 1995: 247).

56   The article in *Life*, 'The Liberation of Gertrude Stein', was by Frank Gervasi (1944). Stein wrote an article for *Life* entitled 'Off We All Went to See Germany' (1945b). See Whittier-Ferguson (2001).

57   For example, the monthly magazine *Confluences*, begun in July 1941 in Lyon, published Stein, as well as Max Jacob, Louis Aragon, Jean-Paul Sartre, André Malraux and André Gide, all 'key members of the intellectual resistance'. Stein and Toklas were close to the magazine's editor, René Tavernier, a friendship that was considered dangerous for them (Wagner-Martin 1995: 247–8; Galvin 2016: 263).

Chapter 3

1   From Paul Auster's 'Foreword' to Esther Allen (2007). A more succinct version is used by Alexandra Lopes as an epigraph to her 2015 article, 'Notes on World Literature and Translation'. Similar sentiments were expressed by Mo Yan, recipient of the 2012 Nobel Prize in literature, when he spoke at the Nobel Banquet, 10 December 2012: 'I also want to express my respect for the translators from

various countries who have translated my work. Without you, there would be no world literature. Your work is a bridge that helps people to understand and respect each other', http://www.nobelprize.org/nobel_prizes/literature/laureates/2012/yan-speech_en.html#not, accessed 21 January 2016.

2   This assessment of Auster's prolific and varied output has been widely quoted. It is drawn from a review by Daniel Dyer that first appeared in the *Plain Dealer* (Cleveland) in January 2006. Since the book review was first published, the quote has appeared, among other endorsements, in the front matter for the 2005 novel, *The Brooklyn Follies*, and has been put into circulation on the numerous websites advertising the book. See, for example: http://www.powells.com/book/brooklyn-follies-9780312426231 and even the German Amazon site, http://www.amazon.de/The-Brooklyn-Follies-Paul-Auster/dp/0312426232, both accessed 19 January 2016.

3   Other autobiographical works include: *The Art of Hunger* (1992) and *Hand to Mouth: A Chronicle of Early Failure* (1997a). Paul Auster was kind enough to invite me to his elegant brownstone in the Park Slope area of Brooklyn, where, one steamy day in June 2013, we chatted at length about writing and translation. Much of what he had to say on the topic had already appeared in published interviews (In *Collected Prose* and *Conversations with Paul Auster*, for example). Fresh insights or new information quoted from the interview is followed by the designation 'PA-int'.

4   In addition to the information provided by Auster during our interview, I have relied on two obituaries, the first published on the website of Wake Forest University, http://inside.wfu.edu/2011/11/retired-professor-allen-mandelbaum-dies/, and the second in *The New York Times* by William Grimes, http://www.nytimes.com/2011/11/06/arts/allen-mandelbaum-translator-of-divine-comedy-dies-at-85.html?ref=obituaries&_r=0, both accessed 29 January 2016. During our interview, Auster added that in his (then) forthcoming autobiographical book (*Report from the Interior*, 2013), his uncle is 'mentioned by name' suggesting that this will be the first time. This is not entirely accurate as the name 'Allen' appears in the 1989 interview mentioned in the previous note, as well as in a later one (Campbell 2005). However, the 2013 memoir not only refers to Allen Mandelbaum by name; Auster also provides a substantial biographical endnote, which concludes with an almost surprising sanctification of the uncle, 'May his name be hallowed forever' (*Report from the Interior*, 219).

5   See, for example, the 1989 *Mississippi Review* interview with Larry McCaffery and Sinda Gregory, reprinted in *Collected Prose* (542), and a 2010 interview with Helena de Bertodano published in *The Telegraph*.

6   In addition to the *Little Anthology*, *The Random House Book of Twentieth-Century French Poetry* and Clastres's *Chronicles*, which will be discussed in greater detail later in this chapter, Auster's main published works as a translator are: *Fits and Starts: Selected Poems of Jacques Dupin* (1974); *The Uninhabited:*

Selected Poems of André du Bouchet (1976); *Life/Situations: Essays Written and Spoken* (1977); *A Tomb for Anatole* (1983); *The Notebooks of Joseph Joubert* (1983); *Vicious Circles: Two Fictions and 'After the Fact'* (1985); and *Joan Miró: Selected Writings and Interviews* (1986). A collection of previous translations, simply entitled *Translations* (1997b), brings together the work of Joubert, Mallarmé, du Bouchet, and Petit.

7   In the context of Hans Vermeer's *skopos* theory, the 'commissioner' participates in the translation process. See 'Skopos and Commission in Translational Action' in Venuti (2000).

8   The publication in this series has been called a kind of 'translation' in that it is an adaptation, or a popularization, of Clastres's original academic work. I am grateful to Christine York for sharing with me her excellent unpublished study of this translation in the context of Mona Baker's theory of 'framing' (2013: 1–2).

9   At the end of the book, Clastres provides a brief guide to pronunciation in the Ache language and a few remarks about the simplified system of transcription that he uses (Clastres 1972: 353).

10 *L'Éphémère* was a French magazine dedicated to poetry and art, founded in 1967 by Yves Bonnefoy, Louis-René Des Forêts, Jacques Dupin and André du Bouchet. Auster also names Michel Leiris and Paul Celan. The last issue, in which Clastres's piece appeared, was published in 1972.

11 See also the website of Guayakí Sustainable Rainforest Products, http://guayaki.com/about/134/The-Guayak%26iacute;-Story.html, accessed 27 January 2016.

12 As reported by Paul Auster in PA-int, and confirmed by Zone Books on their website, http://www.zonebooks.org/titles/CLAS_CHR.html, accessed 18 January 2016.

13 Geertz (2000) is quoted by York (2013: 7), who has brought my attention to several of these reviews.

14 See https://mitpress.mit.edu/books/chronicle-guayaki-indians, accessed 21 January 2016.

15 *Library Journal*, cited on the Amazon web site advertising the book, http://www.amazon.ca/Chronicle-Guayaki-Indians-Pierre-Clastres/dp/0942299787, accessed 21 January 2016.

16 Clastres uses quite a few Ache terms such as 'Yva javu' (with no glossary to explain them), along with proper names such as 'Chono' (sometimes accompanied by its translation 'Thunder'), which he leaves in roman type. They are used often enough that they are understandable from the context or the gloss provided by the author. Auster draws attention to the foreignness of the terms by using italics.

17 See Rainier Grutman (2018) and Dennis Barone (1995).

18 See Walter Benjamin, 'The Task of the Translator', first printed as an introduction to the translation of Baudelaire's *Tableaux parisiens*, 1923; translated by Harry

Zohn, reprinted in Venuti (2000: 17): 'The life of the originals attains in them [translations] to its ever-renewed latest and most abundant flowering', reaching, through such survival, what Benjamin calls 'the age of its fame'.

19 André du Bouchet, *Openwork. Poetry and Prose*, Selected, translated and presented by Paul Auster and Hoyt Rogers (2014). The dedication to du Bouchet is in the acknowledgements (x). Auster had referred to this forthcoming publication in the 2013 interview. The book was included on the Three Percent Best Translated Book Award Poetry Longlist for 2015, http://www.rochester.edu/College/translation/ threepercent/index.php?id=13972, accessed 8 January 2016.

20 Biographical information on Hoyt Rogers is taken from *Openwork* (320) and the website of *The Fortnightly Review* to which he is a contributor, http:// fortnightlyreview.co.uk/the-editors-and-contibutors/, accessed 19 January 2016.

21 The poems that Auster has translated are drawn from two collections by André du Bouchet, *Dans la chaleur vacante* (*In the Vacant Heat*, 1961) and *Où le soleil* (*Where the Sun*, 1968). Named after one of the poems, Auster's first compilation was titled *The Uninhabited: Selected Poems of André du Bouchet*, published by Living Hand editions, a publishing house Auster started with Lydia Davis. The poems were subsequently reprinted in *Translations* (1997b). Auster's preface to *The Uninhabited* is also reprinted, along with a variety of other prefaces, in *Collected Prose*.

22 James Joyce (1962). See O'Neill (2005): 'The earliest translated extracts from any language were those from *Anna Livia Plurabelle* translated into French in 1931 by Samuel Beckett and others … the first major (if still very partial) translation from the *Wake* in any language was André du Bouchet's 1962 collection of extracts in French translation entitled *Finnegans Wake: Fragments*' (2005: 27–8). Bio-bibliographic information on du Bouchet is taken from Rogers's introduction (OW, xi–xliii) and from the 'Select Bibliography' at the end of the book (OW, 311–13). Du Bouchet was the subject of a special edition of the journal *Europe* (June/July 2011) edited by Victor Martinez, who interviewed Paul Auster about his friendship and working relationship with du Bouchet.

23 The versions in *Openwork* have been carefully compared with those of *The Uninhabited* (1976), reprinted subsequently in *Translations* (1997b).

24 False friends (or *faux-amis* in French) are words in two languages that look or sound similar, but actually have different meanings. In this case, the words do not even have the same etymological origin since *écorcher* has a Latin root – *excorticare*, which means to remove the envelope – whereas the English word 'scorch' likely derives from the Old Norse *skorpna*, meaning 'to shrivel up'.

25 Repeated in a slightly different form in Delabastita (2009: 111), quoted by Kaindl (2014: 2).

26 The collection *Transfiction: Research into the Realities of Translation Fiction* (Kaindl and Spitzl 2014) resulted from a conference held in Vienna on the topic 'Fictional

Translators' in 2011. A follow-up conference, 'Beyond Transfiction: Translators and (Their) Authors', took place in Tel Aviv in 2013, resulting in a special edition of *Translation and Interpreting Studies* (Ben-Ari *et al.* 2016). A third conference, 'Transfiction 3: The Fictions of Translation', was hosted by Concordia University in Montreal (Woodsworth 2018).

27 Auster doesn't seem to think there are a lot of translators in his work. 'The only real translator, the only one who is described as such', he says, is Zimmer in *The Book of Illusions*. When I continue to probe, and mention that Quinn (*City of Glass*) is a former translator, he replies, 'Yes, but you don't know much about what he did'. When I mention *Invisible*, he concedes and remembers that he translated excerpts of the poetry of Bertran de Born for the novel. I ask whether he has consciously put in the French references – for instance, the girlfriend called Patty French and the French windows. His response is, 'I'm not going to say. But you're a very attentive reader, which is very nice' (PA-int).

28 The other two are *Ghosts* (1986) and *The Locked Room* (1986).

29 'Prelapsarian' pertains to the period before the fall of Adam and Eve, and a kind of direct language that is no longer possible. Milton is said to have portrayed prelapsarian and postlapsarian language in *Paradise Lost*. An interest in questions of pure language can be traced to the French poets, to Walter Benjamin, translator of Baudelaire, and to related thinkers whom Auster would have encountered in the course of his studies and subsequent years in France. To cite just two examples of links between translation and Babel, one of the most celebrated works on translation theory and history is *After Babel* by George Steiner, and the journal of the Fédération Internationale des Traducteurs is named *Babel*.

30 His emphasis on 'boys' got Auster into a bit of hot water in the press: he was challenged by the Huffington Post (Daniel 2014) and then 'defended' (Dean 2014).

31 Auster published an early work, *Squeeze Play* (1982), under the pseudonym 'Paul Benjamin'. Here, as in other novels, many details are borrowed from Auster's actual circumstances: the Riverside Drive apartment; the few years spent in France; studies at Columbia; a first wife called Delia (for Lydia), with whom he broke up in 1978; a second wife named 'Iris' (Siri spelled backwards); and a son called 'David' (Auster has a son named Daniel).

32 'NYC=USA' was originally published as 'The City and the Country' in *The New York Times*, 9 September 2002; reprinted in *Collected Prose*, 520–2.

33 Published not long after Chateaubriand's death in 1848, the *Mémoires* have been called 'Memoirs from Beyond the Grave' or 'Memoirs from Beyond the Tomb', but are titled 'Memoirs of a Dead Man' here (62). Auster's version in this novel differs from the widely circulated English translation by Robert Baldick (originally published by Hamish Hamilton in 1961 and released in 2014 in a Penguin edition). Baldick's translation includes Chateaubriand's 'Testamentary Preface' of 1833. Auster has based his translation, excerpts of which are quoted in the novel, on the

La Pléaide/Gallimard version, edited by Levaillant and Moulinier (Paris: 1951/1966) (66–8). The La Pléiade edition opens with the 1846 version of Chateaubriand's preface, titled 'Avant-propos' and includes the original 'Préface testamentaire' as an appendix. It is possible that Auster has consulted existing English translations, but, if so, he has made some changes. On pseudotranslation, see, for example, Douglas Robinson (1998). Macpherson's so-called 'translation' was published in 1760. Despite the fact that the Ossianic poems were a forgery, they had a tremendous impact on writers across Europe and were translated into a number of other languages. Robinson distinguishes between the 'found-manuscript conceit' of Cervantes and this classic example of pseudotranslation in which Macpherson, the author, is setting himself up as the translator.

34 Bertran de Born was a medieval troubadour, known for his love songs and political compositions. In Dante's *Inferno,* he is represented as a war-like figure carrying his severed head; Ezra Pound also translated de Born, and modelled some of his original poems after his.

35 The Lycophron incident is partly autobiographical. Auster discovered the ancient Greek poet, in French translation, during his stay in France in the early 1970s; when he returned to New York, he looked up an English translation, although he found one that was excellent instead of the Loeb Classical library translation he writes about in *Invisible* (Martinez 2011b: 21).

36 While Auster admits to knowing Lawrence Venuti, he says he was not at all aware of this particular book on translation (PA-int).

37 See Rosemary Arrojo's exploration of the 'search for authorial mastery' in her sensitive reading of Kafka, Borges, and Kosztolányi (2002).

38 The thirty-two-volume series was produced by Pierre Souvestre and Marcel Allain, followed by several film adaptations including a comic one in the 1960s featuring Louis de Funès and Jean Marais.

39 See http://www.ebooklibrary.org/article/whebn0000025022/paul%20auster and https://en.wikipedia.org/wiki/Plus_One_%282008_film%29, both accessed 22 January 2016.

40 'Je fus orfèvre de mes chaînes' (I was the goldsmith of my chains), *Eupalinos* (*Œuvres* II, 84).

41 Interviewed by Éric Clément for the Montréal Francophone daily, *La Presse*, on 26 April 2016, Auster is quoted as saying, 'C'est toujours difficile. Je m'investis chaque jour dans cette tâche comme je l'ai toujours fait. Après une journée de travail, j'étais si fatigué mentalement et physiquement que je m'écroulais littéralement sur mon lit'. It was reported then that Auster would be releasing a 925-page novel in 2017; the actual publication is 866 pages. It is beyond the scope of the present study to delve into the theme of transfiction in this new novel, but it would certainly merit further investigation. On Valéry's assessment of translation, see the Epilogue.

Epilogue

1   The term 'fictional turn', attributed to Else Vieira, was first used in an academic paper by Adriana Pagano (2000). See Delabastita and Grutman (2005: 28). On the figure of the translator in cinema, see Cronin (2008).

2   'I am you and you are me' is taken from Foer (2003: 214).

3   In her acknowledgements, Cantor cites 'Variations on the *Eclogues*', the English translation of 'Variations sur les *Bucoliques*', which Valéry wrote in 1942 as a preface to his translation of Virgil. In 1956, it was published posthumously along with the translation as *Traduction en vers des Bucoliques de Virgile précédé de variations sur les Bucoliques*, then included in *Œuvres* tome I. The English version, in a translation by Denise Folliot, first appeared in *The Art of* Poetry (London: Routledge & Kegan Paul, 1958) and was later reprinted in Schulte and Biguenet (1992: 113–26). This is the essay in which Valéry famously compared writing to translation: '*Écrire quoi que ce soit* ... est un travail de traduction exactement comparable à celui qui opère la transmutation d'un texte d'une langue dans une autre' (Valéry 1957: 211; emphasis in the original) ('Writing anything at all ... is a work of translation exactly comparable to that of transmuting a text from one language into another' [Valéry 1992: 116–7]).

References

Allen, Esther, ed. (2007), *To Be Translated or Not to Be, PEN/IRL Report on the International Situation of Literary Translation*, Barcelona: Institut Ramon Llull.

Allen, Esther and Susan Bernofsky, eds (2013), *In Translation. Translators on Their Work and What It Means*, New York: Columbia University Press.

Amyot, Eric (1999), *Le Québec entre Pétain et de Gaulle: Vichy, la France libre et les Canadiens français, 1940–1945*, Montréal: Fides.

Arrojo, Rosemary (2002), 'Writing, Interpreting, and the Power Struggle for the Control of Meaning: Scenes from Kafka, Borges, and Kosztolányi', in Maria Tymoczko and Edwin Gentzler (eds), *Translation and Power*, Amherst: University of Massachusetts Press, 63–79.

Auster, Paul, ed. (1982a), *The Random House Book of Twentieth-Century French Poetry*, New York: Random House.

Auster, Paul (1982b), *The Invention of Solitude*, in *Collected Prose*, New York: Henry Holt, 2010, 1–150.

Auster, Paul (1987), *In the Country of Last Things*, New York: Viking.

Auster, Paul (1989), *Moon Palace*, New York: Viking.

Auster, Paul (1989–1990), '*The Mississippi Review*. Interview with Larry McCaffery and Sinda Gregory', in *Collected Prose*, New York: Henry Holt, 2010, 539–68.

Auster, Paul (1991), *The Music of Chance*, London/Boston: Faber and Faber. [c1990].

Auster, Paul (1993), *Leviathan*, New York: Penguin Books. [1992].

Auster, Paul (1994a), *City of Glass* [c1985], in *The New York Trilogy*, Los Angeles, CA: Sun & Moon Press.

Auster, Paul (1994b), *The New York Trilogy*, Los Angeles, CA: Sun & Moon Press. [c1987].

Auster, Paul (1995), *The Red Notebook*, in *Collected Prose*, New York: Henry Holt, 2010, 243–64.

Auster, Paul (1997a), *Hand to Mouth: A Chronicle of Early Failure*, in *Collected Prose*, New York: Henry Holt, 2010, 151–240.

Auster, Paul (1997b), *Translations*, New York: Marsilio.

Auster, Paul (2002a), 'NYC=USA', in *Collected Prose*, New York: Henry Holt, 2010, 520–2.

Auster, Paul (2002b), *The Book of Illusions: A Novel*, New York: Henry Holt.

Auster, Paul (2003a), *Oracle Night*, New York: Henry Holt.

Auster, Paul (2003b), '*The Paris Review*. Interview with Michael Wood', in *Collected Prose*, New York: Henry Holt, 2010, 569–89.

Auster, Paul (2006), *The Brooklyn Follies*, New York: Henry Holt. [c2005].

Auster, Paul (2008), *Man in the Dark*, New York: Henry Holt.

Auster, Paul (2009), *Invisible*, Los Angeles/New York: Picador (Henry Holt).

Auster, Paul (2010a), *Sunset Park*, New York: Henry Holt.

Auster, Paul (2010b), *Collected Prose*, New York: Henry Holt.

Auster, Paul (2012), *Winter Journal*, New York: Henry Holt.

Auster, Paul (2013), *Report from the Interior*, New York: Henry Holt.

Auster, Paul (2014), 'Auster on Poe: A Conversation with Paul Auster and Isaac Gewirtz', 16 January, LIVE from the New York Public Library (copresented with The Morgan Library & Museum). Transcript available at: http://www.nypl.org/events/programs/2014/01/16/auster-poe-conversation-paul-auster-and-isaac-gewirtz?nref=121031 (accessed 8 February 2016).

Auster, Paul (2017), *4321: A Novel*, New York: Henry Holt.

Auster, Paul and Lydia Davis, eds and trans. (1972), *A Little Anthology of Surrealist Poems*, New York: Siamese Banana Press.

Baker, Mona and Gabriela Saldanha, eds (2009), *Routledge Encyclopedia of Translation Studies*, London/New York: Routledge.

Barnstone, Willis (1993), *The Poetics of Translation: History, Theory, Practice*, New Haven, CT: Yale University Press.

Barone, Dennis, ed. (1995), *Beyond the Red Notebook. Essays on Paul Auster*, Philadelphia: University of Pennsylvania Press.

Barthes, Roland (1968), 'The Death of the Author', trans. Richard Howard, Ubu Webb papers. Available at: http://www.tbook.constantvzw.org/wp-content/death_authorbarthes.pdf (accessed 21 July 2013).

Bellos, David (2013), 'Fictions of the Foreign: The Paradox of "Foreign-Soundingness"', in Esther Allen and Susan Bernofsky (eds), *In Translation. Translators on Their Work and What It Means*, New York: Columbia University Press, 31–43.

Ben-Ari, Nitsa, Patricia Godbout, Klaus Kaindl and Shaul Levin, eds (2016), 'Beyond Transfiction: Translators and (Their) Authors', *Translation and Interpreting Studies*, 11 (3).

Benjamin, Walter (2000), 'The Task of the Translator', in Lawrence Venuti (ed.), *The Translation Studies Reader*, London/New York: Routledge, 15–25. (First printed as an introduction to the translation of Baudelaire's *Tableaux parisiens*, 1923; reprinted in *Illuminations*, trans. Harry Zohn; ed. & intro. Hannah Arendt [New York: Harcourt Brace Jovanovich 1968], 69–82).

Benstock, Shari (1986), *Women of the Left Bank. Paris, 1900–1940*, Austin: University of Texas Press.

Bentley, Eric (1957), *Bernard Shaw, 1856–1950*, New York: New Directions.

Berman, Antoine (1992), *The Experience of the Foreign: Culture and Translation in Romantic Germany*, trans. Stefan Heyvaert, Albany, NY: SUNY Press. [English translation of *L'Épreuve de l'étranger*, 1984].

Bernstein, Charles, ed. (2012), 'Gertrude Stein's War Years: Setting the Record Straight. A Dossier', *Jacket2*, 9 May. Available at: https://jacket2.org/feature/gertrude-steins-war-years-setting-record-straight (accessed 3 August 2013).

Bertodano, Helena de (2010), 'Interview with Paul Auster', *The Telegraph*, 16 November. Available at: http://www.telegraph.co.uk/culture/books/authorinterviews/8128941/Paul-Auster-interview.html (accessed 20 July 2013).

Bhabha, Homi K. (1994), *The Location of Culture*, London/New York: Routledge.

Bishop, Janet, Cécile Debray, and Rebecca Rabinow, eds (2011), *The Steins Collect. Matisse, Picasso, and the Parisian Avant-Garde*, New Haven/London: San Francisco Museum of Modern Arts in association with Yale University Press.

Blanchot, Maurice (1985), *Vicious Circles: Two Fictions and 'After the Fact'*, trans. Paul Auster, Barrytown, NY: Station Hill.

Bridgman, Richard (1971), *Gertrude Stein in Pieces*, New York: Oxford University Press.

Brieux, Eugène (1921), *Three Plays*, trans. Charlotte F. Shaw, St. John Hankin, and John Pollock, foreword Charlotte F. Shaw, preface Bernard Shaw, London: Jonathan Cape. [c1911].

Brinnin, John Malcolm (1959), *The Third Rose: Gertrude Stein and Her World*, Boston, MA: Little, Brown.

Brion, Marcel (1930), 'Le Contrepoint poétique de Gertrude Stein', *Échanges*, 3: 122–28.

Broadwayworld.com (2008), 'Photo Coverage: Project Shaw's Jitta's Atonement', 19 November. Available at: http://www.broadwayworld.com/article/Photo-Coverage-Project-Shaws-JITTAS-ATONEMENT-20081119 (accessed 23 April 2016).

Brodzki, Bella (2007), *Can These Bones Live? Translation, Survival, and Cultural Memory*, Stanford, CA: Stanford University Press.

Brooks, Peter (1983), 'Re-Imagined in English', *The New York Times*, 23 January. Available at: https://www.nytimes.com/books/99/06/20/specials/auster–french.html (accessed 2 February 2016).

Burns, Carol, moderator (2003), 'Off the Page: Paul Auster', online interviews with Auster moderated by Burns, published in *The Washington Post*, 16 December; reprinted in James M. Hutchisson (ed.), *Conversations with Paul Auster*, Jackson, MS: University Press of Mississippi, 2013, 132–48.

Burns, Edward, ed. (1970), *Gertrude Stein on Picasso*, afterword by Leon Katz and Edward Burns, New York: Liveright.

Burns, Edward (2011), 'Alice Toklas and the Gertrude Stein Collection, 1946–1967', in Janet Bishop, Cécile Debray, and Rebecca Rabinow (eds), *The Steins Collect. Matisse, Picasso, and the Parisian Avant-Garde*, New Haven/London: San Francisco Museum of Modern Arts in association with Yale University Press, 259–65.

Burns, Edward (2012), 'Gertrude Stein: A Complex Itinerary, 1940–1944', in Charles Bernstein (ed.), 'Gertrude Stein's War Years: Setting the Record Straight', *Jacket2*. Available at: https://jacket2.org/article/gertrude-stein-complex-itinerary-1940%E2%80%931944 (accessed 3 August 2013).

Burns, Edward and Ulla E. Dydo (1987), 'Three Lives', letter to the editor, *The Nation*, 245 (19): 666.

Burns, Edward and Ulla E. Dydo, eds, with William Rice (1996), *The Letters of Gertrude Stein and Thornton Wilder*, New Haven, CT: Yale University Press.

Butor, Michael (1974), 'Travel and Writing', trans. John Powers and K. Lisker, *Mosaic*, 8 (1): 1–16.

Campbell, James (2005), 'The Mighty Quinn', *The Guardian*, 12 November. Available at: http://www.theguardian.com/books/2005/nov/12/fiction.shopping (accessed 30 January 2016).

Caneda Cabrera, M. Teresa (2008), 'Polyglot Voices, Hybrid Selves and Foreign Identities: Translation as a Paradigm of Thought for Modernism', *Atlantis. Revista de la Asociación española de studios anglo-americanos*, 30 (1): 53–67. Available at: http://www.jstor.org/stable/41055306 (accessed 6 November 2013).

Cantor, Rachel (2016), *Good on Paper*, Brooklyn, NY: Melville House Publishing.

Casanova, Pascale (2007), *The World Republic of Letters*, trans. Malcolm B. DeBevoise, Harvard, MA: Harvard University Press.

Chateaubriand, François-René de (1961), *The Memoirs of Chateaubriand*, selected and translated and with an introduction by Robert Baldick, London: Hamish Hamilton. [Also published as *Memoirs from Beyond the Tomb*, trans. Robert Baldick, London: Penguin, 2014].

Chateaubriand, François-René de (1966), *Mémoires d'outre-tombe*, Maurice Levaillant and Georges Moulinier (eds), Paris: Gallimard.

Clastres, Pierre (1972), *Chronique des Indiens Guayaki*, Paris: Plon.

Clastres, Pierre (1998), *Chronicle of the Guayaki Indians*, trans. and foreword, Paul Auster, New York: Zone Books.

Clément, Éric (2016), 'Un roman de 925 pages signé Paul Auster', *La Presse*, 26 April. Available at: http://www.lapresse.ca/arts/livres/201604/26/01-4975104-un-roman-de-925-pages-signe-paul-auster.php (accessed 11 July 2016).

Compagnon, Antoine (2009), *Le cas Bernard Faÿ: du Collège de France à l'indignité nationale*, Paris: Gallimard.

Conolly-Smith, Peter (2013), 'Well, I'm Dashed! Jitta, Pygmalion, and Shaw's Revenge', *SHAW: The Annual of Bernard Shaw Studies*, 33: 95–121, University Park: The Pennsylvania State University Press.

Cordingley, Anthony, ed. (2013), *Self-Translation: Brokering Originality in Hybrid Culture*, London: Bloomsbury.

Cowley, Malcolm (1976), *Exile's Return: A Literary Odyssey of the 1920s*, New York: Viking Press. [c1934].

Crawford, Fred D. (2000), 'Shaw in Translation', *SHAW: The Annual of Bernard Shaw Studies*, 20: 177–220, University Park: The Pennsylvania State University Press.

Cronin, Michael (2008), *Translation Goes to the Movies*, London/New York: Routledge.

The Daily Telegraph (1930), 'Bernard Shaw "Translates". Comic End to a Serious Play. Unexpected Turn to a German Piece', 1 May.

Daniel, Margaret (2014), 'Paul Auster on Poe, Pynchon, and "Boy Writers"', *Huffpost Books*, 29 March. Available at: http://www.huffingtonpost.com/anne-margaret-daniel/paul-auster-on-boy-writer_b_4670507.html (accessed 10 January 2016).

Davis, Phoebe Stein (1998), '"Even Cake Gets to Have Another Meaning": History, Narrative, and "Daily Living" in Gertrude Stein's World War II Writings', *Modern Fiction Studies*, 44 (3): 568–607.

Dean, Michelle (2014), 'In Defense of Paul Auster on "Boy's Literature"', *Flavorwire*, 30 January. Available at: http://flavorwire.com/436137/in-defense-of-paul-auster -on-boys-literature (accessed 10 January 2016), http://www.telegraph.co.uk/ culture/books/authorinterviews/8128941/Paul-Auster-interview.html (accessed 20 July 2013).

DeKoven, Marianne, ed. (2006), *Three Lives and Q.E.D. by Gertrude Stein: Authoritative Texts, Contexts, Criticism*, New York: W.W. Norton.

Delabastita, Dirk (2009), 'Fictional Representations', in Mona Baker and Gabriela Saldanha (eds), *Routledge Encyclopedia of Translation Studies*, London/New York: Routledge, 109–12.

Delabastita, Dirk and Rainier Grutman (2005), 'Introduction. Fictional Representations of Multilingualism and Translation', in Dirk Delabastita and Rainier Grutman (eds), *Fictionalising Translation and Multilingualism, Linguistica Antverpiensia*, 4: 11–34.

Delisle, Jean and Judith Woodsworth, eds (2012), *Translators through History*, Amsterdam/Philadelphia: John Benjamins. Revised edition. [c1995].

Dennis, Helen May, ed. (2000), *Ezra Pound and Poetic Influence: The Official Proceedings of the 17th International Ezra Pound Conference*, Amsterdam/Atlanta: Rodopi.

Dershowitz, Alan (2012), 'Suppressing Ugly Truth for Beautiful Art', *Huffington Post*, 1 May. Available at: http://www.huffingtonpost.com/alan-dershowitz/met-gertrude -stein-collaborator_b_1467174.html (accessed 29 April 2013).

Dilworth, Thomas and Susan Holbrook, eds (2010), *The Letters of Gertrude Stein and Virgil Thomson: Composition as Conversation*, Oxford: Oxford University Press.

Du Bouchet, André (1976), *The Uninhabited: Selected Poems of André du Bouchet*, trans. Paul Auster, New York: Living Hand.

Du Bouchet, André (2014), *Openwork. Poetry and Prose*, selected, translated, and presented by Paul Auster and Hoyt Rogers, New Haven, CT: Yale University Press.

Dukore, Bernard (1973), *Bernard Shaw, Playwright: Aspects of Shavian Drama*, Columbia, MO: University of Missouri Press, 203–11.

Dupin, Jacques (1974), *Fits and Starts: Selected Poems of Jacques Dupin*, trans. Paul Auster, Weston, CT: Living Hand.

Dupre, Joan Alcus (2007), 'Fighting Fathers/Saving Sons: The Struggle for Life and Art in Paul Auster's *New York Trilogy*', The City University of New York, PhD dissertation. Available at: https://crepuq.vdxhost.com/zportal/zeng ine?VDXaction=DocFetch&docfetch_key=4dc70000aa4dd000&docfetch _user=Okbf5XL8&docfetch_password=w4D6OoxI (accessed 26 January 2016).

Dydo, Ulla E. (1985), '"Stanzas in Meditation": The Other Autobiography', *Chicago Review*, 35 (2): 4–20.

Dydo, Ulla E. (2006), 'Plenty More Stein Work', *Electronic Poetry Center*, 24
   March. Available at: http://epc.buffalo.edu/authors/stein/dydo.html (accessed
   12 July 2016).

Dydo, Ulla E., with William Rice (2003), *Gertrude Stein: The Language That Rises: 1923–
   1934*, Evanston, IL: Northwestern University Press.

Dyer, Daniel (2006), 'Prolific Author Outdoes Himself in Latest Effort', *The Plain Dealer*
   (Cleveland), 15 January (Review of *The Brooklyn Follies* in the Sunday Forum section).

Evans, Thomas F., ed. (1997), *George Bernard Shaw. The Critical Heritage*, London/New
   York: Routledge. [c1976].

Faÿ, Bernard (1966), *Les Précieux*, Paris: Librairie académique Perrin.

Finn, Peter and Petra Couvée (2014), *The Zhivago Affair. The Kremlin, the CIA, and the
   Battle over a Forbidden Book*, New York: Pantheon Books.

Fischer, Heinz-Dietrich, ed. (1994), *The Pulitzer Prix Archive. Vol. 7. American History
   Awards 1917–1991*, Munich: K.G. Sauer.

Flanner, Janet (1944), *Pétain: The Old Man of France*, New York: Simon and Schuster.

Flaubert, Gustave (1900), *Trois Contes*, Paris: Eugène Fasquelle. [c1877].

Flaubert, Gustave (2011), *Correspondance 8ᵉ série. 1877–1880*, eBook.

Foer, Jonathan Safran (2003), *Everything Is Illuminated*, New York: HarperCollins. [c2002].

Ford, Hugh, ed. (1972), *The Left Bank Revisited: Selections from the Paris "Tribune"
   1917–1934*, edited with an introduction by Hugh Ford, foreword by Matthew
   Josephson, University Park/London: The Pennsylvania State University Press.

France, Peter, ed. (2000), *The Oxford Guide to Literature in English Translation*, Oxford:
   Oxford University Press.

Gahan, Peter (2004), '*Jitta's Atonement*: The Birth of Psychoanalysis and the "Fetters of
   the Feminine Psyche"', *SHAW: The Annual of Bernard Shaw Studies*, 24, University
   Park: The Pennsylvania State University Press, 128–65.

Gallup, Donald Clifford (1948), 'A Book Is a Book Is a Book: History of the Writing and
   Publication of Stein's *Three Lives*', *The New Colophon. A Book Collectors' Quarterly*, 1
   (1): 67–80.

Gallup, Donald Clifford, ed. (1953), *The Flowers of Friendship. Letters Written to
   Gertrude Stein*, New York: Alfred A. Knopf.

Galvin, Rachel (2013), 'Gertrude Stein anew. A review of "Stanzas in Meditation: The
   Corrected Edition"', in *Jacket2*. Available at: https://jacket2.org/reviews/gertrude
   -stein-anew (accessed 4 April 2016).

Galvin, Rachel (2016), 'Gertrude Stein, Pétain, and the Politics of Translation', *ELH* (English
   Literary History, Johns Hopkins University Press), 83 (1): 259–92. Available at: http://
   muse.jhu.edu/journals/elh/summary/v083/83.1.galvin.html (accessed 21 March 2016).

Gambier, Yves and Luc van Doorslaer, eds (2014), *Handbook of Translation Studies*,
   Amsterdam/Philadelphia: John Benjamins, 4 vols.

Gambino, Megan (2011), 'When Gertrude Stein Toured America', 13 October. Available
   at: http://www.smithsonianmag.com/arts-culture/when-gertrude-stein-toured
   -america-105320781/?all (accessed 18 February 2016).

Gans, Andrew (2008), 'Project Shaw's *Jitta's Atonement*, with Charles Busch'. Available at: http://www.playbill.com/article/project-shaws-jittas-atonement-with-charles -busch-presented-nov-17-com-155207 (accessed 21 April 2016).

Garland, Henry B. and Mary Garland (1986), *The Oxford Companion to German Literature*, 2nd edition, Oxford: Oxford University Press.

Geertz, Clifford (1998), 'Deep Hanging Out', *New York Review of Books*, 22 October. Available at: http://www.nybooks.com/articles/1998/10/22/deep-hanging-out/ (accessed 21 January 2016).

Geertz, Clifford (2000), *Available Light: Anthropological Reflections on Philosophical Topics*, Princeton, NJ: Princeton University Press.

Genette, Gérard (1997), *Paratexts. Thresholds of Interpretation*, trans. Jane E. Lewin, Cambridge: Cambridge University Press (Originally published in French as *Seuils*, Paris: Éditions du Seuil, 1987).

Gervasi, Frank (1944), 'The Liberation of Gertrude Stein', *Life*, 17: 83–4.

Gibbs, Anthony Matthews (2005), *Bernard Shaw: A Life*, Gainesville, FL: University Press of Florida.

Gilbert, Allan H. (1978), 'Review of *The Violet in the Crucible: Shelley and Translation* by Timothy Webb', *Keats-Shelley Journal*, 27: 158–60.

Gluzman, Michael (1998), 'Modernism and Exile: A View from the Margins', in David Biale, Michael Galchinsky, and Susannah Heschel (eds), *Insider/Outsider: American Jews and Multiculturalism*, Berkeley/Los Angeles: University of California Press, 231–51.

Green, Claire (2014), 'Borges and his Successors', *Sounds and Colours*, 1 December. Available at: https://soundsandcolours.com/articles/argentina/borges-and-his- successors-26356/ (accessed 10 January 2016).

Green, Nancy L. (2014), '(Neither) Expatriates (n)or Immigrants? The American Colony in Paris, 1880–1940', *Transatlantica. Revue d'études américaines. American Studies Journal*, Exile and Expatriation, 1: 2–11. Available at: http://transatlantica .revues.org/6893 (accessed 8 January 2016).

Greenberg, Reesa (2010), 'Restitution Exhibitions: Issues of Ethnic Identity and Art', *Intermédialités* (15): 105–17. Available at: http://id.erudit.org/iderudit/044677ar (accessed 15 February 2016).

Greenblatt, Stephen (1980), *Renaissance Self-Fashioning. From More to Shakespeare*, Chicago/London: The University of Chicago Press.

Greenhouse, Emily (2012), 'Gertrude Stein and Vichy: The Overlooked History', *The New Yorker*, 4 May. Available at: http://www.newyorker.com/online/blogs/ culture/2012/05/gertrude-stein-vichy-regime-the-met.html?printable=true&current Page=all (accessed 8 August 2013).

Grene, Nicholas (1996), 'The Edwardian Shaw or the Modernist that Never Was', in Maria DiBattista and Lucy McDiarmin (eds), *High and Low Moderns. Literature and Culture 1889–1939*, Oxford: Oxford University Press, 135–47.

Grimes, William (2011), 'Allen Mandelbaum, Translator of 'Divine Comedy' Dies at 85', *The New York Times*, 5 November. Available at: http://www.nytimes

.com/2011/11/06/arts/allen-mandelbaum-translator-of-divine-comedy-dies-at-85
.html?ref=obituaries&_r=0 (accessed 29 January 2016).

Grindea, Miron (1956), 'G.B.S. and France', *Adam International Review*, 255/256: 1–14.

Grutman, Rainier (2018), 'The Self-translator as Author: Modern Self-fashioning and Ancient Rhetoric in Federman, Lakhous, and De Kuyper', in Judith Woodsworth (ed.), *The Fictions of Translation*, Amsterdam/Philadelphia, John Benjamins.

Gutkowski, Emanuela (2003), 'Gertrude Stein and Jules Laforgue: A Comparative Approach', *European Journal of American Culture*, 22 (1): 125–38.

Hamon, Augustin Frédéric (1913), *Le Molière du XXe siècle: Bernard Shaw*, Paris: Eugène Figuière.

Harris, Frank (1931), *Bernard Shaw*. An unauthorized biography based on firsthand information with a postcript by Mr. Shaw. New York: Simon and Schuster.

Heim, Michael Henry (2013), 'To Foreignize or Not to Foreignize: From a Translator's Notebook', in Sherry Simon (ed.), *In Translation. Honouring Sheila Fischman*, Montreal: McGill-Queen's University Press, 83–91.

Hemingway, Ernest (2010), *A Moveable Feast: The Restored Edition*, New York: Scribner.

Henderson, Archibald (1918), *George Bernard Shaw. His Life and Works. A Critical Biography (Authorized)*, New York: Boni and Liveright. [c1911].

Henderson, Archibald (1932), *Shaw, Playboy and Prophet*, New York: Appleton.

Henderson, Archibald (1956), *George Bernard Shaw: Man of the Century*, New York: Appleton-Century-Crofts.

Hikind, Dov (2012), 'Stein Collected While Fellow Jews Were Murdered', 1 May. Available at: http://dovhikind.blogspot.ca/2012/05/hikind-demands-metropolitan -museum-of.html (accessed 4 April 2016).

Holroyd, Michael (1988), *Michael Holroyd on George Bernard Shaw*, film originally broadcast as an episode of the *South Bank Show*, narrated by Melvyn Bragg, Princeton, NJ: Films for the Humanities.

Holroyd, Michael (1989), *Bernard Shaw. 1898–1918. The Pursuit of Power*, vol. 2, New York: Random House.

Holroyd, Michael (1997), *Bernard Shaw. The One-Volume Definitive Edition*, New York: Random House (Originally published in 4 vols by Chatto & Windus 1988–1992).

Hugnet, Georges (1933), *Enfances*, Paris: Éditions des Cahiers d'art.

Hutcheon, Linda (2006), *A Theory of Adaptation*, London/New York: Routledge.

Hutchisson, James M., ed. (2013), *Conversations with Paul Auster*, Jackson: University Press of Mississippi.

Imbs, Bravig (1936), *Confessions of Another Young Man*, New York: Henkle-Yewdale House.

Jobey, Liz, ed. (2011), *The New Granta Book of Travel*, London: Granta Books.

Jolas, Eugene (1928), 'Inquiry among European Writers into the Spirit of America', *transition* 13: 248–70.

Jolas, Eugene, ed. (1935), *Testimony against Gertrude Stein*, pamphlet published as a supplement to *transition* 23, 1934–1935, with contributions from Georges Braque, Eugene Jolas, Maria Jolas, Henri Matisse, André Salmon, and Tristan Tzara. Available at: http://www.romanianculture.org/downloads/testimony_against_g _stein.pdf (accessed 10 August 2013).

Josephson, Matthew (1972), 'Foreword', in Hugh Ford (ed.), *The Left Bank Revisited: Selections from the Paris 'Tribune' 1917–1934*, University Park/London: The Pennsylvania State University Press, xix–xxiv.

Joubert, Joseph (1983), *The Notebooks of Joseph Joubert*, San Francisco: North Point Press.

Joyce, James (1962), *Finnegans Wake: Fragments adaptés par André Du Bouchet*, introduction de Michel Butor, trans. Paul Auster, Paris: Gallimard.

Kaindl, Klaus (2014), 'Going fictional! Translators and Interpreters in Literature and Film: An Introduction', in Klaus Kaindl and Karlheinz Spitzl (eds), *Transfiction. Research into the Realities of Translation Fiction*, Amsterdam/Philadelphia: John Benjamins, 1–26.

Kaindl, Klaus and Karlheinz Spitzl, eds (2014), *Transfiction. Research into the Realities of Translation Fiction*, Amsterdam/Philadelphia: John Benjamins.

Karlin, Mark (2011), 'Gertrude Stein's "Missing" Vichy Years', *Truthout*, 11 July. Available at: http://www.truth-out.org/news/item/3608:gertrude-steins-missing -vichy-years (accessed 3 August 2013).

Katz, Daniel (2007), *American Modernism's Expatriate Scene*, Edinburgh: Edinburgh University Press.

Katz, Leon (1963), 'The First Making of *The Making of Americans*: A Study Based on Gertrude Stein's Notebooks and Early Versions of Her Novel (1902–1908)', unpublished dissertation, Columbia University.

Katz, Leon (1973), 'Introduction', in Gertrude Stein, *Fernhurst, Q.E.D., and Other Early Writings*, New York: Liveright, ix–xiii. [c1971].

Kellman, Steven G. (2000), *The Translingual Imagination*, Lincoln: University of Nebraska Press.

Kimmelman, Michael (2012), 'Missionaries', review of *The Steins Collect: Matisse, Picasso, and the Parisian Avant-Garde*; *Unlikely Collaboration: Gertrude Stein, Bernard Faÿ, and the Vichy Dilemma*; *Ida: A Novel*, *The New York Review of Books*, 26 April. Available at: http://www.nybooks.com/articles/2012/04/26/missionaries/ (accessed 3 April 2016).

Knoll, Elisabeth (1992), *Produktive Mißverständnisse: George Bernard Shaw und sein deutscher Übersetzer Siegfried Trebitsch*, Heidelberg: Universitätsverlag Carl Winter.

Laforgue, Jules (1922), *Moralités légendaires*, Éditions de la Banderole (eBook). [c1887].

Laird, Holly A. (2000), *Women Coauthors*, Urbana/Chicago: University of Illinois Press.

Langner, Lawrence (1963), *G.B.S. and the Lunatic. Reminiscences of the Long, Lively, and Affectionate Friendship between George Bernard Shaw and the Author*, New York: Atheneum.

Laurence, Dan H., ed. (1965), *Bernard Shaw: Collected Letters. 1874–1897*, vol. 1, London: Max Reinhardt.

Laurence, Dan H., ed. (1972), *Bernard Shaw: Collected Letters. 1898–1910*, vol. 2, London: Max Reinhardt.

Laurence, Dan H., ed. (1985), *Bernard Shaw: Collected Letters. 1911–1925*, vol. 3, London: Max Reinhardt.

Laurence, Dan H., ed. (1988), *Bernard Shaw: Collected Letters. 1926–1950*, vol. 4, New York: Viking.

Lefevere, André (1984), 'Refraction: Some Observations on the Occasion of Wole Soyinka's *Opera Wonyosi*', in Ortrun Zuber-Skerritt (ed.), *Page to Stage: Theatre as Translation*, Amsterdam: Rodopi, 191–8.

Lefevere, André (1992a), *Translation/History/Culture. A Sourcebook*, London/New York: Routledge.

Lefevere, André (1992b), *Translation, Rewriting, & the Manipulation of Literary Fame*, London/New York: Routledge.

Lefevere, André (2000), 'Mother Courage's Cucumbers. Text, System and Refraction in a Theory of Literature', in Lawrence Venuti (ed.), *The Translation Studies Reader*, London/New York: Routledge, 233–49.

Levett, Karl (2001), 'Jitta's Atonement', *Back Stage*, 9 November, 42/45 (27). Available at: http://0-search.proquest.com.mercury.concordia.ca/docview/868607966/fulltext/369117B037D54E1DPQ/23?accountid=10246 (accessed 21 April 2016).

Levine, Anne-Marie (1999), 'Gertrude Stein's War', in Elizabeth Brunazzi and Jeanine Parisier Plottel (eds), 'Culture and Daily Life in Occupied France', *Contemporary French Civilization*, 23 (2): 223–43.

Life (1923), Review of Shaw's *Jitta's Atonement*, 8 February: 18.

Lopes, Alexandra (2015), 'Notes on World Literature and Translation. From Tradition to Transgression and Back?', in Peter Hanenberg (ed.), *A New Visibility: On Culture, Translation and Cognition*, Lisbon: Universidade Católica Editora, 85–104.

Lord, James (1994), *Six Exceptional Women: Further Memoirs*, New York: Farrar, Strauss, Giroux.

Madeline, Laurence, ed. (2005), *Gertrude Stein – Pablo Picasso. Correspondance*, Paris: Gallimard.

Malcolm, Janet (2006), 'Strangers in Paradise. How Gertrude Stein and Alice B. Toklas Got to Heaven', *The New Yorker*, 13 November. Available at: http://www.newyorker.com/archive/2006/11/13/061113fa_fact_malcolm (accessed 11 August 2013).

Malcolm, Janet (2007), *Two Lives: Gertrude and Alice*, New Haven, CT: Yale University Press.

Mallarmé, Stéphane (1983), *A Tomb for Anatole*, trans. Paul Auster, San Francisco: North Point Press.

Malmkjær, Kirsten and Kevin Windle, eds (2011), *The Oxford Handbook of Translation Studies*, Oxford: Oxford University Press.

Mander, Raymond and Joe Mitchenson (1955), *Theatrical Companion to Shaw. A Pictorial Record of the First Performances of the Plays of George Bernard Shaw*, New York: Pitman Publishing Corporation.

Mann, Thomas (1997), 'Thomas Mann on Shaw as "mankind's friend"', in Thomas F. Evans (ed.), *George Bernard Shaw. The Critical Heritage*, London/New York: Routledge (Originally published in the *Listener*, 18 January 1951, Vol. xlv, 1142, 98 as a reprint of a BBC broadcast talk).

Martinez, Victor, ed. (2011a), *André du Bouchet. Nikolaï Zabolotski. Europe*, 986/987.

Martinez, Victor (2011b), 'La Volonté de prendre des risques. Entretien avec Paul Auster', in Victor Martinez (ed.), *André du Bouchet. Nikolaï Zabolotski. Europe*, Paris, 986/987, 15–24.

Massardier-Kenney, Françoise, Maria Tymoczko, and Brian James Baer (2016), *Translators Writing, Writing Translators*, Kent, OH: The Kent State University Press.

Matlaw, Myron (1979), *Jitta's Atonement: Shaw's Adaptation and the Translation of Trebitsch's Original*, Ann Arbor, MI: University Microfilms International.

McCullough, David (2011), *The Greater Journey. Americans in Paris*, New York: Simon & Schuster.

Meizoz, Jérôme (2007), *Postures littéraires. Mises en scène modernes de l'auteur*, Genève: Slatkine Érudition.

Mellow, James R. (1974), *Charmed Circle. Gertrude Stein & Company*, New York: Praeger Publishers.

Millán, Carmen and Francesca Bartrina, eds (2013), *The Routledge Handbook of Translation Studies*, Milton Park, Abingdon: Routledge.

Miró, Joan and Margit Rowell, eds (1986), *Joan Miró: Selected Writings and Interviews*, trans. Paul Auster, Boston: G.K. Hall.

Monk, Craig (2008), *Writing the Lost Generation: Expatriate Autobiography and American Modernism*. Iowa City: University of Iowa Press.

Moore, Mina (1933), *Bernard Shaw et la France*, Paris: Champion.

Mo Yan (Guan Moye) (2012), 'Speech at the Nobel Banquet in Stockholm, 10 December 2012'. Available online: http://www.nobelprize.org/nobel_prizes/literature/laureates/2012/yan-speech_en.html#not (accessed 21 January 2016).

Murray, Matthew (2001), 'Jitta's Atonement', *Talkin' Broadway*, off-Broadway reviews, 22 October. Available at: http://www.talkinbroadway.com/page/ob/10_22_01.html (accessed 21 April 2016).

Nation and Athenaeum (1930), '"Jitta's Atonement", Arts Theatre Club', 10 May, 172.

The New York Times (1923a), 'Bertha Kalich in New Role: Appears in Comedy, "Jitta's Atonement," Adapted by Shaw', 18 January.

The New York Times (1923b), 'Shaw as Adapter', 11 February.

The New York Times (1926), 'Mr. Shaw Frankly Dons The Cap and Bells: But Even His Collection of "Tomfooleries" Is Not Without Seriousness. Review of *Translations and Tomfooleries* by Bernard Shaw', 31 October 1926.

Norris, Margot (1991), 'Modernist Eruptions', in Emory Elliott, Patrick O'Donnell, Valerie Smith, and Christopher P. Wilson (eds), *The Columbia History of the American Novel*, New York: Columbia University Press, 311–30.

Novey, Idra (2016), *Ways to Disappear*, New York: Little, Brown and Company.

Obourn, Nick (2010), 'Paul Auster on His New Novel, *Invisible*', in James M. Hutchisson (ed.), *Conversations with Paul Auster*, Jackson, MS: University Press of Mississippi, 2013, 203–11.

O'Neill, Patrick (2005), *Polyglot Joyce: Fictions of Translation*, Toronto: University of Toronto Press.

Ormsby, Eric (2003), 'Shadow Language', *New Criterion*, 21 (8): 22–7.

O'Rourke, Meghan (2012), 'These Wild Solitudes. "Winter Journal," by Paul Auster', *The New York Times*, 7 September. Available at: http://www.nytimes.com/2012/09/09/books/review/winter-journal-by-paul-auster.html?_r=0 (accessed 6 February 2016).

Pagano, Adriana S. (2000), 'Sources for Translation Theory: Fiction in Latin America', *ATA Chronicle* 29 (4): 38–44.

Paris, Václav (2013), 'Gertrude Stein's Translations of Speeches by Philippe Pétain', in Charles Berntstein (ed.), 'Setting the Record Straight', 6 May. Available at: https://jacket2.org/article/gertrude-steins-translations-speeches-philippe-petain#1 (accessed 7 September 2013).

Pasternak, Boris (1976), 'From *Notes of a Translator*', trans. Angela Livingstone, in Carl R. Proffer and Joseph Brodsky (eds), *Modern Russian Poets on Translation*, Ann Arbor, MI: Ardis, 96–101.

Pearson, Hesketh (2001), *Bernard Shaw. His Life and Personality*, London: House of Stratus. [c1942].

Pétain, Le Maréchal (Philippe) (1941), *Paroles aux Français. Messages et écrits 1934–1941*, Gabriel Louis Jaray (ed.), Paris: Lardanchet.

Peters, Margot (1997), 'Intersections', review of Stanley Weintraub's *Shaw's People: Victoria to Churchill*, SHAW, 17: 258–61. Available at: http://www.jstor.org/stable/40681478 (accessed 1 June 2016).

Peyret-Chappuis, Charles de (1938), *Frénésie*, *L'Illustration*, 423: 1–26.

Pharand, Michael W. (2000), *Bernard Shaw and the French*, Gainesville, FL: University Press of Florida.

Pollock, Arthur (1923), 'The New Plays', *The Brooklyn Daily Eagle*, 18 January, 6. Available at: http://bklyn.newspapers.com/image/57092860/?terms=Jitta%27s%2BAtonement%2Bshaw (accessed 18 January 2016).

Posman, Sarah (2009), 'The Flowers of Friendship. Les "mauvaises" traductions de Gertrude Stein', trans. K. Andringa, *Transitzone*. Available at: http://www.ny-web.be/transitzone/flowers-friendship.html (accessed 5 July 2015).

Pound, Ezra (1931), *How to Read*, New York: Gordon Press.

Prentki, Nigel (n.d.), 'Comparisons and Bontrasts [*sic*] Between *Madame Bovary* and *Un Cœur Simple*', *Études critiques*, Centre Flaubert CÉRÉdI, Université de Rouen. Available at: http://flaubert.univ-rouen.fr/etudes/prentkigb.php (accessed 22 June 2015).

Putnam, Samuel (1947), *Paris Was Our Mistress*, New York: Viking.

Raffel, Gertrude Stein (1971), 'There Once Was a Family Called Stein', in Gertrude Stein, *A Primer for the Understanding of Gertrude Stein*, Robert Bartlett Haas (ed.), Los Angeles, CA: Black Sparrow Press, 127–38.

Riley, Peter (2015), 'The Apophatic Poetry of André du Bouchet', *The Fortnightly Review*, 7 April. Available at: http://fortnightlyreview.co.uk/2015/04/andre-du-bouchet-riley/ (accessed 10 January 2016).

Robinson, Douglas (1998), 'Pseudotranslation', in Mona Baker (ed.), *Encyclopedia of Translation Studies*, London/New York: Routledge, 183–5.

Rodefer, Stephen (1985), 'Translation', in James M. Hutchisson (ed.), *Conversations with Paul Auster*, Jackson, MS: University Press of Mississippi, 2013, 4–5.

Rogers, Hoyt (2015), 'Translating André du Bouchet. An Exchange with Peter Riley', *Fortnightly Review*. Available at: http://fortnightlyreview.co.uk/2015/06/translating -andre-du-bouchet/ (accessed 10 January 2016).

Rogers, William G. (1971), *When This You See Remember Me. Gertrude Stein in Person*, Westport, CT: Greenwood Press. [c1948].

Rossetti, Gabriel Dante (1992), 'Preface to *The Early Italian Poets*', in Rainer Schulte and John Biguenet (eds), *Theories of Translation. An Anthology of Essays from Dryden to Derrida*, Chicago, IL: The University of Chicago Press, 64–7. [c1861].

Rushdie, Salman (1991), *Imaginary Homelands: Essays and Criticism 1981–1991*, New York: Viking.

Said, Edward W. (1996), *Representations of the Intellectual: The 1993 Reith Lectures*, New York: Vintage Books.

Saint-Pierre, Dominique (2009), *Gertrude Stein, le Bugey, la guerre*, Bourg-en-Bresse: Musnier-Gilbert Editions.

Sanborn, Alvan F. (1912), 'Shaw in Paris', *The New York Times*, 5 May.

Sand, George and Gustave Flaubert (1979), *The George Sand-Gustave Flaubert Letters*, trans. Aimee L. McKenzie, Chicago, IL: Academy Chicago Limited. [c1921].

Sanders, Julie (2006), *Adaptation and Appropriation: A New Cultural Idiom*, London/ New York: Routledge.

Sardin, Pascale (2007), 'De la note du traducteur comme commentaire: entre texte, paratexte et prétexte', *Palimpsestes*, 'De la traduction comme commentaire au commentaire de traduction', 121–36. Available at: http://palimpsestes.revues.org/99 (accessed 29 February 2016).

Sartre, Jean-Paul (1977), *Life/Situations: Essays Written and Spoken*, trans. Paul Auster and Lydia Davis, New York: Pantheon Books.

Schulte, Rainer and John Biguenet, eds (1992), *Theories of Translation. An Anthology of Essays from Dryden to Derrida*, Chicago, IL: The University of Chicago Press.

Schweiger, Hannes (2005), 'Bernard Shaw's Contributions to the Culture and Politics of *Fin de Siècle* Vienna', *SHAW* 25: 135–46. Available at: http://www.jstor.org/ stable/40681714 (accessed 30 mai 2016).

Schweiger, Hannes (2006), 'Habituelle Divergenzen – Siegfried Trebitsch als Übersetzer und Vermittler George Bernard Shaws', in Michaela Wolf (ed.), *Übersetzen – Translating – Traduire: Towards a 'Social Turn'?*, Vienna/Berlin: Lit Verlag, 45–54.

Schweiger, Hannes (2009), 'Between the Lines: George Bernard Shaw as Cultural and Political Mediator', in Grace Brockington (ed.), *Internationalism and the Arts in Britain and Europe at the Fin de Siècle*, Oxford: Peter Lang, 279–99.

Serruya, Teresa, Lieven D'hulst, Alexandra Assis Rosa, and Maria Lin Moniz, eds (2013), *Translation in Anthologies and Collections (19th and 20th Centuries)*, Amsterdam/Philadelphia: John Benjamins.

Shaw, George Bernard (1949), *Translations and Tomfooleries*, Standard edition, London: Constable and Company. [c1926].

Shaw, George Bernard (1970), 'What I Owe to German Culture', *Adam International Review*, 35 (337–9): 5–19 (First published in 1911 as 'Was ich der deutschen Kultur verdanke', his preface to *Dramatische Werke*, the German edition of his plays).

Shaw, George Bernard (1993), *The Complete Prefaces. Vol. 1: 1889–1913*, Dan H. Laurence and Daniel J. Leary (eds), London: Allen Lane.

Shaw, George Bernard (1995), *The Complete Prefaces. Vol. 2: 1914–1929*, Dan H. Laurence and Daniel J. Leary (eds), London: Allen Lane.

Shaw, George Bernard (1997), *The Complete Prefaces. Vol. 3: 1930–1950*, Dan H. Laurence and Daniel J. Leary (eds), London: Allen Lane.

Shaw, George Bernard (2000), 'A Devil of a Fellow: Self-Criticism', *SHAW. Bibliographical Shaw*, 20: 247–52. Available at: http://www.jstor.org/stable/40681624 (accessed 9 November 2015).

Simeoni, Daniel (1998), 'The Pivotal Status of the Translator's Habitus', *Target*, 10 (1): 1–39.

Simon, Sherry (2000), 'Forcer la note: quand la traductrice dépasse les bornes', in Mireille Calle-Gruber and Elisabeth Zawisza (eds), *Paratextes. Études aux bords du texte*, Paris: L'Harmattan, 239–51.

Simon, Sherry, ed. (2013), *In Translation. Honouring Sheila Fischman*, Montreal: McGill-Queen's University Press.

Sloboda, Noel (2008), *The Making of Americans in Paris: The Autobiographies of Edith Wharton and Gertrude Stein*, New York: Peter Lang.

Sommer, Elyse (1996), 'Jitta's Atonement', A *CurtainUp* Berkshire Review. Available at: http://www.curtainup.com/jitta.html (accessed 24 April 2016).

Sprigge, Elizabeth (1957), *Gertrude Stein. Her Life and Work*, New York: Harper and Brothers Publishers.

Stein, Gertrude, *Gertrude Stein and Alice B. Toklas Papers* (YCAL MSS 76) and *Gertrude Stein and Alice B. Toklas Papers* (YCAL MSS 77), unpublished manuscripts, Yale University Library, Beinecke Rare Book and Manuscript Library, Yale Collection of American Literature.

Stein, Gertrude (1929), *Morceaux choisis de la fabrication des Américains. Histoire du progrès d'une famille*, trans. and preface Georges Hugnet, Paris: Éditions de la Montagne.

Stein, Gertrude (1930), *Dix portraits: texte anglais accompagné de la traduction*, trans. Georges Hugnet and Virgil Thomson, preface Pierre de Massot, Paris: Éditions de la Montagne.

Stein, Gertrude (1931a), 'Poem Pritten on Pfances of Georges Hugnet', *Pagany*, 2 (1): 10–37. (With the original French by Georges Hugnet on the left side of the page.)

Stein, Gertrude (1931b), *Before the Flowers of Friendship Faded Friendship Faded/ written on a poem by George Hugnet* [by] Gertrude Stein, Paris: Plain Edition.

Stein, Gertrude (1933a), *Three Lives*, introduction by Carl Van Vechten, New York: The Modern Library. [c1909].

Stein, Gertrude (1933b), 'Left to Right', *Story: The Magazine of the Short Story*, 3 (16): 17–20. [c1931].

Stein, Gertrude (1934), *The Making of Americans: The Hersland Family*, preface by Bernard Faÿ, New York: Harcourt, Brace and Company.

Stein, Gertrude (1937), *Everybody's Autobiography*, New York: Random House.

Stein, Gertrude (1938), *Picasso*, London: B.T. Batsford, Ltd. (Published in French by Librairie Floury, 1938).

Stein, Gertrude (1939), 'My Debt to Books', *Books Abroad*, 13 (2): 306–8 (Published jointly with Roda Roda; Stein's portion, 307–8 only).

Stein, Gertrude (1940), *Paris France*, London: B.T. Batsford, Ltd.

Stein, Gertrude (1945a), *Wars I Have Seen*, New York: Random House.

Stein, Gertrude (1945b), 'Off We All Went to See Germany', *Life* 19: 54–58.

Stein, Gertrude (1947), *Four in America*, New Haven, CT: Yale University Press.

Stein, Gertrude (1961), *The Autobiography of Alice B. Toklas*, New York: Vintage Books. [c1933].

Stein, Gertrude (1970), *What Are Masterpieces*, New York: Pitman Publishing Corporation [c1940].

Stein, Gertrude (1971a), *Américains d'Amérique: histoire d'une famille américaine*, trans. J. Seillière and Bernard Faÿ, Paris: Stock. [c1933].

Stein, Gertrude (1971b), *A Primer for the Understanding of Gertrude Stein*, Robert Bartlett Haas (ed.), Los Angeles, CA: Black Sparrow Press.

Stein, Gertrude (1973), *Fernhurst, Q.E.D., and Other Early Writings*, New York: Liveright. [c1971].

Stein, Gertrude (1989), *Mrs. Reynolds*, Los Angeles, CA: Sun and Moon Press. [c1952].

Stein, Gertrude (1995), *Before the Flowers of Friendship Faded Friendship Faded*, ed. and introduction by Juliana Spahr, Boston: *Exact Change Yearbook*, 1, 41–60.

Stein, Gertrude (1996), 'Introduction to the Speeches of Marechal Pétain', Wanda Van Dusen (ed.), *Modernism/modernity*, 3 (3): 93–6. Available at: http://muse.jhu.edu/journals/mod/summary/v003/3.3stein.html (accessed 24 July 2016).

Stein, Gertrude (1998a), *Writings 1903–1932*, Catharine R. Stimpson and Harriet Chessman (eds), New York: The Library of America.

Stein, Gertrude (1998b), *Writings 1932–1946*, Catharine R. Stimpson and Harriet Chessman (eds), New York: The Library of America.

Stein, Gertrude (2006), *Three Lives and Q.E.D.: Authoritative Texts, Contexts, Criticism*, Marianne DeKoven (ed.), New York: W.W. Norton.

Stein, Gertrude (2010), *Narration: Four Lectures by Gertrude Stein with an Introduction by Thornton Wilder*, Chicago, IL: University of Chicago Press. [c1935].

Steiner, George (1975), *After Babel: Aspects of Language and Translation*, London: Oxford University Press.

Stendhal, Renate (2012), 'Why the Witch-Hunt against Gertrude Stein?', *Tikkun*, 4 June. Available at: http://www.tikkun.org/nextgen/why-the-witch-hunt-against-gertrude -stein (accessed 1 May 2013).

Strümper-Krobb, Sabine (2014), 'Witnessing, Remembering, Translating. Translation and Translator Figures in Jonathan Safran Foer's *Everything Is Illuminated* and Anne Michaels's *Fugitive Pieces*', in Klaus Kaindl and Karlheinz Spitzl (eds), *Transfiction. Research into the Realities of Translation Fiction*, Amsterdam/Philadelphia: John Benjamins, 248–59.

Sutherland, Donald (2006), 'Three Lives', in Marianne DeKoven (ed.), *Three Lives and Q.E.D.: Authoritative Texts, Contexts, Criticism*, New York: W.W. Norton, 263–84.

Sutliffe, Alfred (1887), *The Americans in Paris*, Paris: P. Symonds Printer.

Swarbrick, Katharine and Jane Goldman (2007), '"The Flowers of Friendship": Gertrude Stein and Georges Hugnet', *Papers of Surrealism*, 6: 1–18. Available at: http://www .surrealismcentre.ac.uk/papersofsurrealism/journal6/acrobat%20files/articles/ swarbrickgoldmanpdf.pdf (accessed 1 August 2013).

Switzky, Lawrence (2015), 'Introduction: Enchanted Shaw (and Other Shavian Modernities)', in Lawrence Switzky (ed.), 'Shaw and Modernity', special issue of *SHAW The Journal of Bernard Shaw Studies*, 35 (1): 1–8.

Taylor, John (2014), 'In Quest of the Elemental – André du Bouchet's "Openwork"', *The Arts Fuse*, 13 October. Available at: http://artsfuse.org/114283/fuse-book-review-in -quest-of-the-elemental-andre-du-bouchets-openwork/ (accessed 16 January 2016).

Taylor, Markland (1996), 'Review: "Jitta's Atonement"', *Variety*, 12 August. Available at: http://variety.com/1996/film/reviews/jitta-s-atonement-1200446446/ (accessed 22 April 2016).

Thomson, Virgil (1967), *Virgil Thomson*, New York: Alfred A. Knopf.

The Times (London, England) (1956), 'Dr. Siegfried Trebitsch', Obituary, 4 June. Issue 53548, page 14. Available online: http://0-find.galegroup.com.mercury.concordia.ca/ ttda/infomark.do?action=interpret&docType=LTO&docLevel=FASCIMILE&prodI d=TTDA&fromBookMark=true&tabID=T003&callistoContentSet=UDVIN&type= multipage&version=1.0&pageIndex=1&source=gale&navigation=true&userGroupN ame=concordi_main&docPage=article&docId=CS236017348&contentSet=LTO&fin alAuth=true (accessed 15 May 2016).

Toklas, Alice B. (1963), *What Is Remembered*, London: Michael Joseph.

Toledano Buendía, Carmen (2013), 'Listening to the Voice of the Translator: A Description of Translator's Notes as Paratextual Elements', *Translation & Interpreting*, 5 (2): 149–62. Available at: http://www.trans-int.org/index.php/transint/article/view/209/129 (accessed 5 August 2013).

Toury, Gideon (2012), *Descriptive Translation Studies and Beyond*, Amsterdam/Philadelphia: John Benjamins. Revised edition. [c1995].

Towse, J. Ranken (1923), '"Jitta's Atonement". Queer Mixture. Old Triangle Theme from A Modern Psychoanalytical Point of View. Chaotic Result of George Bernard Shaw's Emendation of the Austrian Author's Original Play', *The New York Evening Post*, 18 January.

Trebitsch, Siegfried (1920), *Frau Gittas Sühne*, Berlin: S. Fischer Verlag.

Trebitsch, Siegfried (1931), 'How I Discovered Bernard Shaw', *The Bookman*, 80 (465): 1–3.

Trebitsch, Siegfried (1953), *Chronicle of a Life*, trans. Eithne Wilkins and Ernst Kaiser, London: Heinemann (First published as *Chronik eines Lebens*, Zürich: Artemis Verlag, 1951).

Valéry, Paul (1927), 'Quelques fragments des *Marginalia*, traduits et commentés par Paul Valéry', *Commerce*, 14: 11–14.

Valéry, Paul (1957), *Œuvres*, tome I, Jean Hytier (ed.), Paris: Pléiade.

Valéry, Paul (1960), *Œuvres*, tome II, Jean Hytier (ed.), Paris: Pléiade.

Valéry, Paul (1992), 'Variations on the *Eclogues*', trans. Denise Folliot, in Rainer Schulte and John Biguenet (eds), *Theories of Translation. An Anthology of Essays from Dryden to Derrida*, Chicago, IL: The University of Chicago Press, 113–26. [c1956].

Van Dusen, Wanda (1996), 'Portrait of a National Fetish: Gertrude Stein's 'Introduction to the Speeches of Maréchal Pétain' (1942)', *Modernism/Modernity*, 3 (3): 69–92.

Van Puymbroeck, Birgit (2015), 'Triangular Politics: Stein, Bernard Faÿ, and Elisabeth de Gramont', in Sarah Posman and Laura Luise Schultz (eds), *Gertrude Stein in Europe: Reconfigurations across Media, Disciplines, and Traditions*, London: Bloomsbury, 85–103.

Venuti, Lawrence (1995), *The Translator's Invisibility: A History of Translation*, London/New York: Routledge.

Venuti, Lawrence, ed. (2000), *The Translation Studies Reader*, London/New York: Routledge.

Vermeer, Hans (2000), 'Skopos and Commission in Translational Action', trans. Andrew Chesterman, in Lawrence Venuti (ed.), *The Translation Studies Reader*, London/New York: Routledge, 221–32.

Wagner-Martin, Linda (1995), *'Favored Strangers': Gertrude Stein and Her Family*, New Brunswick, NJ: Rutgers University Press.

Wake Forest University (2011), 'Retired Professor Allen Mandelbaum Dies', *Inside WFU*. Available at: http://inside.wfu.edu/2011/11/retired-professor-allen-mandelbaum-dies/ (accessed 29 January 2016).

Walker, Jayne L. (2006), '*Three Lives*: The Realism of the Composition', in Marianne DeKoven (ed.), *Three Lives and Q.E.D.: Authoritative Texts, Contexts, Criticism*, New York: W.W. Norton, 339–58.

Webb, Timothy (1976), *The Violet in the Crucible: Shelley and Translation*, Oxford: Clarendon Press.

Weintraub, Stanley, ed. (1969), *Shaw. An Autobiography 1856–1898*, selected from his writings by Stanley Weintraub, vol. 1, London: Max Reinhardt.

Weintraub, Stanley, ed. (1970), *Shaw. An Autobiography 1898–1950: The Playwright Years*, selected from his writings by Stanley Weintraub, vol. 2, London: Max Reinhardt.

Weintraub, Stanley (1996), *Shaw's People: Victoria to Churchill*, University Park: The Pennsylvania State University Press.

Weiss, Samuel A., ed. (1986), *Bernard Shaw's Letters to Siegfried Trebitsch*, Stanford, CA: Stanford University Press.

Weiss, Samuel A. (2000), 'Bernard Shaw's Further Letters to Siegfried Trebitsch', *SHAW. Bibliographical Shaw*, 20: 221–45. Available at: http://www.jstor.org/stable/40681623 (accessed 9 November 2015).

Whittier-Ferguson, John (1999), 'Stein in Time: History, Manuscripts, and Memory', *Modernism/Modernity*, 6 (1): 115–51.

Whittier-Ferguson, John (2001), 'The Liberation of Gertrude Stein: War and Writing', *Modernism/Modernity*, 8 (3): 405–28.

Will, Barbara E. (2004), 'Lost in Translation: Stein's Vichy Collaboration', *Modernism/Modernity*, 11 (4): 651–68. Available at: http://muse.jhu.edu/login?auth=0&type=summary&url=/journals/modernism-modernity/v011/11.4will.html (accessed 24 July 2016).

Will, Barbara E. (2008), 'Gertrude Stein, Bernard Faÿ, and the Ruthless Flowers of Friendship', *Modernism/Modernity*, 15 (4): 647–64. Available at: http://0 gateway.proquest.com.mercury.concordia.ca/openurl?ctx_ver=Z39.88-2003&xri:pqil:res_ver=0.2&res_id=xri:lion-us&rft_id=xri:lion:ft:abell:R04108607:0 (accessed 2 May 2013).

Will, Barbara E. (2011), *Unlikely Collaboration: Gertrude Stein, Bernard Faÿ and the Vichy Dilemma*, New York: Columbia University Press.

Wineapple, Brenda (1996), *Sister Brother. Gertrude and Leo Stein*, New York: G.P. Putnam's Sons.

Wood, Carl (2006), 'Continuity of Romantic Irony: Stein's Homage to Laforgue in *Three Lives*', in Marianne DeKoven (ed.), *Three Lives and Q.E.D.: Authoritative Texts, Contexts, Criticism*, New York: W.W. Norton, 302–13.

Wood, James (2009), 'Shallow Graves', *The New Yorker*, 30 November. Available at: http://www.newyorker.com/arts/critics/books/2009/11/30/091130crbo_books_wood (accessed 24 July 2016).

Woodsworth, Judith (1988), 'Writers and Their Translators: The Case of Mavis Gallant', *TTR: traduction, terminologie, redaction*, 1 (2): 47–57.

Woodsworth, Judith (2000), 'Fragments d'une théorie de la traduction: Paul Valéry traducteur', in Mawy Bouchard, Isabelle Daunais, Anne-Marie Fortier, and Maxime Prévost (eds), *Mélanges à la mémoire de Jean-Claude Morisot. Littératures*, Montreal: McGill University, 21–22: 245–63.

Woodsworth, Judith (2001), 'In the Looking Glass: Bernard Shaw on and in Translation', in Susan Petrilli (ed.), 'Lo stesso altro', Università di Bari, *Athanor*, 4: 128–45.

Woodsworth, Judith (2003), 'In the Looking Glass: Bernard Shaw on and in Translation', in Susan Petrilli and Augusto Ponzio (eds), *Translation Translation*, Amsterdam/ New York: Rodopi, 531–51.

Woodsworth, Judith, ed. (2018), *The Fictions of Translation*, Amsterdam/Philadelphia, John Benjamins.

Wright, Paul (2003), 'George Bernard Shaw', in Paul Poplawski (ed.), *Encyclopedia of Literary Modernism*, Westport, CT: Greenwood Press, 381–3.

Yao, Steven G. (2002), *Translation and the Languages of Modernism: Gender, Politics, Language*, New York: Palgrave.

York, Christine (2013), 'Pierre Clastres's *Chronique des Indiens Guayaki*: Reframing the Narrative through Translation', unpublished paper given at University of Ottawa School of Translation and Interpretation, 15 February 2008.

Zuber-Skerritt, Ortrun, ed. (1984), *Page to Stage: Theatre as Translation*, Amsterdam: Rodopi.

Zulauf, Sander W., and Edward M. Cifelli (1978), *Index of American Periodical Verse: 1976*, Metuchen/London: Scarecrow Press.

Zweig, Stefan (1964), *The World of Yesterday. An Autobiography*, trans. Benjamin W. Huebsch and Helmut Ripperberger, introduction by Harry Zohn, Lincoln: University of Nebraska Press. [c1943].

Index

Note: The letter 'n' following locators refers to notes; entries in bold indicate the most important range of pages for particular authors or translators.